False Friends, Falser Friends, Falsest Friends

A Student's Workbook on Deceptive Resemblances

English–German, German–English

Richard Humphrey

Ernst Klett Sprachen
Barcelona · Budapest · London · Posen · Sofia · Stuttgart

It is but a small part of the genius and powers of language which is to be learnt from dictionaries and grammars. There are innumerable niceties, not only of construction and of idiom, but even in the signification of words, which are discovered only by much reading, and critical attention.
ALEXANDER TYTLER, Essay on the Principles of Translation, *1790*

Nichts ist schlimmer, als wenn einer Wörtlichkeit nimmt, ohne den Sinn zu kontrollieren, und nichts ist gefährlicher als Wörter, die so vertraut klingen, weil man Verwandtschaft spürt: gemeinsame Herkunft ist oft nur die Ursache völliger Verschiedenheit.
HEINRICH BÖLL, „Wort und Wirklichkeit", *1965*

The difference between the almost-right word and the right word is really a large matter – it's the difference between the lightning bug and the lightning.
MARK TWAIN, letter to an unknown clergyman, *n. d.*

Bibliographische Information der Deutschen Bibliothek.
Die Deutsche Bibliothek verzeichnet diese Publikation in der Deutschen Nationalbibliographie; detaillierte bibliographische Daten sind im Internet über http://dnb.ddb.de abrufbar

1. Auflage A 1 5 4 3 2 1 | 2007 2006 2005 2004 2003

Internetadresse | http://www.klett-verlag.de
Bildnachweis | © Helmut Minkowski. *Vermutungen über den Turm zu Babel.* Mit freundlicher Genehmigung des Luca-Verlages. Freren 1991

Redaktion | Margit Künzel
Umschlaggestaltung | Christine Schneyer
Satz | Steffen Hahn GmbH, Medienservice, Kornwestheim
Druck | Ludwig Auer GmbH, Donauwörth. Printed in Germany.
ISBN 3-12-939613-6

Inhalt

Vorwort

Der falsche Freund

Es ist bei den Sprachen wie auf dem Lebensweg: Kaum einer fügt einem mehr Schaden zu als der falsche Freund. Dem naiven Vertrauen, das man in ihn setzte, entsprechen die Untiefen der Enttäuschung, die einsetzt, wenn er einen verrät. Falsche Freunde sind maliziös, ihre Fallstricke sind nicht immer von der harmlosen Art.

Begriffsbestimmung

Als ‚falsche Freunde' oder *faux amis* des Spracherwerbs werden gemeinhin solche Wort- oder Idiompaare bezeichnet, die in zwei Sprachen zwar ähnlich erscheinen, aber unterschiedliche Referenzbereiche aufweisen. In dem Sprachenpaar Deutsch-Englisch gibt es zahlreiche solche Scheinentsprechungen, wobei es zum Wesen der Sprachentwicklung wie des Spracherwerbs gehört, dass die Zahl weder endgültig fixierbar noch konstant ist.

Begriffsentwirrung

Dabei sind die ‚falschen Freunde' der Sprachen streng genommen weder ‚Freunde' noch ‚falsch'. Nicht sie verraten uns, sondern wir verraten uns selbst und sie, indem wir mit ihnen undifferenziert umgehen.

Umfang

Der vorliegende Band versteht sich als Übungs- und Lernbuch zum Thema für Studierende der Anglistik in sämtlichen Studiengängen und -richtungen inkl. Übersetzen und Fachübersetzen. Bedingt durch dieses Zielpublikum vermittelt er etwa 1150 lexikalische falsche Freunde Deutsch-Englisch, also weitaus mehr als vergleichbare Bände. Der in 30 Sachgebiete eingeteilte Band geht dafür auf alle Lebens- und Wissensbereiche ein, die mit einer modernen, weltoffen-liberal aufgefassten Anglistik zu tun haben, und berücksichtigt auch das literarische Register. Einige der simpleren Wortpaare werden stillschweigend vorausgesetzt.

Didaktik

In der Frage nach der Anzahl der falschen Freunde ist die Frage nach deren Didaktik inhärent. Denn so unverzichtbar und verdienstvoll die einander ablösenden Wörterbücher der falschen Freunde, so unzureichend erweisen sie sich in der Lernpraxis. Auflisten ist noch lange nicht vermitteln, differenzieren noch lange nicht einprägen. Der vorliegende Band geht folglich neue Wege, um seine Inhalte an sein Zielpublikum zu bringen.

Konzept

Wie seine Vorgänger in der Serie ist auch dieses Werk den didaktischen Prinzipien Piagets verpflichtet. Das Dozieren weicht dem Für-sich-Entdecken, das Vorexerzieren dem vorwissenaktivierenden Differenzierenlernen. Hauptmerkmale der neuen Übungstypologie des Bandes sind: Irritation, Reflexion, Rätseln, aber auch Einprägsamkeit und Mnemotechnik.

Sowohl für universitäre Veranstaltungen als auch für das Selbstlernen bietet der Band eine Fülle an Übungs- und Lernmaterial an. Auch für den anspruchsvollen Leistungskurs Englisch dürften geneigte Lehrkräfte hier Geeignetes vorfinden.

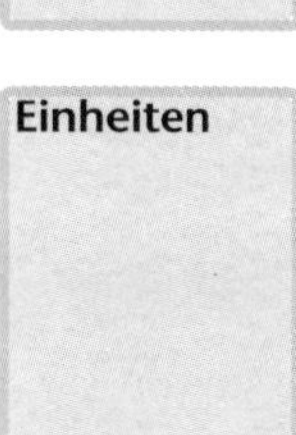

Die 30 Einheiten des Bandes sind alle in sich geschlossen und können in beliebiger Reihenfolge vorgenommen werden. Jede Einheit nimmt sich einen separaten Lebens- oder Sachbereich vor, die Palette reicht vom Lebensweltlichen über die Wirtschaft und Technik bis hin zum Literarischen und Gedanklichen. Jede Einheit teilt sich wiederum in einzelne Übungen, die jeweils einen Teilbereich des Gebiets behandeln.

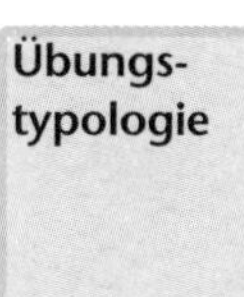

Bei den Übungen handelt es sich zum Teil um neue Übungsformen, die allerdings alle in der hochschuldidaktischen Praxis erprobt worden sind. Dass es sich hier häufig um diffiziles Vexiermaterial handelt, ist weder unüberlegt noch zufällig, sondern unvermeidbar. Bewusst ist auch das Einbeziehen von ‚wahren Freunden' in die Übungs- und Lernstrategien. Gäbe es nämlich die nicht, so gäbe es die falschen ebensowenig.

Zwischenkapitel

Die vier translationswissenschaftlichen Zwischenkapitel führen konzis in ausgewählte Aspekte der Problematik ein.

Antwortteil

Im ausführlichen Antwortteil werden zur Selbstkontrolle die Lösungen zu sämtlichen Übungen sowie auch detaillierte Auflistungen der involvierten Wortpaare angeboten. Der Antwortteil enthält ebenso Angaben zu mehreren zusätzlichen Wortpaaren, die nicht in den Übungen vorkommen, sowie auch zu der ‚Biographie' *('Language Lineage')* ausgewählter Wortpaare.

Aktualität

Der Band ist auf dem neuesten Stand und bezieht auch jüngere und jüngste Sprachentwicklungen ein. Die neuesten Wörterbücher der Neuprägungen wurden mit berücksichtigt, wie auch die aktuelle Fassung des *OED* auf CD-ROM. Redaktionsschluss war März 2003.
Die Aktualität ist ein Gebot der Sache. Denn: Wer meint, die Zahl der „falschen Freunde" sei infolge der globalisierenden Zeitläufe eher abnehmend, unterliegt gleich einer zweiten Täuschung. Im smarten Diskurs der Postmoderne fällt es zunehmend schwer, die denglische Spreu vom genuin englischen Weizen zu trennen. Gerade während und wegen der großen Wanderungen unseres Zeitalters, zu deren Hybridisierungen auch eine Migration der Bedeutungen gehört, verdient der Problembereich „Falsche Freunde" ein Höchstmaß an Aufmerksamkeit.

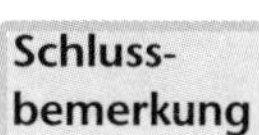

„Falsche Freunde" sind weder eine bloße Lach- noch eine unerforschliche Vexiernummer, sondern die unerbittliche Realität der interkulturellen Kommunikation, zumal im multilingualen Europa. Sich mit

ihnen auseinanderzusetzen und ihre Entwicklungen aufmerksam zu verfolgen, ist Pflicht jedes seriösen Fremdsprachenerwerbs. Nach wie vor gilt: Wer wahrer Freund einer Fremdsprache sein möchte, muss mit deren falschen Freunden innig vertraut sein.

Danksagung

Der besondere Dank des Autors gilt dem sperberäugigen und sprachkundig-differenzierten Klaus Schaeffler.

Field 1: The World of Matter

Area 1: The Physical World

Your Task

The ten word-pairs below are all false friends from the physical world around us. Distinguish between the pairs by matching each word on the left with the person or object on the right most associated with it. The correct answers are to be found on page 102.

Word Pairs

A. blank		1. wet chewing gum
B. blank		2. a pill for a sea-sick stomach
	C. blasen	3. a high mountain or noble thought
	D. to blaze	4. polished furniture or parquet flooring
E. blenden		
F. to blend		5. the Pacific
		6. deep, deep water
	G. blubbern	
	H. to blubber	7. a river at its source
		8. a sheet of paper still unwritten
I. breit		
J. bright		9. a raging fire or fiery anger
		10. a trumpeter or the West wind
	K. luftig	
	L. lofty	11. the Great Wall of China
		12. a badly ventilated room
M. massiv		
N. massive		13. a tobacco-merchant or a painter
		14. an old oak table
	O. plombieren	
	P. to plumb	15. a bubbling liquid
		16. a morning in early summer
Q. quellen		
R. to quell		17. a dazzling light
		18. a bad tooth
	S. stickig	
	T. sticky	19. a crying, sobbing child
		20. a windy English hill-top

Als falsche Freunde bezeichnet man v. a. morphologische und idiomatische Entsprechungen zwischen zwei Sprachen, wenn sich zwei Wörter oder Wendungen scheinbar entsprechen, aber unterschiedliche Referenzbereiche haben.

Metzler Lexikon Sprache, hg. von Helmut Glück, Stuttgart 1993

Area 2: States, Qualities and Quantities

Your Task

Fill in the gaps in the sentences below, choosing the appropriate word from the list beneath. Of the words in brackets only four have 'true friends' in English. Correct answers are to be found on page 102.

Sentences

1. While the *(Brand)* _____ was at its fiercest, the *(Qualm)* _____ was too thick to allow potential rescuers to enter the building.
2. Careful! The recipe says 'a *(Prise)* _____ of salt' – not a handful!
3. The sculpture, an imposing figure in *(Bronze)* _____, was a (*Geschenk*) _____ of its creator, a local artist.
4. In extreme *(Feuchtigkeit)* _____ *(Fäulnis)* _____ can develop.
5. She felt no *(Skrupel)* _____ as she poured a nice little quantity of *(Gift)* _____ into his bedtime drink.
6. One can always tell when you've had a shower. There's so much *(Dampf)* _____ in the bathroom, it's like the fog in a Dickens novel.
7. The soldiers threw *(Feuerbrände)* _____ into the straw huts and watched as the village burned to the ground.
8. They tried to force the door open with a metal bar, but there was no room to get sufficient *(Hebelwirkung)* _____.
9. At very first *(Blick)* _____ you could see the quality of the material: it *(glänzen)* _____, having a fine *(Glanz, Schimmer)* _____.
10. Sometimes a large *(Kerbe)* _____ had been made in a tree trunk and sometimes a *(Büschel)* _____ of grass had been left on the path.
11. She could not stand the *(Schmutzigkeit)* _____ of their language and it was her fate to spend two weeks with them on the 'Dreamboat'.
12. They soon learned that it was no easy task: the sacks of *(Kalk)* _____ were a terrible burden, even over the short distance from the *(Randstein)* _____ to the back-yard.
13. In the early morning sun, the white *(Kreide)* _____ of the cliffs seemed like specks of *(Kristall)* _____ dancing on the far horizon.
14. Last year she went to Italy and brought back some *(Lava)* _____ from Mt. Vesuvius. This year she's been to France and brought back a *(Fossil)* _____ from the Dordogne.
15. 'You must stop being so modest. You must stop hiding your light under the proverbial *(Scheffel)* _____.'

Options

brand	bronze	bushel	chalk
crystal	damp	fire	fossil
foulness	gift	glance	kerb
lava	lime	notch	pinch
poison	prise	qualm	rottenness
sheen	shine	smoke	steam
tuft			

Area 3: Man-Made Substances and States

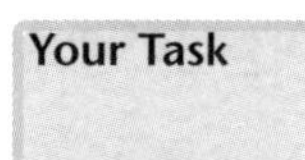

Complete the crossword below, which is made up of nine pairs of false friends from the field of man-made substances. The clues are the words underlined. Correct answers are to be found on page 103.

Crossword

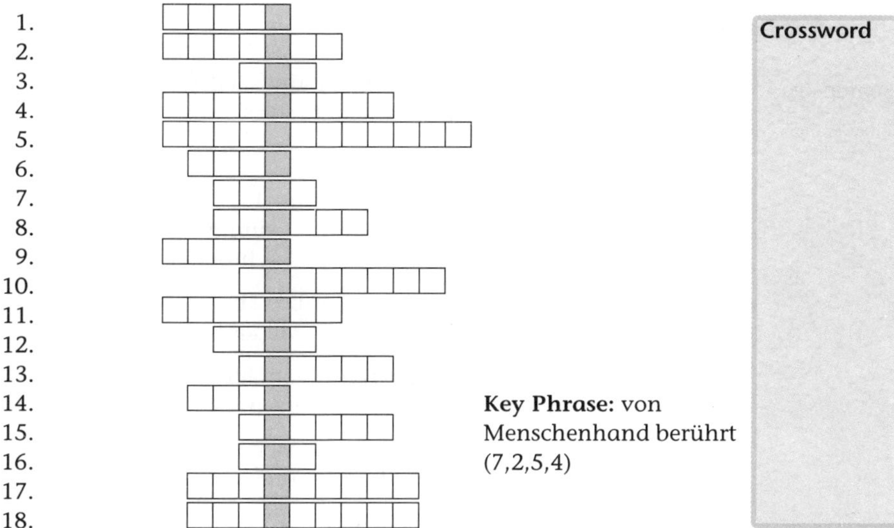

Clues

1. Die Holzplatte wies einen Riss auf, einen richtigen Sprung (5).
2. Behrens' Meisterwerk ist wohl die AEG-Turbinenfabrik (7).
3. Der Klebstoff (3) hielt nicht, war völlig unwirksam.
4. Beim Abkochen entstand ein leicht süßlich riechender Sud (9).
5. Gottseidank, dass die schon mit Splitt (7,5) gestreut haben!
6. Wir benötigen auch unbedingt Büro- bzw. Papierleim (4).
7. Das Seifenwasser bildete eine weißliche, leicht klebrige Lauge (4).
8. 'Kannste mir deinen Gummi leihen, deinen Radiergummi (6)?'
9. An den Fenstern der Villa war der Kitt (5) abgebröckelt.
10. Nur wo nicht gehobelt wird, fallen keine Späne (8).
11. Man fand auch Spuren von Holz- oder Nagellack (7).
12. Ich benötige Kalk (4) zur Herstellung von Zement, genau: *CaO_2*.
13. Görlitz war die Stoffstadt, spezialisiert auf Görlitzer Tuch (6).
14. Die Stützweite (4) der Brunel'schen Brücke war für die damaligen Verhältnisse schier atemberaubend.
15. Schon die Ausrüstung (3) macht das Skifahren enorm teuer, die Sessellifte kommen erschwerend hinzu. (mit Artikel).
16. Die Füllung schmeckte wie (Kinder)Brei (3).
17. Kaum fährst du das Auto, schon ist ein Kratzer im Lack (9)!
18. Erstaunlich, dass ein Postpaket aus Pappe (9) so robust ist.

Field 2: Geography and Topography

Area 1: General Topography

Your Task

Distinguish between the following pairs of ill-translated sentences, each of which contains one or more pairs of false friends from the realm of general topography. For the correct answers see page 104.

Sentences

1. a) Er lief den niedrigen Damm entlang zu den Schleusen.
   *b) He walked along the low dam to the sluices.
2. a) Sie holten sich Torf vom Moor.
   *b) They fetched turf from the moor.
3. a) Schon vor dem Herbst wurde das Grummet geerntet.
   *b) Before the harvest the grummet was brought in.
4. a) Der Anger wurde von allen Dorfbewohnern geteilt.
   *b) The anger was shared by all the villagers.
5. a) Es wuchs an den Saatrillen sowie im Ried am Feldrain.
   *b) It grew by the rills and in the reeds in the rain.
6. a) Being near a stream meant at least freshwater.
   *b) Die Nähe zum Strom bedeutete zumindest frisches Wasser.
7. a) There was mist over the fell.
   *b) Auf dem Fell lag Mist.
8. a) They crossed the brook and went on to the hide.
   *b) Sie überquerten die Brücke und liefen weiter in die Heide.
9. a) Each farm consisted on average of a hundred acres.
   *b) Auf jede Farm kamen durchschnittlich hundert Äcker.
10. a) They waded through the slick by the shore.
    *b) Sie wateten durch den Schlick an der Küste.
11. a) Strolling the Strand Kipling's soldier dreamt of a far sea.
    *b) Beim Strandspaziergang träumte Kiplings Soldat vom fernen See.

Interference is the translator's worst problem, as it is the language learner's. Failure to recognize [it] makes him look most foolish.

PETER NEWMARK, *Approaches to Translation*. Oxford 1981

Area 2: The Whole Wide World

Your Task

Read the passage below, paying especial attention to the key words from world geography, sixteen of which are false friends. Then consider the statements beneath.

Text

Onkel Vince, hoch aufgeschossen, leicht schlaksig, war der Vagabund unserer eher seßhaften Familie. Das Ausländische zog ihn zeitlebens an. Nichts, pflegte er zu sagen, sei ihm fremder als das Insulare. Ihm war jede Reede eine Aufforderung zum baldigen Aufbruch, jede Förde eine Einladung zur Überquerung. Wo wir in den tristen Nachkriegsjahren in den ebenso tristen englischen Badeorten Urlaub machten, bereiste er bereits Skandinavien und das Baltikum, war an der Adria, später am Golf, dann unterwegs im „schwarzen Kontinent", danach, bevor die Diktatoren an die Macht kamen, in Südamerika. 'Vinny' war Kosmopolit. Zu seinen Freunden zählten Isländer und Schweden, Wallonen und Romanen, später Afrikaner, Nachfahren der ersten Buren. Bei ihm paarten sich Reiselust und Erzähltalent. Er wußte von der Elfenbeinküste wie von Brasilien zu erzählen, von Bergen und Klippen, Strudeln und Klammen. Wie er sein Reisepensum schaffte? Auf hoher See pflegte er die Überfahrt ‚abzuverdienen', an Land verließ er sich gerne auf Schusters Rappen. Wie er sich durchschlug? Durch Sprachbegabung. Der Weltenbummler sammelte Sprachkenntnisse wie Stubenhocker Briefmarken. Nichts verachtete er so sehr wie die *little Englanders*. Wo dem Engländer bereits der Ire ein Rätsel blieb, war Vince jeder Völkerstamm verwandt, ja sogar die Germanen. Dem Novalis-Satz, wonach jeder Engländer eine Insel sei, hielt er seinen Lieblingsspruch entgegen: „Das Menschenleben ist keine Insel, sondern ein Archipel."

Statements

In the light of the above passage, which of the following statements are definitely true? Correct answers are to be found on page 105.

1. For Uncle Vince the outlandish was a perpetual attraction.
2. He counted boors and Afrikaners among his friends.
3. He could tell stories of bergs and strudels, cliffs and clams.
4. 'Vinny' knew the Baltic, the Adriatic and was familiar with golf.
5. He knew Scandinavia, the Ivory Coast and Brasilia.
6. He viewed reeds as a challenge and crossed every ford he came to.
7. Islanders and suèdes were among his acquaintances . . .
8. . . . as were Walloons and Romans.
9. He disliked the insular and was a cosmopolitan.
10. The English do not understand ire.
11. Even the Germans Uncle Vince liked.
12. Human life, for 'Vinny', was an archipelago.

Area 3: The British Countryside

Your Task

Read the texts below, paying especial attention to the words underlined, eight of which are false friends from the area of the British countryside. Then consider the statements below.

Texts

1. Arthur Ransome's renowned children's novels *Swallows and Amazons* (1931), *Pigeon Post* (1936) and *The Big Six* (1940) contain memorable portrayals of sailing on the English meres.
2. Firths naturally feature in Scottish literature. Scott's *Quentin Durward* (1815) takes place on the Solway Firth and the hero of R. L. Stevenson's *Kidnapped* (1886) is abducted on the Firth of Forth.
3. George Orwell's *Coming Up for Air* (1939) is a superb evocation of the rapidly changing relationship between London and its hinterland.
4. Raymond Williams's *Border* trilogy takes place in the Welsh Marches with their line of Norman castles built between 1086 and 1200 and subsequently held by the Marcher Lords.
5. Rugged Glastonbury Tor is one of the settings in John Cowper Powys's *Glastonbury Romance* (1932).
6. In the 'Palice of Honour', Gavin Douglas (1475?–1522), the first great poet in Scots, characterises life as 'this loch of cair'.
7. William Cobbett's socially exploratory *Rural Rides* (1822–26) take the reader through – among other areas – the changing green landscapes of the Kent and Sussex Weald.
8. *Cider With Rosie* (1959) is Laurie Lee's resonant depiction of a Cotswolds childhood. The Lincolnshire Wolds still await their poet.
9. Graham Swift's early novel *Waterland* (1982) is located in the flatlands of the East Anglian fens.
10. In *The Spectator* of 28 November 1712, Joseph Addison is looking for 'a convenient Place where I may build an Alms-house [...] for a Dozen superannuated Husbandmen.'

Statements

In the light of the above passages, which of the following statements are definitely true? Correct answers are to be found on page 106.

1. In der schottischen Literatur spielt die Furt eine wesentliche Rolle.
2. Die Romanze von Powys spielt zum Teil am Stadttor.
3. Cobbett schilderte u.a. den sozialen Wandel im Wald von Kent.
4. Swifts *Waterland* ist ein Roman des Flachlands und des Venns.
5. Ransome war Meeresdichter.
6. Addison wollte auf der Alm bauen.
7. Douglas fasste das irdische Dasein als kummervolles Loch auf.
8. Orwell schilderte eindringlich das alte Hinterland von London.
9. Laurie Lee war Walddichter.
10. Die Romane von Williams spielen in einer Marschlandschaft.

Field 3: Flora and Fauna

Area 1: The Animal World I

Your Task

This exercise contains twelve pairs of false friends from the animal world. Discover them by translating the sentences below, as in the example. Correct answers are to be found on page 107.

Example

Je mehr Schnee**flocken** fielen, desto weniger sah man die Schafherde.
*The more snowflakes fell, the less you could see the **flock** of sheep.*

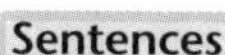

Sentences

1. Die Trappe lag regungslos in der Falle. Ein Martyrium.

2. Immer noch keine Spur. Er spornte das Pferd an. Weiter, weiter.

3. Während der Lord auf Moorhuhnjagd in den Hochlandtälern war, fütterte die Lady lieber die gemeinen Teichhühner am Schloßweiher.

4. Das kläffende Untier ist kein Hund mehr, sondern ein Köter!

5. Zu der Vogeltränke kamen allerlei Vögel angeflogen: Kohlmeisen, Finke, Tannenmeisen und Rotkehlchen.

6. Die englische Dogge schnüffelte forsch an jedem noch so kleinen Hund herum.

7. Die Natter schlich, vom ihrem Geschwätz gestört, leise davon.

8. Was als Schülerstreich anfing, endete tragisch in den Pranken des Löwen.

9. Bereits bei der 8000-Euro-Frage ließ ihn seine Bildung im Stich. Gehörte es zu der Familie der Lurchen oder zu der der Kriechtiere?

10. Der Halter ließ das Halfter verzagt fallen. Das Pferd war nicht zu dressieren.

11. Ob männliches Füllen oder weibliches, der Nachwuchs des renommierten Rennpferdes war immer begehrt.

Übersetzungen sind nichts anderes als Namengebung an fremde, bislang namenlose Wesen. Die Übersetzer schaffen diese Urbedingung des Zusammenlebens.

Karl Dedecius, *Vom Übersetzen*. Frankfurt/M., Suhrkamp 1986

Area 2: The Animal World II

Your Task

Read the passage below, paying especial attention to the key words from the world of fauna, ten of which are false friends. Then deal with the statements below.

Text

Es war heiß in Le Tholonet, salamanderheiß, unter der Hitzeglocke der Haute Provence.

Der Falke hatte seine kreisenden Patrouillen eingestellt. Selbst die Lerche war vor dem Anmarsch der Sonne zurückgewichen.

Am Feldrain der schrille Wetzstein der Grillen, in der Luft die flimmernde Geometrie der Mücken, hin und wieder der jähe Pfeil einer Libelle. Ansonsten Stille, Regungslosigkeit, Lichtglanz: eine Welt, die im Banne des Mittags innehielt. Thymian, Salbei, Heu.

Im Schatten des Obstgartens ein Gaul. An der Tränke zwei Stiere. Auf dem Berghang eine in sich gekehrte Schafherde.

Die Welt glich einem Esel, einem Maultier. Nein, sie war noch träger. Sie glich einer Schnecke. Nein, sie war noch langsamer. Sie glich einem Igel. Nein, sie war noch geborgener. Sie glich einem Schäferhund, hingegeben-zufrieden eingeschlafen auf heißer Schwelle.

„Ohne Bedenken der Zukunft“, schrieb Erhart Kästner, „das ist der Hund in der Sonne“. Er schrieb dies wohl mißbilligend, aber Le Tholonet wußte es besser. Man soll nicht immer flink wie das Wiesel, umtriebsam wie der Hamster sein. Der Hitze huldigend, das Jetzt auskostend, eingedenk eines geschätzten Jetzts die Zukunft würdigend – *das* ist der Hund in der Sonne.

Statements

In the light of the above passage, which of the following statements are true? The answers are to be found on page 107.

1. There was a <u>Gaul</u> in the orchard.
2. The world that day was more secure than an <u>eagle</u>.
3. One should not always be as swift as a <u>weasel</u>.
4. There was a <u>shepherd</u> on the hillside.
5. Beside the field there were <u>grilles</u>.
6. The <u>falcon</u> had stopped its patrolling.
7. The author describes the world as ‘slower than a <u>snake</u>’.
8. There were two <u>steers</u> at the water-trough.
9. The world of Le Tholonet was more indolent than a <u>muleteer</u> or an <u>easel</u>.
10. Even the <u>lark</u> had fled the sun.
11. There was some <u>muck</u> and <u>libels</u> in the air.
12. One should not always be as busy as a <u>hamster</u> either.

Area 3: Flora

Your Task

The fifteen word-pairs below are all false friends from the world of flora. Distinguish between the pairs by matching each word on the left with its definition on the right. The correct answers are to be found on page 108.

Word Pairs

A. der Baum
B. the beam
C. das Beet
D. the beet
E. das Blatt
F. the blade
G. die Blume
H. the bloom
I. das Bukett
J. the bucket
K. die Ferne
L. the fern
M. die Föhre
N. the fir
O. der Klee
P. the clay
Q. die Knolle
R. the knoll
S. das Korn
T. the corn
U. die Ragwurz
V. the ragwort
W. die Rüster
X. the rooster
Y. die Schote
Z. the shoot
AA. der Splint
BB. the splint
CC. der Trunk
DD. the trunk

1. coloured, seed-bearing part of plant
2. stiff viscous earth
3. perennial plant with wood stem
4. green trefoil, at times four-leafed
5. the (far) distance
6. plant with feathery fronds
7. tuber, thick root or stem of plant
8. pine tree, Scotch fir
9. elm tree
10. long piece of squared timber
11. domestic cock (crowing at dawn)
12. EngE wheat, ScE, IrE oats
13. type of (insect-like) orchid, ophrys
14. garden plot for plants
15. pod
16. single flower; flowering
17. young branch or sucker
18. plant with edible roots, e.g. sugar ~
19. stem of tree
20. drink, draught
21. organ of plant springing from its side
22. evergreen coniferous tree
23. seed, grain (of cereal)
24. bunch of flowers
25. wooden or metal water-container
26. sap wood
27. flat leaf of grass and cereals
28. groundsel, sometimes of herb value
29. appliance to hold firm wounded part
30. small hill, hillock

Field 4: The Human Being and Health

Area 1: The Human Body

Your Task

The twenty-eight pairs of words below all derive from the field of the human body, only nine of them, however, being genuine equivalents. Find the true friends and then distinguish between the false. The correct answers are to be found on page 109.

Word Pairs

die Achsel – the axle
die Aorta – the aorta
die Backe – the back
der/die Ballen – the balls
der Buckel – the buckle
der Deltamuskel – the deltoid
der Gaumen – the gums
der Grind – the grind
das Gut – the gut
die Haare – the hairs
der Humeruskopf – the head of humerus
die Kniescheibe – the kneecap
der Körper – the corpse
die Koteletten – the cutlets
die Lunge – the lunge
der Nacken – the neck
die Nervenfaser – the nerve fibre
der Papillarmuskel – the papillary muscle
der/die Pickel – the pickles
der Pony – the ponytail
die Pore – the pore
die Rippe – the rib
der Rist (am Fuß) – the wrist
der Rumpf – the rump
der Spleen – the spleen
der Teint – the tint
die Tresse – the tress
die Warze – the wart
die Wimper – the whimper

Examples [of false friends] are legion among most European languages and they represent one of the main stumbling blocks to inexperienced translators, particularly if their little knowledge has not taught them the dangers of guessing.

IAN F. FINLAY, *Translating*. Edinburgh 1971

Area 2: Health and Medicine

Your Task

Study the sixteen mini-biographies below, all but two of which contain false friends from the field of medicine, and then consider the statements beneath.

Biographies

Ärmste Annabella mußte schnell in die Ambulanz.
Anwalt Andreas hatte eine akute Angina.
Nach der Dialyse ging es Dana immer dreckig.
Ines war mehr als 'indisponiert': OP Indikation!

Iris blieb irre lange auf der Intensivstation in Island.
Die Ingeborg litt fast immer an Ischias.
Katharina, unsere ewige Kranke, hatte die Farbe von Kondensmilch.
Auch der kreidebleiche Kai war der kränkliche Typ.

Der lausgeplagte Laurens ließ sein Leben im Lazarett.
Lederhäutige Lea ließ sich zum elften Male liften.
Patrick war fast permanent ambulanter Patient.
'Poppiger' Pierre hatte immer ein paar Präservative in petto.

Riccardo legte das Rezept rechtzeitig der Krankenkasse vor.
Samuel, die schöne Seele, war Samariter.
Sorgengeplagt ließ Susanne das Sekret untersuchen.
Der stoische Stefan blieb lange auf der Station.

Statements

In the light of the above mini-biographies, which of the following statements are true? The answers are to be found on page 110.

1. Andreas suffered from angina.
2. Stefan was at the station for a lengthy time.
3. Katharina was a crank.
4. Pierre was never without preservatives.
5. Sam was a Samaritan.
6. Laurens died in a lazaret.
7. Lea liked being lifted.
8. Annabella had to go by ambulance.
9. Kai was a cranky type.
10. Ingeborg had an itch.
11. Dana suffered after every dialysis.
12. Susanne had a secret that needed to be investigated.
13. Iris spent a long time in the intensive care unit.
14. Patrick was an ambling patient.
15. Riccardo took the receipt to his medical insurance office.
16. Ines was 'indisposed': there were indications of an operation.

Area 3: Medicine and Pain

Your Task

Distinguish between the following pairs of ill-translated sentences, each of which contains one or more pairs of false friends – but also the occasional 'true friend' – from the realm of medicine and pain.

Sentences

1. a) Gerade in Zentralafrika war das gelbe Fieber virulent.
   *b) Precisely in Central Africa the yellow fever was virulent.

2. a) Die Schwester hatte einen langen Arbeitstag im Uniklinikum.
   *b) The sister had a long working day in the university clinic.

3. a) Sie war für ihre Absencen mittlerweile bekannt.
   *b) She had become well-known for her absences.

4. a) Er hatte Fieber. 40°. War es nur etwas Gastrisches oder sollte er bald wieder vom Fieber geschüttelt werden?
   *b) He had a fever. 40°. Was it only something gastric or was he soon to be shaken by fever again?

5. a) Keine Frage. Der Mann war psychisch krank.
   *b) No question about it. The man was psychically ill.

6. a) Die Akupunktur half tatsächlich gegen ihre Migräne.
   *b) The acupuncture really helped to combat her migraine.

7. a) Nach der Rosenkohlcremesuppe rumorte es am ganzen Tisch. Eine fatale Wahl?!
   *b) After the cream of Brussels sprouts soup, there were rumours all round the table. A fatal choice?!

8. a) Der Schwarze Tod der Jahre 1348–51 – die schlimmste Pest des Mittelalters – machte für Millionen Menschen das Leben zur Pein.
   *b) The Black Death of the years 1348–51 – the worst pest of the Middle Ages – made life a pain for millions of people.

9. a) Die Schnaken waren eine Plage. Nie hatten sie solche Stiche bekommen.
   *b) The snakes were a plague. Never had they had such stitches.

10. a) Er war nur ein Quacksalber mit den landesüblichen Placebos. Weder bei Rachitis noch bei Tuberkulose wußte er Rat.
    *b) He was just a quack with the customary placebos. Neither for rickets nor for tuberculosis did he have any real answer.

Field 5: Eating and Drinking

Area 1: Market Day

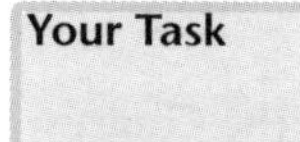

Study Tina's shopping list below, which contains almost twenty false friends – but also some 'true friends' – from the field of essential foodstuffs, and then consider the statements beneath.

Wochenmarkt

2 x Gurke
1 Salat
Cherry-Tomaten
Mange-tout
4 x Zucchini
2 Stangen Porree
1 x Sellerieknolle
1 Limone
Minze

Naturkostladen

Backpflaumen
Apfelmus
Kakao
Rosinen
Mehl
Puffermischung
Gries
Yoghurt (verschiedene Aromas)
Sauerkirschmarmelade

Bäcker/Supermarkt

Toastbrot u. Biskuitboden
Berliner (gefüllt), Kekse od. Printen

Fleischer

Broiler

In the light of the above shopping list, which of the following statements are true? The answers are to be found on page 112.

1. At the market, Tina intends to buy a salad, two gherkins and celery.
2. She is planning to cook with grease, resins and meal.
3. Perhaps she will serve puffers with apple mousse or baked plums.
4. From the baker's she wants toast, cakes (or prints) and Berliners.
5. She is also hoping for a biscuit flan to be still available there.
6. Porridge is on the list, as is cacao.
7. She wants cherry tomatoes, mange-tout and zucchinis.
8. Mince she should have listed under 'butcher's' with her broiler.
9. Tina likes yoghurts with varying aromas.
10. Not least, she wants some marmalade, and a lemon.

L'intérêt de l'examen des interférences n'est pas de nous renseigner sur ce qu'est la traduction, mais de démontrer ce que celle-ci ne peut pas être: une transposition pure et simple des composantes du signifié.

MAURICE PERGNIER, *Les fondements socio-linguistiques de la traduction.* Lille 1993

Area 2: On the Menu

Your Task

The Lutzke family is eating out to celebrate Uncle Ernst's eighty-fifth. Study their choices below and the comments they make on the food, and then consider the statements opposite/overleaf.

The Choices

Onkel Ernst (85)
Panierter Flußkrebs mit Hummersauce auf Austern
Sein Kommentar: „Mein lieber Schieber, das war nicht bekömmlich!"

Tante Sofie (91)
Gebratene Gans mit Rotkohl und Sudetenland-Klößen
Ihr Kommentar: „Schön knusprig, schön kross."

Dieter (62)
Doradenfilets in Bärlauch-Sauce auf Marktgemüse mit Basmati-Reis
Sein Kommentar: „Hervorragend, köstlich! Ein Genuß!"

Margot (61)
Lammkoteletts in Rosmarinjus mit Speck-Butterbohnen u. Kartoffelgratin; danach: Französische Käseplatte
Ihr Kommentar: „Reichhaltige Portionen. Kann man nichts sagen."

Marion (39)
Menü II: Krabbencocktail; Schollenfilets auf Provençale-Ratatouille; Pistazien-Pudding mit Creme
Ihr Kommentar: „Tut mir leid, dies sagen zu müssen, aber: fade."

Alfred (59)
Pochierter Schellfisch mit einer Champignonfarce auf Spinat-Tagliatelli
Sein Kommentar: „Ganz schön raffiniert. Und jetzt, Mädchen, ein Stück Torte – aber bitte mit Sahne"

Danni (29)
Kartoffel-Brokkoli-Auflauf gratiniert mit Bechamel-Sauce
Ihr Kommentar: „Adäquat, aber nicht berauschend"

Felix (10)
Dt. Beefsteak mit Pommes und Ketchup; danach: Nougat-Torte
Sein Kommentar: „Lecker!"

Michel (8)
Kindermenü I: Chili con Carne mit Maischips; danach: Feuerbowle-Eisbecher
Sein Kommentar: „Wow! Ganz schön scharf, Felix!"

Statements

In the light of the above choices and reactions, which of the following statements are true? The answers are to be found on page 113.

A. *The Dishes*

1. Dieter, the fish-lover, ate a dorado.
2. Uncle Ernst's food was panned.
3. Marion chose a dish with ratatouille as vegetable.
4. Both she and Ernst ate a form of crab.
5. Alfred opted for shellfish.
6. His fish was poached.
7. Margot's potato dish was cooked *au gratin*.
8. Danni's dish, on the other hand, was grated.
9. Young Felix ate beefsteak.
10. His subsequent *Torte* contained nougat.
11. Both Marion and young Michel ate a menu.
12. Marion's main course was fillet of sole.
13. She was the only grown-up to eat a pudding.
14. It included cream.
15. Michel, as youngsters tend to do, chose a meal with chips.
16. Felix, however, went for ketchup.
17. Margot's dish was served with butter beans . . .
18. . . . on which there were specks of bacon.
19. Her lamb dish was spiced with rosemary.
20. Thereafter she was still hungry enough to tackle a plate of cheese.
21. Alfred's dish involved a farce.
22. The two young (great-)nephews both ate a tart, as did Alfred.

B. *The Reactions*

23. Dieter's chosen dish was costly.
24. Michel considered his chili con carne really sharp.
25. Uncle Ernst felt that his chosen meal was not becoming.
26. Danni stated that her meal was adequate.
27. Margot was satisfied with her two portions.
28. Alfred judged his chosen meal to be refined.
29. Aunt Sofie was delighted with her goose because it was cross.
30. Marion was the most disappointed: her food was faded.

Area 3: In the Glass

Your Task

Read the passage below, paying especial attention to the key words from the world of drinking and alcohol, thirteen of which are false friends. Then consider the statements beneath.

Text

„Essen ist ein Bedürfnis des Magens, Trinken ein Bedürfnis des Geistes." Im schneegesegneten, sonnengetränkten Wallis war Beat Bonvin diese Erkenntnis aufgegangen. Dabei war Bonvin, der Belesene, der Nietzsche-Kenner, alles andere als ein Trunkenbold. Er hielt es mit seinem Meister: „Alkoholika sind mir nachteilig". Bereits ein Bier am Tag mache das Leben zum Jammertal. Der Sekt tauge höchstens zum Schiffetaufen.

Spirituosen waren erst recht nicht nach Bonvins Gusto. Ihn zog es weder in die Beiz zur Bowle noch in die Pinte zum Punsch. Whisky pur? Das schlimmste Männerparfüm. Rum? Hilft höchstens beim Samba-Tanzen. Likör? Die perfideste Kompensation für schlechte Küche.

Trotzdem lag Bonvin nichts ferner als Nietzsches Abstinenz. So sehr er das Gebraute verabscheute, so sehr schätzte, ja brauchte er das Gekelterte. Mittags ein Fendant hell wie ein Sommertag, zum Diner ein Sonnenuntergangs-Burgunder. Wie er mit Flaschen hantierte, ihr Etikett musterte, ihr Bukett bereits am Korken ergründete, hatte etwas Feierliches, Priesterliches an sich. Auch das unterschied ihn von Nietzsche. Nannte dieser den Alkohol und das Christentum die zwei großen europäischen Narkotika, waren für Beat die feinen Weine eher eine Versöhnung mit dem Dasein. Der Wein war Vergangenheit, Weite, Kontaktaufnahme. Wie er da stand, drahtig wie ein Weinstock, sonnenvergnügt wie ein Rebhang, konnte man es fast glauben: „Wer da trinkt Walliser Wein, dem schaut Gott ins Herz hinein".

Statements

In the light of the above passage, which of the following statements are true? The answers are to be found on page 114.

1. Nietzsche disliked alcoholics.
2. Bonvin, who liked a fendant, was not in favour of abstinence.
3. One bier a day can make life a misery.
4. A sect, liquor and pure whisky are little better.
5. Bonvin liked a Burgundy in the diner.
6. He studied wine etiquette, handling flasks with religious care.
7. Beat looked like a vine stock.
8. A pint and a bowl were not to his liking.
9. Nor did he drink spirits such as rum with gusto.
10. He could tell a bucket of a wine from its cork.
11. For Nietzsche, alcohol and Christianity were narcotics.
12. Bonvin, however, respected fine vines.

Field 6: Human Perception and Action

Area 1: Perceiving

Your Task

The ten word-pairs below are all false friends from the field of human perception. Distinguish between the pairs by matching each word on the left with the person or thing on the right most associated with it. The correct answers are to be found on page 115.

Word Pairs

A. behalten
B. to behold

C. bewahren
D. to beware

E. glotzen
F. to gloat

G. irritieren
H. irritate

I. der Klang
J. the clang

K. klingen
L. to cling (to)

M. riechen
N. to reek (of)

O. schmecken
P. to smack of

Q. tasten
R. to taste

S. unsichtbar
T. unsightly

1. a fish market at high noon
2. invisible ink
3. a fishy business inviting suspicion
4. the metallic sound of a prison door
5. a puzzling, confusing perception
6. a family heirloom
7. sth. to be kept in mind, remembered
8. the sound of a musical instrument
9. an escapee feeling his way forward
10. a Sixties housing block, ugly as sin
11. a wine-tester or tea-merchant
12. a delicious *haute cuisine* dish
13. over-inquisitive neighbours
14. an itching pullover
15. an enjoyer of another's misfortune
16. a person taking precautions
17. the shepherds seeing the angel
18. a floating mast after a shipwreck
19. two glasses chinking together
20. a glorious perfume

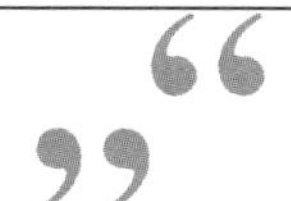

Gleichartigkeiten verführen dazu, sie auch in Fällen als gegeben anzunehmen, in denen Verschiedenartigkeit zutrifft.

PETER SCHIFKO, ‚Morphologische Interferenzen im Bereich des fachsprachlichen Wortschatzes', 1992

Area 2: Doing, Overdoing, Outdoing

Your Task

Fill in the gaps in the sentences below, choosing the appropriate word from the list beneath. Of the words in brackets only two have 'true friends' in English. Correct answers are to be found on page 116.

Sentences

1. Annabel was A1 at algebra! Who'd *(überreichen)* _____ her prize?
2. Beer-loving Bert could *(besiegen)* _____ anyone at bar billiards.
3. Caroline did not care much for cars. She thought most people could and should *(auskommen)* _____ without them.
4. Daniel didn't dare. He could not *(überwinden)* _____ his dread.
5. Exams exhausted Evelyn. She simply *(sich überanstrengen)* _____.
6. Foolish Felix fell over, *(übersehen)* _____ the flower-pots.
7. Gerta asked Graham to *(wiederholen)* _____ the grammar with her.
8. Hard-of-hearing Hamish had *(überhören)* _____ the request.
9. Ines felt injured and insulted on *(zufällig hören)* _____ the remark.
10. Jonathan got the job. Jealous Julian felt *(übergangen)* _____.
11. Kay was croquet-crazy. She insisted they *(zu Ende spielen)* _____.
12. Lazybones Lionel was late. He had *(‚sich verschlafen')* '_____'.
13. Muddled Mirabel could not make up her mind. She went to bed to *(sich überschlafen)* _____ the problem.
14. Never-satisfied Neville was again *(überarbeiten)* _____ his novel.
15. Olive's office was completely *(überheizt)* _____, 'orribly 'ot.
16. Pessimist Percival predicted mankind would *(untergehen)* _____.
17. Queenie felt queasy. Should she *(sich outen)* _____?
18. Rupert's school was really rotten at rugby. Their rugger team always *(unterliegen)* _____ to even ropy opposition.
19. Stella couldn't stomach slimy sea-food. She decided to *(verzichten auf)* _____ the oily oysters.
20. Terry was terrified. Tess had to *(vorausgehen)* _____ him.
21. Unfortunate Ursula had to *(sich unterziehen)* _____ an operation.
22. Vernon was vexed. What *(zugrundeliegen)* _____ the disaster?
23. Wretched Winifred had *(überdrehen)* _____ her wrist-watch.
24. Xavier made extraordinary exertions. But this time he had really *(sich überfordern)* _____ himself.
25. Yvonne's sister Eve *(überschatten)* _____ even Eve's evil-doing.
26. Zealous, zestful Zebedee enjoyed *(beaufsichtigen)* _____ slaves.

Options

come out	fail to hear	forgo	go ahead of
go over	lose (to)	manage	neglect
outplay	overcome	overhear	overheat
overlook	overreach	oversee	overshadow
oversleep	over-wind	overwork	perish
play to the finish	present	revise	sleep on sth.
	undergo	underlie	

Area 3: Essential Actions

Your Task

Distinguish between the following pairs of ill-translated sentences, each of which contains one or more pairs of false friends – but also the occasional 'true friend' – from the realm of basic human actions.

Sentences

1. a) The airline was effectively grounded in 1997.
   *b) Effektiv wurde die Fluggesellschaft 1997 gegründet.
2. a) The Chancellor seemed hemmed in, unable to handle the situation.
   *b) Der Kanzler wirkte gehemmt, handlungsunfähig.
3. a) They built a new movement.
   *b) Sie bildeten eine neue Bewegung.
4. a) He stemmed the flood.
   *b) Er stemmte sich gegen die Flut.
5. a) For heaven's sake, please stop whining! And kids, stop jabbering!
   *b) Um Gottes willen, hör bitte auf zu weinen! Und Kinder, hört auf, zu jammern!
6. a) The frolicking children were suddenly hushed.
   *b) Plötzlich huschten die frohlockenden Kinder hinein.
7. a) He was continually hustling.
   *b) Er war ständig am Hüsteln.
8. a) It was not difficult to lug round the corner.
   *b) Es war nicht schwer, um die Ecke zu lugen.
9. a) They did it by robbing and grabbing what they could.
   *b) Sie erreichten es dadurch, daß sie robbten und gruben, was das Zeug hielt.
10. a) Your job is to stick the emblems on.
    *b) Ihre Aufgabe besteht darin, die Embleme anzusticken.
11. a) It was flattering. He flustered her.
    *b) Es flattere, flüsterte er ihr zu.
12. a) At the first opportunity, they took their revenge.
    *b) Sie nahmen die erste Gelegenheit wahr, sich zu revanchieren.

Translation Theory I: What Are False Friends?

Initial Definitions

'False friends' or *faux amis* are habitually characterized as 'words or expressions which have the same form in two or more languages but convey different meanings' (Baker, 1992, p. 25). Such a definition covers the many cases such as 'rank'/rank where the form is indeed the same, but fails to include the even more cases such as 'officious'/*offiziös* where the form is – however slightly – different. A preferable formulation, therefore, would be that 'false friends' are 'those words in various languages which resemble in appearance words in other languages, but have a meaning quite different from the words they resemble' (Finlay, 1971, p. 112). This second definition, however, also fails to do justice to the subject in that its concentration on individual words ignores the many deceptive expressions such as 'red tape'/*roter Faden*. A more sensitive formulation again, therefore, would be that the term 'false friend' is a 'standard term used to describe SL and TL items which have the same or very similar form but different meanings, and which consequently give rise to difficulties in translation (and indeed interlingual communication in general)' (Shuttleworth, 1997, 57f.). A similarly inclusive German definition reads: 'Als falsche Freunde bezeichnet man v.a. morphologische und idiomatische Entsprechungen zwischen zwei Sprachen, wenn sich zwei Wörter oder Wendungen scheinbar entsprechen, aber unterschiedliche Referenzbereiche haben (Glück, 1993). Equally judicious and admirably elegant is the characterization of 'false friends' as 'Scheinentsprechungen im Wortschatz'(Kupsch-Losereit, 1998).

Types of False Friends

None of the above definitions, however, is particularly satisfying in that none of them states in what ways the 'false friends' resemble one another. There are, essentially, four possibilities:

- the 'false friends' can look identical such as 'qualm'/*Qualm* or 'hub'/*Hub*;
- the 'false friends' can look alike such as 'sheen'/*Schein* or 'vicar'/ *Vikar*;
- the 'false friends' can sound alike, such as 'plight'/*Pleite* or 'reek'/*riechen*;
- the 'false friends' can be structurally alike, such as 'to lead by the nose'/*an der Nase herumführen*.

In each of the four groups, the apparent similarity can lead to assumed yet illusory familiarity.

Total and Partial

In addition, there is a much-remarked further distinction which must be made between types of illusory resemblances. There are the 'total' and the 'partial' 'false friends' – those that are always and those that are merely often 'false'. The former group is large and includes such pairs as 'ewer'/*Ewer* or 'nut'/*Nut*. The latter group is larger and includes such word pairs as 'moral'/*Moral*, 'epitaph'/*Epitaph* or 'caricature'/*Karikatur*. Precisely such partial 'false friends' are often viewed as the most malicious. As a further proviso to the above definitions, therefore, one must add that it is only correct to speak of 'false friends' as of 'interlingualen Homonymen, also formal ähnlichen Wörtern, die inhaltlich teilweise [. . .] oder ganz verschieden sind' (Kupsch-Losereit, 1998).

Fuller Definition

A fuller definition of 'false friends', therefore, and one underlying the present volume, would be that 'false friends' are deceptive resemblances between two languages – pairs of words or expressions which look, sound or structurally seem alike and yet have different, or partially different, meanings.

History of the Term

Published interest in *faux amis* goes back at least as far as the mid-18th century, when Eléazar de Mauvillon published his *Remarques sur les germanismes* (1747), subtitled *Ouvrage utile aux Allemands, aux François, et aux Hollandais*. Henri Portitor's *Petit traité de gallicismes et germanismes* (1788) was the first of many followers. But it was only in 1923 with Veslot and Blanchet's *Les traquenards de la version anglaise* that attention turned to English.

Other terms

It is perhaps a symptom of the innate difficulty in dealing with the material that it is habitually treated in, often misleading, metaphorical terms. '*Falsi amici' 'falsos amigos' 'falsaj amikoj', 'falske venner'* and the variants *'faux cousins', 'faux frères'* and the like are as uninformative as their source term. Alternative expressions such as *'Sprachfallen', 'Stolpersteine', 'mots-pièges', 'mots perfides',* 'pitfalls' also tend to misallocate the blame. The linguistic term 'deceptive cognates' at least stresses perception.

Quantifying False Friends

Matters of nomenclature and definition are not incidental to any work on the subject: the number of 'false friends' a work includes will depend in part on its assumed audience but in part also on which definition it adopts. The question as to how many 'false friends' there are between any two languages is, however, as unanswerable as it is important. As long as languages and meanings develop and alter, so will the number shift and change. And given that 'false friends' are a matter of perception, there is an irreducible subjective element involved.

Parkes and Cornell (1989–93) deal, admirably, with some 650 'false friends'. Pascoe and Pascoe (2001) marshal, also excellently, some 800. Hill's standard European *Dictionary of False Friends* (1981) gives some 1000 examples for German-English, some albeit very basic. The present volume, with its different audience, goes on to some 1150. But all the authors involved readily acknowledge that there are a good many more 'false friends' afoot, especially of the 'partial' variety. The subject is perhaps inexhaustible – and certainly liable to exhaust any who take it to its final conclusion.

Field 7: Clothing and Accessories

Area 1: Special Attire

Your Task

Study the fourteen mini-biographies below, all but one of which contain false friends from the field of special attire, and then consider the statements beneath.

Biographies

1. Belinda liebte es, ein Brillant-Bouton am Ohr zu haben
2. Bergsteiger Bernd ging nur im blauen Blouson ins Gebirge.
3. Carolas Cut konnte die Aufmerksamkeit der Kerle gewinnen.
4. „Dribbelkönig" Daniel trug Fußballdress wie Deisler.
5. Die partygeile Gerlinde warf sich gerne in Gala.
6. Gabriele gefiel die aufsehenerregende Gaze an ihrem Gucci-Kleid.
7. Hausmeister Henry hatte die Hosen an im Heim.
8. Mackie Messer erschien nur in einen Mantel vermummt.
9. Miriam war noch im Morgenmantel, ihr Michael im Morgenrock.
10. Unter seinem Plüschpulli hatte Patrick noch einen Pullunder an.
11. Fast sämtliche Studis trugen den gestreiften College-Schal.
12. In seinem samtweichen Smoking sah Sam beinahe sinatrahaft aus.
13. Die vier Vettern aus Fritham kamen alle in Frack und Zylinder.
14. Als versierter Weinkellner trug Wiktor die obligate Weste.

Statements

In the light of the above, which of the following statements are true? The answers are to be found on page 118.

1. The students all wore <u>shawls</u>.
2. Gertrud liked the <u>gaze</u>.
3. Patrick had a <u>pulley</u> and a <u>pullunder</u>.
4. The four cousins all wore <u>frocks</u> and <u>cylinders</u>.
5. Wiktor wore a <u>vest</u> when serving wine.
6. Michael was wearing <u>morning-dress</u>, Miriam a <u>morning-coat</u>.
7. Carola attracted glances for the <u>cut</u> of her clothes.
8. Sam and Sinatra had one thing in common: <u>smoking</u>.
9. Young Daniel enjoyed wearing a <u>dress</u>.
10. Mac the Knife wrapped himself in a <u>mantle</u>.
11. Henry wore <u>hose</u>.
12. Gerlinde threw herself into the <u>gala</u>.
13. Belinda wore a <u>button</u> in her ear.
14. Bernd always dressed in a blue <u>blouson jacket</u>.

Man muß eben nicht nur ein Lexikon, man muß auch Fingerspitzen haben. Die meisten haben nicht einmal ein Lexikon.

KURT TUCHOLSKY, ‚Der Übersetzer' (1927)

Area 2: Fashion and Accessories

Your Task

Read the passage below, paying especial attention to the twenty-one words underlined, seventeen of which are false friends from the field of fashion and accessories. Then consider the statements beneath.

Text

In der Konfektionsabteilung konnte man fast alles kaufen, vom Slipper bis zum Slip, vom T-Shirt bis zum Tweedanzug, vom Blazer bis zur Brosche, vom Kostüm bis zum Kimono.

Auch die Kundschaft war entsprechend buntscheckig.

Aufgedonnerte Damen mit einer Vorliebe für Ohrringe, Colliers, Armbänder und allerlei Klunker erkundigten sich aufgeregt nach den neuesten Moden und Mustern.

Ein distinguierter Herr hielt nach einer neuen Fliege Ausschau, seine seidene Krawatte und aparte Brieftasche zeugten von seiner Kaufkraft.

Ein selbstbewußtes Mädchen zog einen gescheckten Pullover über und schaute sich lange im Spiegel an, bald mit Gürtel, bald ohne.

Und ein Student in mehrfach geflickten Jeans zog schüchtern seinen juckenden, fleckigen, mit Buttons geschmückten Pulli aus, um auch mal den Reiz des Modischen zu probieren.

Statements

In the light of the above passage, which of the following statements are definitely true? The correct answers are to be found on page 119.

1. The gentleman was wearing a silk cravat.
2. Slippers were on sale.
3. The student's sweater had buttons on it.
4. The gentleman had a briefcase with him.
5. You could buy almost anything in the confectionery department.
6. Among the garments on sale were T-shirts.
7. Blazers were equally available, as were costumes.
8. The girl was trying on a checked pullover.
9. The women had a liking for earrings.
10. And they were fond of colliers too.
11. The student's pullover was yucky.
12. The girl, surprisingly, tried on a girdle.
13. You could buy slips in the department.
14. The women were wearing arm-bands.
15. They liked musters.
16. Brooches could be bought.
17. The student had often flicked his jeans.
18. His sweater was flecked.
19. The women were interested in modes.
20. The gentleman needed a new fly.

Field 8: Human Nature and Characteristics

Area 1: Basic Character

Your Task

Study the ten quotations below, paying especial attention to the key words of character underlined. Suggest translations for them and then translate also their false friends, listed below. Correct answers are to be found on page 120.

Quotations

1. Genie ist das säkulare Wort für Apostel und umgekehrt.
GOTTFRIED EDEL

2. Mut: Abfallprodukt der Angst. RUDOLF ROLFS

3. Die Gelassenheit ist eine anmutige Form des Selbstbewußtseins.
MARIE V. EBNER-ESCHENBACH

4. Man muß nicht jedem Spleen der Globalisierer folgen.
WOLFGANG ROSE

5. Sympathie ist eine Allegorie der Seele. OTTO MICHEL

6. Trost und Rat sind, unter anderem, auch eine Maske der Distanz.
LUDWIG MARCUSE

7. Die Lust am Schönen, am Rührenden, am Erhabenen stärkt unsere moralischen Gefühle. FRIEDRICH V. SCHILLER

8. Vorsicht ist die Einstellung, die das Leben sicher macht, aber selten glücklich. SAMUEL JOHNSON

9. Ich finde seine kulturelle Vergangenheit vor allem in seinen literarischen Vorlieben und in seinem Faible für Malerei.
ANNE-SOPHIE MUTTER über André Previn

10. Genialität ist persönliches Erlebnis der Welt, Talent Widerspiegelung der Welt. HANS LOHBERGER

False Friends

genie – foible – geniality – lust – mood – self-consciousness – spleen – sympathy – trust – foresight

Fremdwörter haben fast immer etwas Gesteigertes. Nun wir reden noch davon.

LOUIS FONTANE, zitiert in: Theodor Fontane, *Meine Kinderjahre* (1894)

Area 2: Essential Characteristics

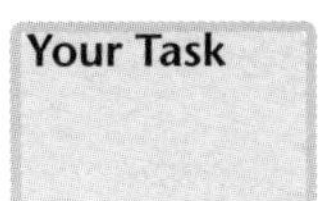

Complete the crossword below, which is made up of twenty-three of the essential false friends from the field of human character. Then turn to the further questions in the second part beneath. Correct answers are to be found on page 121.

Crossword

1.
2.
3.
4.
5.
6.
7.
8.
9.
10.
11.
12.
13.
14.
15.
16.
17.
18.
19.
20.
21.
22.
23.

Key Phrase: 'I have a dream that my four little children will one day live in a nation where they will be judged not by the colour of their skin but by the … (7,2,5,9)'
Martin Luther King

1. plump 2. lustig 3. adrett 4. kleinlich 5. streng 6. eitel 7. heftig 8. kühn 9. genial 10. faul 11. rüstig 12. famos 13. rasch 14. brüsk 15. glücklich 16. brav 17. groß 18. skrupellos 19. sauber 20. graziös 21. keusch 22. schmal 23. exaltiert

Your Task

State the meaning of the words below, which are the incorrect – false friend – answers to the questions above.

False Friends

adroit – brave – brisk – cleanly – coy – exalted – famous – foul – genial – gracious – gross – hefty – idle – keen – lucky – lusty – plump – rash – rusty – scrupulous – small – sober – strong

Area 3: Positive Characteristics

Your Task

Read the 'lonely hearts' ad below, paying especial attention to the many epithets of character, and then consider the statements beneath.

Text

Ein Mann, dessen Name und Herkunft für sich sprechen, Dr. Jur., int. tätig, Ende 50/186
ein mehr als gutauss., attraktiver, männlicher Typ mit Wohnsitz Zürich (Traumvilla am See, Yacht) und London, eine prominente Persönlichkeit aus einer der führenden Unternehmerdynastien unserer Zeit, beruflich voll engagiert und erfolgreich, mehr als gutsituiert, ein „Gewinner" eben, und dennoch integer, humanistisch geprägt und sensitiv, ein romantischer Realist, ein durch und durch sympathischer, sinnlicher, kultivierter, musisch interessierter Weltmann mit Phantasie und Kreativität, mit Stil, Niveau und apartem Geschmack, charmant und mit gewinnendem Lachen, hat sich fest vorgenommen, dieses Jahr seine Traumfrau zu finden. Er sucht eine temperamentvolle, sprühende, schlanke, feminin-verführerische, mutig-initiative SIE (bis 35) mit selbstbewußtem, souveränem Auftreten, eine adäquate junge Firstlady mit Background, die in Jeans und Abendkleid gleichermaßen parkettsicher ist, gewohnt zu repräsentieren, open-minded, sensibel, mit Sinn für alles, was das gute Leben ausmacht, vom Reisen, Reiten und Geselligsein über den sinnlichen Genuß (Kaninchen in Balsamico) bis zur Liebe zu den „sonnigen Gefilden". Fühlen Sie sich angesprochen? Dann sollten Sie nicht zögern! Rufen Sie an bei
Cordula Pommel-Pfühl GmbH
Argentinien-Haus, Am Fleet, Hamburg

Statements

In the light of the above passage, which of the following statements are definitely true? The correct answers are to be found on page 122.

1. He is integrated.
2. She must be temperamental and moody.
3. He has musical interests, his taste being a thing apart.
4. She should be able to represent and should be initiative in person.
5. He is a man of fantasy.
6. She needs to be self-conscious and sensible.
7. He is sensitive, cultivated and humanist in his orientation.
8. She must be adequate.
9. He is sympathetic.
10. She should be the feminine type.
11. He is well-situated and engaged.
12. She should be sovereign.
13. He is the manly type.
14. She should combine 'bubbliness' with background.

Area 4: Problematic Characteristics

Your Task

Study the sixteen mini-biographies below, all but two of which involve false friends from the field of human character, and then consider the statements beneath.

Biographies

Der amusische Andy hatte keine Ahnung von Arien und Arpeggios
Das Benehmen von Bodo war des öfteren bäurisch
Die cholerische Christina kanzelte ihre Kunden ab
Der feiste Franz erzählte vorwiegend frivole Geschichten

Grimmig griff der aggressive Gregor seine Gegner an
Der lethargische Leo war der allergrößte Lahmarsch
Lulu war ein launisches Luder: bald Lamento, bald Lebenslust
Otto erzählte ostentativ ordinäre Witze über seine Mitoffiziere

Shlomo war kein Schlemihl, sondern ein Schuft und ein Schurke
Der etwas schrille Sascha erzählte skurrile Storys
Stephan schuftete stur an den stupiden Steuererklärungen
Die süffisante Susanne sagte, sie sei schon im sicheren Hafen

Unsympathisch wie er war, unterstrich Urs unsere „Unfähigkeit"
Die unverschämte Ulla unterstellte uns Untreue und Unzucht
Nach den Wochen in der Wüste wirkte Verena völlig verwildert
Wolfram entpuppte sich als Windbeutel mit wildem Lebenswandel

Statements

In the light of the above mini-biographies, which of the following statements are true? The answers are to be found on page 123.

1. Shlomo was a <u>shirker</u>.
2. Franz was the <u>frivolous</u> type.
3. Bodo's basic behaviour was downright <u>boorish</u>.
4. Stephan's work was simply <u>stupid</u>.
5. Aggressive Gregor was a <u>grimy</u> figure.
6. Lackadaisical Leo was <u>lethargic</u>.
7. Wild-living Wolfram was a <u>windbag</u>.
8. Ostentatious Otto was an <u>ordinary</u> officer.
9. Ulla was <u>unashamed</u>.
10. Sascha's stories were <u>scurrilous</u>.
11. Verena became <u>bewildered</u>.
12. Andy was <u>amusing</u>.
13. Loose-living Lulu was rather <u>loony</u>.
14. Urs was <u>unsympathetic</u> in underscoring our inability.
15. Susanne spoke <u>sufficient</u>.
16. Christina was <u>choleric</u>.

Area 5: The Kaleidoscope of Character

Your Task

The fifteen word-pairs below are all further false friends from the world of human character. Distinguish between the pairs by matching each word on the left with the person on the right most associated with it. The correct answers are to be found on page 124.

Word Pairs

A. artig		1. a long-legged lass or lad
B. arty		2. a pious and prayerful priest
	C. devot	3. a highly humane humanist
	D. devout	4. a benevolent old benefactor
E. feist		5. a well-behaved child
F. feisty		6. a normal 'nerd'
	G. fröhlich	7. a submissive servant
	H. frolicsome	8. a genteel, well-bred gentleman
I. gelenkig		9. a smelly stinker, madly malodorous
J. lanky		10. a person of artistic pretensions
	K. gentil	11. a semi-official representative
	L. gentile	12. a lord never late for launch or lunch
M. human		13. a formidable fighter for a cause
N. human		14. a slender slimmer
	O. kindlich	15. a suave and civil city-dweller
	P. kindly	16. fat and greasy citizens
Q. mondän		17. a gloriously gifted guitarist
R. mundane		18. capering, cavorting children
	S. offiziös	19. a small, insubstantial soul
	T. officious	20. a happy inhabitant of this earth
U. pünktlich		21. a person not of Jewish blood
V. punctilious		22. a moral man, a person of probity
	W. rank	23. an agile athlete
	X. rank	24. a high society socialite
Y. schlicht		25. a child-like creature
Z. slight		26. an over-zealous officer or official
	AA. urban	27. a town-bred townie
	BB. urban	28. a drudge addicted to detail
CC. virtuos		29. a humble hermit, sat in a simple cell
DD. virtuous		30. fallible folk full of faults and failings

Area 6: Character Mix

Distinguish between the following pairs of ill-translated sentences, each of which contains one or more pairs of false friends – but also the occasional 'true friend' – from the realm of human characteristics.

Your Task

Sentences

1. a) Er war ausgesprochen rüde
   *b) He was outspokenly rude.

2. a) Der deftige Humor des Dozenten belebte das Seminar.
   *b) The lecturer's deft humour enlivened the seminar.

3. a) Sie war häufig blau, wobei sie apathisch, phlegmatisch wirkte.
   *b) She was often blue, seeming apathetic and phlegmatic.

4. a) Der Lehrer hatte offensichtlich einen Knacks. Was für eine Art, mit Schülern umzugehen! Und so penetrant!
   *b) The teacher clearly had the knack. What a way of dealing with schoolchildren! And so penetrating.

5. a) Ja, sein Vater war einst ein sehr akkurater Handwerker gewesen. Nunmehr war er tatterig, ein Tattergreis.
   *b) Yes, his father had once been an very accurate craftsman. Now he had become tatty, a tatty old man.

6. a) Man nahm sich vor ihm in acht. Er war eher der kräftige Typ.
   * b) People took care in dealing with him: he was rather a crafty type.

7. a) Ihre Mutter war erschreckend proper in allem.
   *b) Her mother was terribly prim and proper about everything.

8. a) Die geborene Forscherin war sie nicht: selten konzentriert, häufig desinteressiert.
   *b) She was not the born researcher: rarely concentrated, often disinterested.

9. a) Das herzige Kind wird später gutherzig.
   *b) The hearty child becomes in later life good-hearted.

10. a) Viele meinten, er hätte für seine Galanterie eine Medaille gewinnen sollen.
    *b) Many said he should have won a medal for gallantry.

11. a) Ja, der Filmtitel stimmte: Deutschland war eine bleiche Mutter.
    *b) Yes, the film title was correct: Germany was a bleak mother.

Field 9: Inter-Human Relationships

Area 1: Human Interaction

Your Task

The twenty-four pairs of words below all derive from the field of human interaction and human assessment, only two of them, however, being genuine equivalents. Find the true friends and then distinguish between the false. The correct answers are to be found on page 125.

Word Pairs

sich arrangieren
to arrange oneself

das As
the ass

belügen
to belie

der 'Bonze'
the bonze

der Bubi
the booby

der Crack
the crack

der Depp
the dep.

der Flirt
the flirt

der Gaffer
the gaffer

herzen
to hearten

herumpoppen
to pop around

die Koryphäe
the coryphaeus

das Kraut
the kraut

die Mätresse
the mistress

nagen
to nag

necken
to neck

die Nutte
the nutter

der Pimpf
the pimp

der Puff
the pouf

eine Runde schlafen
to sleep around

der/die Senior(in)
the senior

der Spanner
the spanner

der Strohwitwer
the grass widower

wanken
to wank

Heute ziehen wir wörtliche Übersetzungen vor; tatsächlich akzeptieren viele von uns nur wörtliche Übersetzungen, weil wir jedem gerecht werden wollen. Den Übersetzern vergangener Zeiten wäre das als Verbrechen *erschienen.*

JORGE LUIS BORGES, *Das Handwerk des Dichters.* München 2000

Area 2: Relating to Relations

Read the letter below, paying especial attention to the key terms concerning relatives and relationships, twenty of which are false friends. Then consider the statements beneath.

Your Task

Text

Liebe Sanni,

endlich! Endlich ist diese Hochzeit vorüber! Sei froh, daß Du nicht dabei warst. Schauderhaft! Der Tag war fast eine einzige Blamage. Nicht wegen dem Kirchenritual oder dem Essen – beide waren sogar auf hohem Niveau –, sondern aus familiären Gründen.

Da war zunächst die eingebildete Base mit ihren Allüren. Sie hielt einige Gäste offensichtlich für Bagage (ihr Wort!). Ihre hochnäsige Art und ihr Spott waren unausstehlich.

Dann mußte natürlich der kahlköpfige, für Fauxpas und ewiggestrige Gesinnung geradezu berüchtigte Pate da sein. Mit seinen Tratsch-Einlagen und Indiskretionen hat er etliche Gäste verletzt. Björns toll aussehende neue Freundin aus Kamerun nannte er sogar ‚Bimbo'!!!

Und dann: Der eine Onkel war scharf auf die Brautjungfern. Der Schwiegervater – unsensibel, wie er oft ist – widmete sich mehr seiner hübschen Nichte als seiner Frau. Der greise Großvater versuchte, die Braut zu ‚beraten' bzw. belabern. Unsere lieben Eltern schwindelten wie immer, was das Zeug hält. Peinlich! Und die arme Kerstin, unsere kesse Braut, wurde von ihren jungen Vettern umschwärmt, sie konnte sich kaum von ihnen losmachen. Kurz: Es hat sich fast jede(r) blamiert.

Kerstin blieb allerdings ein Trost: Sie hat gut gewählt, ihr Zukünftiger ist eine gute Partie. Sie hat vielleicht doch den besten Mann geheiratet!

Wenn es nur Hochzeiten ohne Hochzeitsgäste geben könnte …

Deine familiengeschädigte Dagmar

Statements

In the light of the above passage, which of the following statements are definitely true? The correct answers are to be found on page 127.

1. The day failed for <u>familiar</u> reasons, leading to much <u>blame</u>.
2. The aunt had <u>allure</u>, despite her unbearable <u>spot</u>.
3. The godfather was renowned for his <u>faux pas</u> and <u>indiscretions</u>.
4. The parents <u>swindled</u>, which was <u>painful</u>.
5. The granddad tried to <u>berate</u> or <u>belabour</u> the bride.
6. She, in turn, could hardly free herself from her <u>fetters</u>.
7. The aunt, really <u>base</u>, thought some guests were <u>baggages</u>.
8. The godfather spoke <u>trash</u>, calling Björn's girlfriend a '<u>bimbo</u>'.
9. The father-in-law was often <u>insensible</u>.
10. One guest had a bald <u>pate</u>.
11. One uncle was <u>sharp</u> on the bridesmaids.
12. Everyone <u>blamed</u> himself or herself.
13. But after all, Kerstin married the <u>best man</u> – a good <u>party</u>.

Field 10: House, Home and Hearth

Area 1: Domestic Architecture

Your Task

Read the passage below, paying especial attention to the twenty-five words underlined, all but six of which are false friends from the field of domestic architecture. Then consider the statements beneath.

Text

Old houses are not older than their old families but their oldness is more present. They are living mausoleums with all the plunder, all the bric-à-brac of the centuries. You know the type of house – its rooftops all high gables and mansards. Its walls all orioles, balustrades and balconies. Down in the hall dark-stained wood-panelling, in the living rooms thick tapestries, in the studies bureaux, on the floors leading to the estate office ancient majolica tiling. Upstairs now to the oaken landing, to the bedrooms with their Victorian closets, in some forgotten corner an ancient commode. Up further to the attic, full of chests and chests of drawers, book-shelves and broken stools. Then down the echoing back stairway to the cellar, all musty, with an out-used oven, a battered wash-stand, a rolled-up marquee. On the veranda with its tattered canopy the air is fresher. Let's go into the garden, walk to the bower. Oh yes, a magnificent house in a magnificent area, a superb locale. But, like all mausoleums, stifling.

Statements

In the light of the above passage, which of the following statements are definitely true? The correct answers are to be found on page 128.

1. Das Haus mit seinem wunderbaren Areal wäre ein schönes Lokal.
2. Auf der Veranda steht ein zerfetztes Kanapee.
3. Das Dach ist gabelförmig angelegt mit mehreren Mansarden.
4. Die große Halle hat Holzpanelen, das Wohnzimmer dicke Tapeten.
5. Im Garten befindet sich ein Vogelbauer.
6. Im Keller stehen ein alter Ofen, ein Wäscheständer, eine Markise.
7. Der Flur, der zur Office führt, ist mit Majolikafliesen ausgelegt.
8. Die Arbeitszimmer dienten als Büros.
9. An den Außenwänden gibt es Balkone und Balustraden.
10. Die Schlafzimmer haben ein eigenes Klosett und Kommoden
11. Nach oben führt ein Geländer aus Eiche, auf dem Dachboden stehen alte Stühle.
12. Ja, ein altes Haus ist ein Mausoleum voller Plunder.

Die Interferenz stellt sich im Überschneidungsbereich von Identitäten und Differenzen ein.

PETER SCHIFKO, ‚Morphologische Interferenzen im Bereich des fachsprachlichen Wortschatzes', (1992)

Area 2: The Household

Your Task

This exercise contains fifteen pairs of false friends from the world of the household. Discover them by translating the sentences below, as in the example. Correct answers are to be found on page 129.

Sentences

Eine scheußliche Wohnung: höllisch **laut** und mit penetranter Tapete.
A ghastly flat – hellishly noisy and with **loud** *wallpaper.*

1. Seine Eifersucht malte aus, was hinter den Jalousien passierte.

2. Im Gartenschuppen stand allerlei Gerät: Spaten, Rechen, Besen, Hacken, ein Reisigbesen für Herbstlaub, Scheren, Gartenscheren, ein Rasenmäher.

3. Der Spiegelsaal, die illustren Gäste, die vielen Lüster – alles verlieh dem Ballabend einen eigenen Glanz.

4. Auch die mit Efeu bedeckte Mauer war mit Wimpeln geschmückt.

5. Es war ein fast verwaistes Viertel: Trümmergrundstücke, abgerissene Häuser, Industriebrachen, eine demolierte Tankstelle.

6. Die Stövchen lagen unter den Tisch- und Geschirrtüchern in der Schublade am Herd.

7. Nur mit einem Zauberstab waren solche Wände und Mauern zu überwinden.

8. Was immer man suchte, es befand sich im einzigen Küchenschrank: Dosen und Büchsen, Tabletts und Tabletten, die Kaffeekanne …

9. Im Salon benimmt man sich doch nicht wie in einer Bar im amerikanischen Westen!

10. Die Wohnung war voll klimatisiert. Trotzdem dauerte es Tage, bis sie sich an die Hitze des amerikanischen Südens gewöhnt hatten.

11. In einem Zimmer des lange unbewohnten Trakts fand man etliche Papiere, Predigten, erbauliche Traktate, Gelegenheitslyrik.

12. Das Postamt befand sich in einem kleinen, schnuckeligen Tante-Emma-Laden, in dessen Rundfenstern vergilbte Stores hingen.

Field 11: The Built Environment

Area 1: Cities

Your Task

In each of the sentences below, the sense is disturbed by at least one grave misuse of word concerning cities. Replace the offending terms by correct alternatives. The answers are to be found on page 130.

Sentences

*1. Jenners, with its ornate frontage, is the best-known warehouse on Princes Street, Edinburgh's main shopping thoroughfare.
*2. London is not criss-crossed by wide alleys such as Haussmann created in nineteenth-century Paris.
*3. Meadowhall on the outskirts of Sheffield is said to be Britain's most-frequented shopping passage.
*4. The magnificent, many-towered City Chambers on George Square – superb Victorian architecture – are Glasgow's council house.
*5. The many courts and cloister-like quadrangles which make up the Cambridge colleges are known for their fountains, lawns and plaster.
*6. The pilgrims in Chaucer's *Canterbury Tales* set out from the Tabard guest-house in Southwark, a hostelry on London's south bank.
*7. St. Paul's dome, with its famous cupola, took so long to build that the saying emerged 'as slow as a St. Paul's workman'.
*8. Few British towns have a more attractive city than Norwich, with its narrow lanes, tiny shops and carefully sanitized houses.
*9. Unlike Germany with its heritage of *Kleinstaaterei*, Britain does not have many towns of residence.
*10. Beneath the London Embankment lies not only the underground railway but also the famous canalization built by Joseph Bazalgette, the great drainage engineer, from 1855 to 1865.
*11. No British city is as famous for its messes and exhibition halls as are Hanover or Leipzig.
*12. British seaside towns such as Blackpool or Ramsgate used to be full of little pubs and pensions, hotels and hostels.
*13. The three new towns of Edinburgh are renowned for their crescents, gardens, places and mews.
*14. Norman fortifications develop from mere castles, as at Gloucester or Portchester, to complex designs with bastions and baileys, walls and warts, parapets and palaces, as at Beaumaris.

Der Übersetzer befindet sich ständig zwischen zwei Polen, die man als assimilatorischen und distanzhaltenden Umgang mit dem zu übersetzenden Text bezeichnen kann.

WOLFRAM WILSS, ‚Zur Praxisrelevanz der Übersetzungswissenschaft' (1991)

Area 2: Downtown

Your Task

Study the sixteen mini-biographies below, all but one of which contain false friends from the field of life downtown, and then consider the statements beneath.

Biographies

Barry's battalion – bless 'em – was better in the barracks than in battle
Bluett's bungalow was still blighted from the blitz
Bob and Beth met over beef-burgers at the bus-station
Chris and Cath could always be found in the caff

Emma could not ever resist the excitement of an excellent emporium
Goofy Gus fell down the gully. He was a goner. Oh golly!
Hal's Honda caused a horrible hullabaloo all along the High Street
Carping Kitty couldn't get on with her colleagues in the kitchen

Laddish Lawrence liked meeting all the likely lads at the local
Lew liked life especially when it meant that lovely local lager
Mirabel and Matthew met at Mensa – a meeting of minds
Sanguine blacksmith Sam always went smilingly to the smithy

Sceptical superintendent Sue said the stadium was still not safe
Samantha always settled for a seat in the stalls
Ted and Tina took the utmost trouble to avoid the toll-house
Thomas the town-crier took up position outside the town hall

Statements

In the light of the above mini-biographies, which of the following statements are true? The answers are to be found on page 131.

1. Lawrence traf seine Kumpel im Lokal.
2. Hal verursachte viel Lärm auf der Hochstraße.
3. Emma war gerne auf der Empore.
4. Mirabel und Matthew lernten sich in der Mensa kennen.
5. Ein sicheres Stadium war es laut Sue nicht.
6. Samantha saß gerne im Stall.
7. Barry und Kohorten wohnten in Baracken.
8. Gus starb tragisch bei einem Sturz ins Gully.
9. Kitty kam mit den Insassen im Kittchen nicht klar.
10. Bluetts Bungalow war vom Blitz beschädigt worden.
11. Sam arbeitete gerne in seiner Schmiede.
12. Bob und Beth trafen sich an der Busstation.
13. Tom nahm vor der Stadthalle Stellung.
14. Lew gefiel das Lagerleben.
15. Ins Tollhaus wollten Ted und Tina nicht.
16. Chris und Cath waren immer im Kaff.

Field 12: The Media and Communications

Area 1: On the Air

Your Task

The nine word-pairs below are all false friends from the world of broadcasting, film and communications. Distinguish between the pairs by matching each word on the left with its definition on the right. The correct answers are to be found on page 132.

Word Pairs

A. die Antenne
B. the antenna

C. das Fernsehspiel
D. the screenplay

E. der Gaffer
F. the gaffer

G. das Handy
H. the handy

I. der/die Moderator(in)
J. the Moderator

K. das Erste Programm
L. the first programme

M. der Recorder
N. the recorder

O. der Sender
P. the sender

Q. der Spot
R. the spot

1. Channel One
2. the cassette recorder
3. the gawper, gaper
4. the broadcaster, transmitter
5. the first broadcast
6. the TV drama
7. the dispatcher (of a letter/parcel)
8. the woodwind instrument
9. the easily available
10. the speck, stain, eruptive mark
11. the aerial
12. the mobile, mobile phone, cell phone
13. the film text
14. the Head of the Church of Scotland
15. the lighting expert on a film set
16. the sensory organ of an insect; temporary outside aerial
17. the presenter
18. the commercial, ad; party political broadcast

> *Solche Sprachen mit gemischtem Wörtervorrath theilen sich wieder in verschiedene Classen, je nachdem die eingedrungenen Wörter entweder ihre fremde Natur mehr geltend machen, oder sich mehr der einheimischen angestalten.*

Wilhelm v. Humboldt, *Ueber die Verschiedenheiten des menschlichen Sprachbaues*, (1827–29)

Area 2: Communication

Your Task

Fill in the gaps in the sentences below, choosing the appropriate word from the list beneath. Of the words in brackets only two have 'true friends' in English. Correct answers are to be found on page 132.

Sentences

1. He *('Schiss kriegen')* _____ and simply ran away.
2. The report was swiftly *(dementiert)* _____ by the government.
3. At last they both had time, time for a good meal together, time for a good glass of wine, time to *(parlieren)* _____.
4. Desperately the ship tried to *(funken)* _____ the coastguards, and then to *(funken)* _____ an SOS.
5. The shocking thing was that the elected representatives had no real opportunity to *(debattieren)* _____ the issue.
6. Their reaction seemed crazed, *(wahnsinnig)* _____.
7. Her uncle *(zuzwinkern)* _____ at her. No, he was not serious.
8. In view of the political situation, it was decided not to *(senden)* _____ the contentious programme just then.
9. The Red Indian chiefs met to *(verhandeln)* _____ over the proverbial pipe of peace.
10. The broadcasting network quickly *(schicken)* _____ two reporters.
11. Their job was to *(sondieren)* _____ the mood of the populace.
12. The parents *(winken)* _____ until the train had disappeared into the far distance and the rain.

Options

to broadcast – demented – denied – to debate – to despatch – to funk – to parley – to send out – to sound out – to talk – to wave – to wink – to wire

Area 3: The Press

Your Task

The ten pairs of words below all derive from the field of the press and printing, only three of them, however, being genuine equivalents. Find the true friends and then distinguish between the false. The correct answers are to be found on page 133.

Word Pairs

das Comic – the comic
das Exemplar – the example
das Feature – the feature
das Impressum – the impression
die (Gast)Kolumne – the (guest) column
die Karikatur – the caricature
der Leitartikel – the leading article
das Magazin – the magazine
die Rezension – the recension
die Rubrik – the rubric

Translation Theory II: How do False Friends Emerge?

Mythologically speaking, 'false friends' are a product of the confusion of languages after Babel. Linguistically speaking, they are a product of borrowing and meaning shift. Sociologically speaking, they are a product of the great migrations of ideas and of people that have marked the world since the Renaissance, perhaps most notably in our own post-war and postmodern ages.

After Babel

If there ever was 'one world and one language', then 'false friends' are among the more eloquent tokens that this is no longer so. Lexical items such as 'barracks', 'band' or 'armature' can have among the European languages eight, ten or even fifteen distinct meanings (Hill, 1981).

Germane, not the Same

The English and German vocabularies often have a common root in early stages of language such as OFris, OHG, MLG or MHG and have both been markedly influenced by Latin and French. They are thus germane, related, languages – and as language students we have many reasons to be grateful for this. But from a common root very different branches can grow, and the same Latin or French item can be influential in many different ways. What is germane is by no means always the same.

From the Same Root

Examples of differing English and German items emerging from the same root are word-pairs such as 'beam'/*Baum* or 'Weald'/*Wald*. In each case the current meanings are far enough apart to cause little confusion, but the same cannot always be said of 'wall'/*Wall*, 'moor'/*Moor*, 'crank'/*krank*, 'ordeal'/*Urteil* or 'lust'/*Lust* and numerous others.

Calques from Latin/ Greek

Lexically and grammatically, English and German both owe much to Latin. But one has only to think of terms such as 'Mensa'/*Mensa* or 'primus'/*Primus* to see how different the end-result can be. Even such basic shared Latin roots as *'castellum'* or *'vallum'* can lead to such varying offshoots as 'castle'/*Kastell* or 'wall'/*Wall*. The same can, of course, hold true for words of Greek root such as the renowned 'gymnasium'/*Gymnasium*.

Calques from French

A similar process has operated with French. Take a classic case such as Fr. *parole*. Long before its modern meaning in Saussurean linguistics, it took on from *c.* 1616 in English the sense of 'word of honour', with 'to obtain parole' coming in by 1667 and the modern legal 'parole system' being established in the United States in 1876. The sense of 'password' existed briefly from 1777–1844, but never had the political sense of the German *Parole*. Parallel developments can be traced with terms as various as Fr. *billet, cravate, engagement, gratiner, nougat, parquet, polytechnique, rente* and countless more.

More surprising, and for some more deceptive, are the many calques in modern German from English or American – terms such as *City*, *Flipper* or *Oldtimer* – which are again distinct from their originals.

Anglicisms

But the peregrinations of language in the postmodern age do not stop there. Yet more surprising, even bizarre, is the array of pseudo-anglicisms which modern German also boasts: words such as *Chesterkäse, Dressman, Showmaster* or *Twen*, which never have existed in English or American. Only for the last does the *OED* have an entry – but then exclusively in the long extinct meanings of 'twain' and 'of tow'.

Pseudo-Anglicisms

There are fewer examples of such borrowings into English from German. But terms such as 'b/Blitz', *'lieder'*, and 'strafe' reveal the same process working in the reverse direction.

Germanisms

Such word-pairs are often fascinating windows onto social developments – as the 'language lineage' boxes below hope to demonstrate.

Windows

In the case of the many partial 'false friends', the potential confusion derives not only from the above processes but from polysemy or multiple meaning: whereas the word-pair may share one sense, one or both of them may have other senses which are not shared. Representative examples here would be 'fusion'/*Fusion*, 'tariff'/*Tarif*, 'smelt'/*(ein)schmelzen*.

Polysemy

A further possibility, perhaps the logical conclusion of the meaning-movements detailed above, is that a once 'false friend' can in the course of time become 'true'. The more often a word is (mis)-used in its 'false' sense, the more likely that sense is to establish itself. The word 'hopefully' has shifted over the last thirty years – probably under the influence of German-speakers emigrating to the United States – to take on the sense of *hoffentlich*, which it did not formerly have. In a similar way, 'oversight' is assuming in AmE the sense of *Übersicht* and the words 'slip' and 'sympathetic' are also shifting in the German/French direction.

From False to True

It is essential, however, not to let these last developments seduce one into a false sense of security or a mood of 'anything goes'. It is true that in the postmodern world of multiple varieties of English more 'goes' than ever before. But there is still the bath-water and there are still the many delicate babies of meaning.

Caveat

Field 13: The World of Work

Area 1: Essential Professions

Your Task

Complete the crossword below, which is made up of fifteen false friends (and three true) from the field of professions. Then turn to the further questions in the second part beneath. Correct answers are to be found on page 133.

Crossword

1.
2.
3.
4.
5.
6.
7.
8.
9.
10.
11.
12.
13.
14.
15.
16.
17.
18.

Key Phrase: 'Without work, all life goes rotten, but when work is soulless, (4,7,3,4)'
Albert Camus

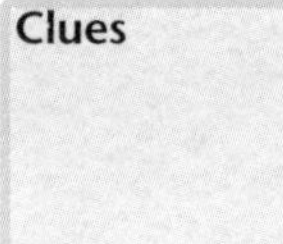

Clues

1. Personalchef 2. (Auto)Mechaniker 3. Personalarzt 4. Kompagnon 5. Physiker 6. Administrator 7. Controller 8. Finanzier 9. Grossist 10. Kontrolleur 11. Kommissionär 12. Laborant 13. Unternehmer 14. Produzent 15. Dekorateur 16. Konstrukteur 17. Hausmeister 18. Chef

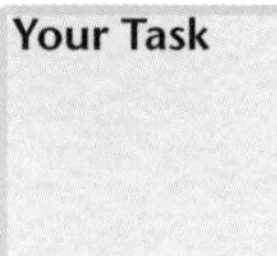

Your Task

State the meaning of the words below, which are the incorrect – false friend – answers to the questions above.

administrator – chef – commissionaire – companion – constructor – controller – decorator – grocer – house-master – labourer – personal chef – personal doctor – physician – undertaker

Semantically speaking the problem is caused by polysemy. One of the meanings of these words, but not all, can be translated by a formally corresponding TL-word.

PAUL KUßMAUL, *Training the Translator*. Amsterdam, 1995

Area 2: Puzzling Professions

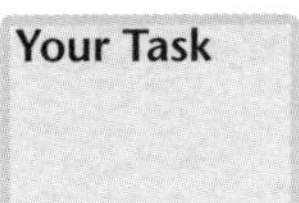

The twelve word-pairs below are all false friends from the world of jobs and professions. Distinguish between the pairs by matching each word on the left with its definition on the right. The correct answers are to be found on page 134.

Word Pairs

A. Akquisiteur
B. acquisitor

C. Aktuar
D. actuary

E. Börsianer
F. bursar

G. Dealer
H. dealer

I. Expedient
J. expedient

K. Hausmann
L. houseman

M. Knacker
N. knacker

O. Malermeister
P. master painter

Q. Pikkolo
R. piccolo

S. Prokurist
T. procurator

U. Propagandist
V. propagandist

W. Volontär
X. volunteer

1. junior/assistant doctor in hospital
2. treasurer, esp. of a college
3. stock-jobber, Stock Market player
4. one who voluntarily offers his services
5. person who disseminates propaganda
6. skilful, talented painter
7. buyer, purchaser
8. clerk of court, registrar
9. expert on insurance risks
10. trader in goods
11. small flute
12. drug peddler
13. trainee journalist
14. commercial traveller, representative
15. representative of a firm
16. chief clerk, confidential clerk
17. miser, skinflint; 'old fogey'
18. a contrivance, device
19. husband who does the housework
20. buyer and slaughterer of old horses
21. agent, proxy with power of attorney
22. house painter
23. apprentice waiter
24. forwarding clerk

Area 3: Office Work

Your Task

Fill in the gaps in the sentences below, choosing the appropriate word from the list beneath. Of the words in brackets only two have 'true friends' in English. Correct answers are to be found on page 135.

Sentences

1. 'Oh, no! I simply can't *(tippen)* _____ this morning! That's the fourth time I've hit the wrong *(Taste)* _____ in as many minutes! Thank goodness for the *(Del-Taste)* _____!'
2. 'Hey, Doris, could you take this *(Stapel)* _____ of incoming *(Formulare)* _____ to room 218 please?'
3. 'We must order more *(Heftklammern)* _____, more self-adhesive *(Kuverts)* _____, a few *(Minen)* _____for biros and, above all, more paper for the *(Fotokopierer)* _____ and laser printer.'
4. 'Phone the printer to say that our *(Prospekt)* _____ must at all costs be ready by 1 May. If there is no *(Aussicht)* _____ that he can have it done by then, then we'll have to give the job to somebody else.'
5. 'You're going in the *(Richtung)* _____ of the *(Expedition)* _____, aren't you Doris? Could you please show them this *(Reklamation)* _____? Ask them if their *(Verpackungsmaterial)* _____ is okay.'
6. 'Could you please deal with this *(Inserat)* _____, Doris? We decided at the last meeting to *(inserieren)* _____ in both local newspapers and in the trade journal. A big *(Annonce)* _____.'
7. 'Oh, Doris, the *(Direktion)* _____ is meeting on Thursday afternoon at 2.30. Could you please be there and take down the *(Protokoll)* _____? You do it so well.'
8. 'I want you to *(einfügen)* _____ this paragraph in the middle of the page. And then at the very bottom of the page we must have the phrase 'for further information see *(Rückseite)* _____.'
9. 'Doris, hot news! We are planning to bring out a new *(Marke)* _____ in the autumn. Could you please contact our design people and ask them to design a new *(Etikett)* _____? Here are the details.'
10. 'If I *(bekommen)* _____ one more order today I shall go up the wall and round the bend!! I'll just check these *(Posten)* _____, *(heften)* _____ all those papers together and then I'm off. TGIF. See you on Monday, folks!'

Options

advertisement / ad / advertise / announcement / backside / become / board / brand / clip / complaint / cover / del- / direction / envelope / etiquette / expedition / form / formula / forwarding dept. / get / insert / item / key (2x) / label / leaflet / mark / mine / minutes / overleaf / packing material / packaging material / photocopier / pile / pin / possibility / post / prospect / prospectus / protocol / reclamation / re-fill / reproducer / staple / taste / tip / type / write

Field 14: Business, Industry and Commerce

Area 1: Big Business

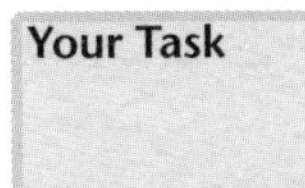

In the headlines below, twelve of the sixteen words underlined are false friends from the field of business and industry. Translate each word in its context, choosing your version from the options beneath. The correct answers are to be found on page 136.

Headlines

1. Elektronik bleibt Wachstumsbranche
2. Den Mittelstand zieht es ins Ausland
3. Konkurse und Vergleiche
4. **Online-Broker zwischen Integration und Fusion**
5. **Fiat macht Toro-Verkauf perfekt**
6. Royal Bank of Scotland erweitert Präsenz in Deutschland
7. Sparkassen sind größer und rentabler als Kreditgenossenschaften
8. Bieterkonsortien werfen das Handtuch
9. **RWE verzichtet auf globale Ambitionen**
10. Sortimentserweiterung bewährte sich
11. **„Wir konkurrieren auf allen Weltmärkten"**
12. Kontingente ausgeschöpft
13. ***Fangquoten stark reduziert***
14. **Philips baut konzernübergreifendes, globales Marketing auf**
15. **Commerzbank forciert den Stellenabbau**
16. Waggons nach Nürnberg expediert

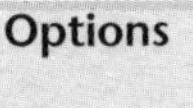

ambition – assortment – availability – bankruptcy – branch – compete – complete – concern – concourse – concur – concurrence – consortium – contingent – expedite – fabric – force – goal – group – integration – involvement – marketing/product mix – medium-sized firms – middle class – overtake – perfect – presence – profitable – quota – quote – rentable – sector – ship

Usually, both true and false friends are grecolatinisms which are found in large numbers both in cognate and non-cognate languages.

PETER NEWMARK, *More Paragraphs on Translation*. Clevedon, 1998

Area 3: Company Development

Your Task

The two stories below contain some fifteen or more false friends from the realm of company development. The story on the right is a bad – a very bad – translation of the story on the left. Find as many errors as you can. The answers are to be found on page 137.

Stories

Die Firmenpleite	**The Firm's Plight**
Anfangs war an der Bonität der Firma nicht zu zweifeln.	At first, the bounty of the firm was not in doubt.
Davon zeugte die neue Fabrik.	The new fabric was proof.
Von der neuen Technik war viel zu erwarten. Neue Patente!	Much could be expected of the new technique. New patents!
Aufstocken. Neue Arbeitsplätze.	Stocking up. New work-places.
Zukunftsorientiert das Unternehmen.	Future-oriented the undertaking.
Aber dann: Der Doppelschlag.	But then – the double whammy.
Es kommt zu einem Tarifkonflikt.	There is a conflict over tariffs.
Nur anfangs wollen die Neuen im Akkord arbeiten.	Only at first do the new men work in accord.
Die Fabrikationskosten steigen. Die Rentabilität!?	The fabrication becomes more costly. Rentability!?
Und die verdammte Konkurrenz!	And the damn concurrence!
Neue Exportaktionen starten?	Start new export actions?
Sich übernehmen lassen? Eine Fusion?!	Allow oneself to be overtaken? A fusion?!
Man analysiert die Aktiva und Passiva. Kann man konkurrieren?	They study the actives and passives. Can they concur?
Nein, die Pleite läßt sich nicht abwenden. Eine Misere.	No, there is no escaping the plight. Misery.

Field 15: Technology and the Natural Sciences

Area 1: Do-It-Yourself

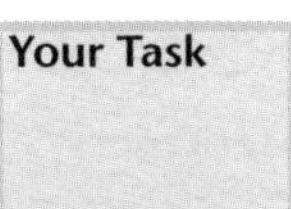

Complete the crossword below, which is made up of eighteen false friends, and one true, from the field of do-it-yourself. Then turn to the further questions in the second part beneath. Correct answers are to be found on page 138.

Crossword

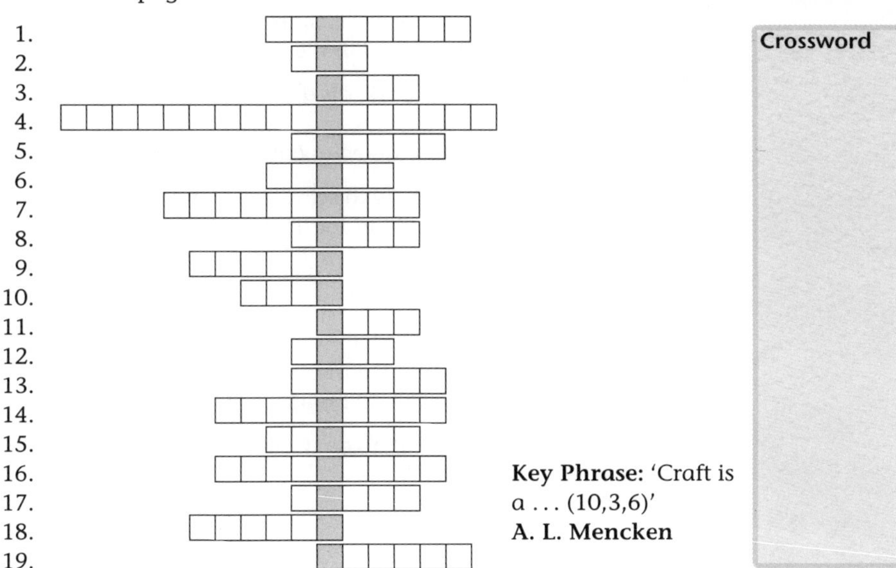

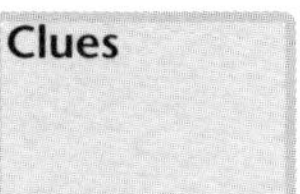

1. isolieren 2. Mutter 3. Bolzen 4. Engländer 5. Hub 6. Bohrer 7. Isolierung 8. Lineal 9. Holzhammer 10. pflastern 11. Kabel 12. Last 13. <u>Nut</u> und Feder 14. Lot 15. Winkel 16. Plane 17. Angel 18. Knopf 19. Metall<u>winkel</u>

Your Task

State the meaning of the words below, which are the incorrect – false friend – answers to the questions above.

False Friends

angle – bore – cable – Englander – hammer – hub – isolate – isolation – knob – last – lineal – lot – mutter – nut – plane – plaster – winkle

> *Once a word or expression is borrowed into a language, we cannot predict or control its development or the additional meanings it might or might not take on.*

MONA BAKER, *In Other Words*. London and New York, 1992

Area 2: In the Lab

Your Task

Distinguish between the following pairs of ill-translated sentences, each of which contains one or more pairs of false friends from the realm of the natural sciences.

Sentences

1. a) *Das Quantum, der Abgott der Neuzeit* (Buchtitel)
   *b) The quantum, the idol of the modern age (book title)
2. a) Im Laborprozess konnte es leicht hergestellt werden.
   *b) It could easily be produced in the labor process.
3. a) Die Glut war noch zu stark, als dass man hätte handeln können.
   *b) The glut was still too marked to allow any action.
4. a) Das neue Glas bestach durch seine Härte und Bruchfestigkeit.
   *b) The new glaze was striking for its hardness and break-resistance.
5. a) Sie hatten noch etwas Petroleum zum Heizen und Kochen.
   *b) They still had some petroleum for heating and cooking.
6. a) Die Theorie schien alles Quark zu sein.
   *b) The theory seemed to be all quarks.
7. a) Ein Pond (1 p) wird leicht als das Gewicht der Masse von einem Gramm (1 g) definiert.
   *b) One pound (1 lb) is easily defined as the weight of the mass of one gram (1 g).
8. a) Etwa bei dieser Temperatur wird die Substanz einschmelzen.
   *b) Around this temperature the substance will smelt.
9. a) Das Quant bewegte offensichtlich viel.
   *b) The quant clearly moved a great deal.
10. a) Was tun mit dem Rest? Der Rest ist ja Schweigen.
    *b) What was to be done with the rest? The rest is silence.

Field 16: Money, Economics and Finance

Area 1: The Public Purse

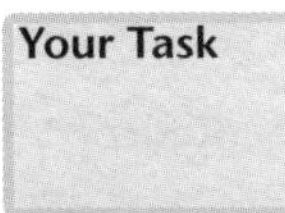

Your Task

In the headlines below, twelve of the fourteen words underlined are false friends from the field of business and industry. Translate each word in its context, choosing your version from the options beneath. The correct answers are to be found on page 140.

Headlines

1. **Sozialausgaben bilden den größten Etatposten**
2. **Jetzt streikt auch noch die Konjunktur**
3. **Lohnopfer bei der Credit Suisse**
4. FDP: Viele Existenzen gefährdet
5. Der erfundene Spender
6. Industrie und Handel aufgeschreckt
7. **Gewerkschaft sagt Rabatt den Kampf an**
8. **Befreiung der Existenzgründer von Regelungen**
9. ***Hochschulen buhlen um Spenden***
10. **Haushaltskonsolidierung**
11. **„Wir kommen durch die Rezession ohne Verlust"**
12. **Größter Ausgabenblock ist die Rente**
13. **Subventionen für Werften noch nicht entschieden.**
14. **Diäten werden in aller Ruhe erhöht**

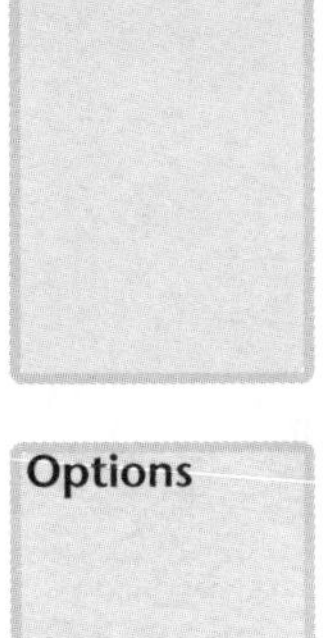

Options

allowance – budget (2x) – charitable gifts – conjuncture – diet – discount – donations – donor – downswing – economy – estate – existence – founder of new business – giver to charity – handle – livelihood – loan – pension – rebate – recession – rent – retail trade – spender – spending – subvention – subsidy – wage(s)

In the development of languages, the meanings will change. Some or all of the semantic features of the source language word may be lost. They may retain one special feature or may change meaning completely.

Mildred L. Larson, *Meaning-Based Translation*. Lanham 1984

Area 2: You and Your Money

Your Task

Fill in the gaps in the sentences below, choosing the appropriate word from the list beneath. Of the words in brackets only three have 'true friends' in English. Correct answers are to be found on page 141.

Sentences

1. Why is it that the state *(Stipendium)* _____ is always totally inadequate?
2. How am I going to pay the *(Miete)* _____!?
3. And soon I'll be an ERASMUS student in Britain! It's even more expensive there: sometimes you have to pay *(Gemeindesteuern)* _____ or whatever the new form is.
4. Heavens, I'm totally and utterly *(blank)* _____. I'm still waiting for that *(Rückvergütung)* _____ from the online booksellers. I wonder if I can *(pumpen)* _____ some dough from dear old Dad ?
5. Officially, of course, we're supposed to take out a *(Darlehen)* _____. But that's like a *(Hypothek)* _____ on my future.
6. After all, as a teacher or clergyman you get only a modest *(Gehalt)* _____ in comparison to other economic sectors. Why didn't I study Business? Or Law?
7. No wonder I can't make two ends meet! These food prices are exorbitant! I'm paying through the nose! The restaurants are not just *(profitieren)* _____, they're *(Wuchergeschäfte machen)* _____.
8. And there's always a catch in the small print: 'No (Rabatt) _____ available if payment is made in *(Raten)* _____.'
9. I'm convinced the government should *(Finanzspritze geben)* _____ a lot of *(Kapital)* _____ into the education system. It's all our futures!
10. Yes, a state loan – no, better a state *gift* – at the *beginning* of life! Much more important than a *(Rente)* _____ at the end!
11. It's time the government *(bitten)* _____ young people for creative ideas and then *(bieten)* _____ a genuine, big prize for the best ways out of the financial *(Krise)* _____. Radical thinking, yes. That's what's needed. Tap the hidden *(Ressourcen)* _____, the latent wells of talent!
12. Hey, what's this in my post-box!? Brilliant! Wow! Good old Dad! Now I've got money to *(ausgeben)* _____, money to *(sparen)* _____ and money *(übrig)* _____, perhaps to *(spenden)* _____.
13. I'll *(spendieren)* _____ everyone a round at the pub tonight, you bet I will! I feel really my genuine, *(spendabel)* _____ self now!

Options

ask – bid – borrow – broke – capital – cash – crisis – discount – funds – give to charity – generous – grant – hypothec – instalments – lend – loan – mortgage – offer – pension – profit – profiteer – pump – quandary – rates – rebate – rent – resources – save – to spare – spend – spendable – stand – stipend

Area 3: Hey, Big Spender

Your Task

Fill in the gaps in the sentences below, choosing the appropriate word from the list beneath. Of the words in brackets only four have 'true friends' in English. Correct answers are to be found on page 142.

Sentences

1. Working at the counter for *(Sorten)* _____ she had to be careful always to give the right *(Kurs)* _____. And so many people wanted *(Devisen)* _____, even after the Euro! Very tricky.
2. His Lordship was one of the biggest holders of *(Obligationen)* _____ in the entire country. No wonder he could often give his servants a nice little *(Gratifikation)* _____. He knew how to *(honorieren)* _____ long service and devotion. Very generous.
3. Brokers watch every *(Emission)* _____ with care. Very prudent.
4. He received not only his salary, but also a *(Provision)* _____ of 15 % on all company products he was able to sell. Very nice.
5. Only 24 hours after the launch, the shares were being *(notiert)* _____ at more than double the issue price. Very tempting.
6. Her – highly successful – portfolio was made up of many *(Arten)* _____ of shares and *(Effekten)* _____. Very wise.
7. What will be the *(Auswirkung)* _____ of the budget? To spread *(Einkommen)* _____ and increase *(konsumtive Ausgaben)* _____ or to reduce unemployment and fuel *(Inflation)* _____? Very debatable.
8. With her will she started a *(Fonds)* _____ for the education of deserving girls from deprived backgrounds. Very splendid.
9. Before buying any new share, his *(Verfahrensweise)* _____ was to *(beobachten)* _____ its *(Kurs)* _____ for some months. Very savvy.
10. The judge ordered that the husband should pay *(Alimente)* _____ of several hundred pounds per month. Very just.
11. The taxi-driver received no *(Rekompensation)* _____ at all after his contretemps with drunken right-wing passengers. Very rough.
12. The substantial *(Fund)* _____ of ancient coins led to a court case to decide who was the rightful owner. Very contentious.
13. Like all wise investors they had made *(Vorkehrungen)* _____ for a crash, but even they were taken by surprise by Black Wednesday. Very unlucky.
14. The thieves failed to open the *(Tresor)* _____, thus missing the chance to carry off a major *(Schatz)* _____. Bloody incompetent.

Options

alimony – commission – compensation – consumer spending – course – debentures – devices – effects – emission – find – foreign currency – foreign notes and coins – fund – gratification – gratuity – honour – income – inflation – new issue – note – obligations – price – provision(s) – quoted – (exchange) rate – recompense – recognise – safe – sorts – stocks – treasure

Field 17: Travel and Transport

Area 1: Means of Transport

Your Task

The twenty-one pairs of words below all have to do with means of transport or their parts, only eight of them, however, being genuine equivalents. Find the true friends and then distinguish between the false. The correct answers are to be found on page 143.

Word Pairs

der (Auto)skooter – the scooter
der Bagger – the bagger
die Batterie – the battery
das Benzin – the benzine
der Blinker – the blinker
der Caravan – the caravan
das Coupé (Auto) – the coupé
die Hupe – the hoop
der Katalysator – the catalyst
der Kühlergrill – the grille
der Kipper – the kipper
der Kompressor – the compressor
die Limousine – the limousine
der Minibus – the minibus
der Oldtimer – the oldtimer
das Pickup – the pickup truck
das Profil – the profile
der Roller – the roller
das Schneemobil – the snowmobile
das Tachometer – the tachometer
das Vehikel – the vehicle

Where the linguistic and cultural differences between source and receptor codes are least, one should expect to encounter the least number of serious problems, but as a matter of fact if languages are too closely related one is likely to be badly deceived by the superficial similarities, with the result that translations done under these circumstances are often quite poor.

EUGENE NIDA, *Toward a Science of Translating*. Leiden 1964

Area 2: Travel

Your Task

Read the passage below, paying especial attention to the fourteen words underlined, all but three of which are false friends from the field of travel. Then consider the statements beneath.

Text

Dear Mum and Dad

Wrong! Quite wrong!

What did you say our walking holiday would be like? Wandering aimlessly like a boat without a rudder! Only tramps for company!

Wrong! Quite wrong!

Yesterday, for example, Sam and I were waiting at a level crossing when we were offered a lift by a farmer. Today, we were tramping through the Scottish Borders when along came a limousine, with a yacht in tow, and asked for the pleasure of our company. We put our backpacks in the boot, climbed aboard, and soon we were sailing through Selkirk and Peebles. In Selkirk itself we hopped out, swanked into a restaurant for a meal and soon found a B&B for the night.

And no trouble about fares. No hassle with tickets valid only midweek. No bother about overhauling bikes or cars. Far, far better than tanking down the motorway with the hoi polloi. 'Sweep on, you fat and greasy citizens' (Shakespeare!), we say.

Edinburgh next stop! Highlands and Islands here we come! With a rucksack on your back the world is at your feet. And sometimes you can put your feet up too. Ah, the joys of wanderlust!

Greetings to you stay-at-homes and stick-in-the-muds,

Lynn

Statements

In the light of the above passage, which of the following statements are definitely true? The correct answers are to be found on page 144.

1. Lynn und Sam trampen durch Schottland.
2. Die autofahrende, an Autobahnen tankende Mehrheit mögen sie nicht unbedingt.
3. An einer Kreuzung wurden sie von einem Landwirt mitgenommen.
4. In Selkirk schwankten sie in ein Restaurant hinein.
5. Lynns skeptische Eltern meinten, sie würden ziellos wandern wie ein Boot ohne Ruder und würden nur mit Trampern verkehren.
6. Um Fähren mußten sich die beiden nicht kümmern.
7. Beim Überholen von Autos und Radfahrern hatten sie keine Probleme.
8. Mit nur mittwochs gültigen Fahrkarten ebenfalls nicht.
9. Das Auto, das sie mitnahm, zog eine Yacht hinter sich her.
10. Sie legten ihre Rucksäcke ins Boot.
11. Hast du einen Rucksack auf dem Rücken, steht dir die Welt offen.
12. Die Wanderlust birgt manche Freude.

Field 18: Ships and Navigation

Area 1: Messing About in Boats

Your Task

Distinguish between the following pairs of ill-translated sentences, each of which contains one or more pairs of false friends – but also the occasional 'true friend' – from the realm of boats and boating.

Sentences

1. a) Das Schiff lag draußen in der Reede vor Anker an einer Boje.
   *b) The skiff was anchored out in the reeds by a buoy.
2. a) Der Ewer war effektiv bei kleineren Transportaufgaben.
   *b) The ewer was good for minor transportation jobs.
3. a) Es saß sich gut auf der Back oder am Bug.
   *b) It was pleasant to sit at the back or on the bug.
4. a) Das Stag stützte den Mast.
   *b) The stag held up the mast.
5. a) Ja, es handelte sich um einen außerordentlich großen Fang.
   *b) Yes, it was an extraordinarily large fang.
6. a) Because of the haar, he could hardly see the sterns.
   *b) Wegen des Haars sah er kaum die Sterne.
7. a) He was sitting in the fore of the galleon, working on the tackle.
   *b) Er saß vorne an der Galion und arbeitete am Takelwerk.
8. a) They desperately needed some kind of floss.
   *b) Sie benötigten dringend eine Art Floß.
9. a) The jolly-boat took them out into the roads.
   *b) Die Jolle brachte sie in die Reede.
10. a) Was there a haven nowhere, nowhere?
    *b) Befand sich nirgends ein Hafen?
11. a) There were several fish swimming languorously at the heck.
    *b) Am Heck schwammen träge mehrere Fische.

Mental models can [. . .] differ considerably across cultures. The problem arises as to how these covert models can be identified.

JEAN AITCHISON, 'Taming the Wilderness: Words in the Mental Lexicon', in: Gunilla Anderman et al. ed., *Words, Words, Words.* Clevedon 1996.

Area 2: Voyages

Your Task

Read the texts below, paying especial attention to the eleven words underlined, seven of which are false friends from the area of sea voyages. Then consider the statements below.

Texts

1. The Lyme Regis Cobb, which features in John Fowles's *The French Lieutenant's Woman* (1969) and in Jane Austen's *Persuasion* (1818), is British literature's most famous mole.
2. The rise of C. S. Forester's Hornblower, from below decks to helm, from midshipman to admiral, parallels that of Lord Nelson.
3. Coleridge's 'Ancient Mariner', with his beady eye and bewitching, gaia-sustaining tale, is the most famous of literary sea-dogs.
4. 'The blown spume and the flung spray and the seagulls crying' – in the poems of John Masefield you can almost smell the tang of the sea.
5. As the *Euphrosyne* leaves London in Virginia Woolf's *The Voyage Out* (1915), its characters standing and taking symbolic leave by the railing, so the British novel sets sail into the uncharted waters of modernism.
6. George Blake's novel *The Shipbuilders* (1935) takes one to the wharves and yards, banks and berths of Glasgow in the Depression.
7. In Julian Barnes's *A History of the World in 10½ Chapters* (1989), a major motif is the fragile hull of ships and of life.
8. In *Strumpet City* (1969) James Plunkett superbly evokes the labour of the Dublin docks on the eve of the First World War.
9. As his fiction from *The Nigger of the Narcissus* (1897) to *Typhoon* (1903) so memorably shows, Joseph Conrad, perhaps the greatest seafarer among writers in English, was long at the rudder.
10. Even in British children's literature, such as Kenneth Grahame's *The Wind in the Willows* (1908), watercraft play a major role.

Statements

In the light of the above passages, which of the following statements are definitely true? Correct answers are to be found on page 146.

1. Hauptmotiv und -metapher bei Barnes ist die Hülle des Daseins.
2. Blakes Roman spielt in den Glasgower Werften.
3. Woolf läßt ihre Hauptfiguren symbolträchtig an der Reling stehen.
4. Bei Masefield atmet man den würzigen Geruch des Seetangs.
5. In der britischen Kinderliteratur ist das Thema Wasserkraft zentral.
6. Hornblower trägt am Schluß den Helm eines Admirals.
7. Conrad, ein großer Seefahrer, hat viel gerudert.
8. Wichtiger Schauplatz von Fowles' Roman ist eine Mole.
9. Plunkett schildert das Arbeitsleben der Dubliner Docks.
10. Hauptfigur beim naturnahen Romantiker Coleridge ist ein Seehund.

Translation Theory III: Categories of False Friends

On the Alert One of the main tasks of any course on 'false friends' must be not just successfully to pinpoint the 'false' items but to alert the language student also to those language areas where they are liable to occur. Of such areas at least the following deserve highlighting.

French Origin Perhaps the most fruitful lexical item to be sensitive to is the word of French origin. The profound and early impact of French on English from the Norman conquest onwards and its later impact on the German world make this a highly vexed area. From such basic words as 'actual'/*aktuell* via the well-known 'billet'/*Billett* and 'menu'/*Menü* to the more subtle 'foible'/*Faible* and 'spleen'/*Spleen* this is a rich hunting ground.

Latin Origin Suspicion is also often called for with German words that flaunt their Latin origin. From 'angina'/*Angina* via 'crux'/*Crux*, 'ratio'/*Ratio* and 'senior'/ *Senior* to 'terminus'/*Terminus* there are here often good grounds for wariness.

Germanic Root Very striking is also the number of words of Germanic root – often monosyllables and often among the basic words of the language – that have drifted apart in sense: the English terms 'clang', 'craft', 'deer', 'dish', 'meal', 'mere', 'mood', 'moor', 'pain' and 'pest' stand for many more.

Yiddish The strong presence of Yiddish in both BrE and AmE since the Jewish diasporas of the last centuries has also led to a clutch of 'false friends' ranging from 'spiel'/*Spiel* through 'zaftig'/*saftig* to 'glitch'/*Glitsche* and 'shmuck'/*Schmuck*.

Verb Groupings If one focuses not on languages of origin but on word-types, some very precise warnings can be given. Of the many verb prefixes in English and German, for example, the pairs 'over-'/*über-*, 'out-'/*aus-*, 'under-'/ *unter-* and 'for(e)-'/*vor-* can frequently lead to confusion. Another significant grouping is verbs beginning with 'be-'/*be-*, including 'berate', 'beset', 'besiege', 'betray'.

Of verb suffixes it is perhaps '-eer'/*-ieren* which should arouse the greatest caution – as with 'commandeer'/*kommandieren*, 'domineer'/*dominieren*, 'profiteer'/*profitieren* and so on. Indeed the very ending *-ieren*, often attached to a French stem and corresponding to the French verb ending *-er*, is of itself a warning light – as with *defilieren, honorieren, promovieren, visitieren* and the like.

Noun Groupings As with verbs, so with substantives: the suffix '-ion'/*-ion*, again denoting French origin, is a frequent sign of illusory resemblance – the examples *Fabrikation, Konfektion, Provision* standing for many others. Similarly, the suffix-pair '-or'/*-eur* as with *Konstrukteur, Kontrolleur,* is deceptive for the selfsame reason. An equal cause for concern are the suffixes '-ic'/*-ik*, as for example in *Charakteristik, Historik, Lyrik* and also '-aph'/*-aph* as in 'lithograph'/*Lithograph* and suchlike.

Adjective Groupings

With adjectives also, it is certain suffixes which need to be treated with circumspection. The pairs '-y'/*-ig* and '-ly'/*-lich* can often deceive, as can '-al'/*al*. 'Hefty', 'lofty', 'lusty' and 'sticky' are just a few salient examples here.

The *Fremdwort*

As much of the above suggests, one of the most helpful pointers to 'false friends' is their frequent status in German as *Fremdwörter*. Whether from Greek or Japanese, whether 'coryphaeus'/*Koryphäe* or 'bonze'/*Bonze* the foreignness of the foreign word is often a token of its possible deceptiveness. Its own migration from language to language presages the migration of its meaning. Is *akkurat* accurately translated by 'accurate'? Is *exakt* exactly 'exact'? As these pages exemplify again and again, the answer is often 'No'.

W. von Humboldt

The early philologists were right here. W. von Humboldt reminds us in his reflections on translating *Agamemnon* that, with the exceptions of words denoting mere physical objects (and, one might add, by no means with all of them) 'kein Wort Einer Sprache vollkommen einem in einer anderen Sprache gleich ist. Verschiedene Sprachen sind in dieser Hinsicht nur ebensoviel Synonymieen; jede drückt den Begriff etwas anders, mit dieser oder jener Nebenbestimmung, eine Stufe höher oder tiefer auf der Leiter der Empfindungen aus‘.

Fr. Schleiermacher

Or as Fr. Schleiermacher put it: 'Nun aber verhält es sich mit allen Sprachen, die nicht so nahe verwandt sind daß sie fast nur als verschiedene Mundarten können angesehen werden, gerade umgekehrt, und je weiter sie der Abstammung und der Zeit nach von einander entfernt sind, um desto mehr so, daß keinem einzigen Wort in einer Sprache eins in einer anderen genau entspricht, keine Beugungsweise der einen genau dieselbe Mannigfaltigkeit von Verhältnißfällen zusammenfaßt, wie irgend eine in einer andern‘ (‚Ueber die verschiedenen Methoden des Übersetzens‘, 1813). In translation, great caution is almost always required. The caution we must bring to 'false friends' is just an extreme case of the broader caution we must generally deploy in the world beyond Babel and beyond equivalences.

Field 19: Politics and Politicking

Area 1: Politicking

Your Task

Distinguish between the following pairs of ill-translated sentences, each of which contains one or more pairs of false friends – but also the occasional 'true friend' – from the realm of political activity.

Sentences

1. a) An ihrem Engagement war nicht zu zweifeln. Engagiert waren sie.
   *b) There was no doubting their engagement. Engaged they were.
2. a) Die Waffenkontrolleure zogen sich trostlos zurück. Eine effektive Kontrolle war Zukunftsmusik.
   *b) The arms controllers beat a disconsolate retreat. Effective control was a thing of the future.
3. a) Der fehlende Rapport stimmte nachdenklich.
   *b) The lack of rapport gave food for thought.
4. a) Kurz darauf traf der Premier mit seiner Entourage ein.
   *b) Shortly after the premier arrived with his entourage.
5. a) Aufgabe der Intelligenz sei es, Staatsorgane zu kontrollieren.
   *b) It was a task of intelligence to control state organs.
6. a) Der Pair nahm an jeder Abstimmung teil.
   *b) The pair was involved in every division.
7. a) In der Postmoderne wissen wir es: Auch Transparente können verfälscht sein.
   *b) In the postmodern age we know that even transparencies can be faked.
8. a) Es gab nach wie vor zu viele Schikanen an der Grenze.
   *b) There were still too many chicanes by the border.
9. a) Die Opposition hatte fleißig plakatiert.
   *b) The opposition had been industrious in placating.

Wie die Sprache ein geschichtliches Ding ist, so giebt es keinen rechten Sinn für sie, ohne Sinn für ihre Geschichte.

Fr. Schleiermacher, ‚Ueber die verschiedenen Methoden des Übersetzens', 1813

Area 2: Political Life

The two stories below contain some twenty or more false friends from the world of politics. The story on the right is a bad – a very bad – translation of the story on the left. Find as many errors as you can. The answers are to be found on page 147.

Your Task

Stories

A Politician Resigns	**Ein Politikus resigniert**
Foreign politics were his hobby, domestic politics his life.	Die Außenpolitik war sein Hobby, die Innenpolitik sein Leben.
His father had been Speaker under Eden.	Sein Vater war unter Eden Parteisprecher gewesen.
He himself was to be a Minister.	Er selbst sollte Minister werden.
A cabinet post! Chancellor?!	Ein Kabinettsposten! Kanzler?!
Why not? He was the born parliamentarian.	Was sprach dagegen? Er war der geborene Parlamentär.
His zeal was clear, his concepts were clearer. Community. The communal.	Seine Ziele waren klar, seine Konzepte klarer. Die Gemeinschaft. Das Kommunale.
He besought, berated.	Er besuchte, beriet.
But in vain. Not even a fraction were in favour.	Aber vergeblich. Nicht mal die Fraktion war dafür.
The basis had crumbled away!	Die Basis war weggebröckelt!
Then – corruption! In the Civil Service! In his own ministry.	Dann: Korruption! Im Zivildienst! Im eigenen Ministerium.
A betrayal! Manifest betrayal!	Betrug! Betrug am Manifest!
And then the smears. A campaign of lies! Besieged by the press. They were the real fiends!	Und dann die Schmiergelder. Eine Lügenkampagne! Von der Presse besiegt. Die waren die eigentlichen Feinde!
He had one last resort. That was it: he resigned.	Er hatte ein letztes Ressort. Das war's: Er resignierte.

Area 3: War and the Military

Your Task

Read the passage below, paying especial attention to the key words of war and the military, twenty-one of which are false friends. Then deal with the statements below.

Text

Jahrhundertelang haben die Dichter den Krieg besungen. *Arma virumque cano.* Erst im historischen Roman der Neuzeit aber, bei Scott, Zschokke und Puschkin, erst recht bei Tolstoj, wird der Krieg in all seiner Erbärmlichkeit dargestellt. Der Krieg des historischen Romans ist weniger der Vater aller Dinge als die Mutter aller Undinge. Die Politiker dirigieren, die Generäle kommandieren, die Offiziere requirieren, die Kriegsgewinnler profitieren. Der gemeine Soldat spurt und hurt. Hauptbestandteile des Krieges sind die Generalität, die nicht versteht, das Kommando, das nicht stimmt, die Schlacht, die nicht zu überblicken ist, und das ‚freundliche Feuer', das recht unfreundlich darniederprasselt. Es wird bombardiert, belagert, besetzt, bestraft. Den Besiegten geht es dabei am schlimmsten, aber auch den Siegern geht es dreckig. Die Granate und die Salve unterscheiden nicht zwischen Soldaten und Söldnern, Leutnants und Laien, Militärs und Mütterchen, Privaten und Pionieren, Patern und Patrouillen. Zu jedem Anschlag gehört der Kollateralschaden, bei allen Repressalien ist der Schweinehund dabei. Zum Krieg gehörte einst auch die Marine, bei der es angeblich gentlemanhafter zuging. Wer das noch glaubt, der lese *Trafalgar* (1881) von Pérez Galdós.

Statements

In the light of the above passage, which of the following statements are true? The answers are to be found on page 148.

1. In war, the besieged fare worst.
2. Generals commandeer and officers require.
3. The common soldier spurs things on.
4. In war, you are bombarded and beleaguered.
5. All repression has its nasty element.
6. 'Friendly fire' is as unfriendly as any other fire.
7. Grenades and salves make no fine distinctions.
8. They hit soldiers and lieutenants alike, privates too.
9. Every onslaught involves collateral damage.
10. In war, no-one can gauge the slaughter.
11. Militaries can be victims of war, as can patrols, even pioneers.
12. War used to involve the marine.
13. In war, you are beset and strafed.
14. A commando is never right.
15. The generality does not understand war.

Field 20: Crime and the Law

Area 1: In the Law Courts

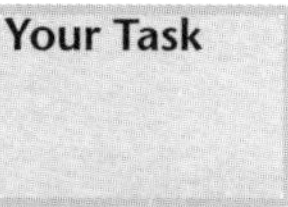

The ten word-pairs below are all false friends from the world of the law courts. Distinguish between the pairs by matching each word on the left with the person or object on the right most associated with it. The correct answers are to be found on page 149.

Word Pairs

A. der Advokat
B. the advocate
C. die Injurie
D. the injury
E. (die) Jura
F. the Jura
G. die Pacht
H. the pact
I. der Paragraph
J. the paragraph
K. die Police
L. the police
M. das Quiproquo
N. the quid pro quo
O. die Revision
P. the revision
Q. visitieren
R. to visit
S. das Zivilrecht
T. civil rights

1. case of mistaken identity
2. to call on, pay s.o. a visit
3. non-criminal law
4. appeal to a court of law
5. the section of a law
6. going over a matter again
7. the officers of law enforcement
8. the youngest Swiss canton
9. Law as a subject of study
10. the public rights of a citizen
11. the insult
12. to 'frisk', to submit to a body search
13. professional pleader in court
14. physical harm
15. document of insurance contract
16. lease
17. person who argues for a cause
18. the compensation, the return made
19. indented body of writing
20. the agreement, covenant

One must keep up with the growth and change of the language, and be up-to-date in all of its nuances and neologisms.

Morry Sofer, *The Translator's Handbook*. Rockville 1996

Area 2: Crime and Punishment

Your Task

The two stories below contain some twenty false friends from the world of crime and the law. The story on the right is a bad – a very bad – translation of the story on the left. Find as many errors as you can. The answers are to be found on page 150.

Stories

The Ordeal	**Das Urteil**
A murder is always gruesome, mused the judge.	Ein Mörder ist ja immer grausam, sinnierte der Richter.
Like the Fall: Cain and Abel.	Wie der Fall Kain und Abel.
Above all when arson is involved.	Vor allem, wo Arsen mitspielt.
The criminals always think that the evidence is gone.	Die Kriminalen meinen immer, es fehle die Evidenz.
They think they're so guileful.	Sie halten sich für voll geil.
But motives remain. And then you suddenly say: 'There it is: that's the clue!'	Es bleiben aber die Motive. Und dann heißt es plötzlich: ‚Das ist es. Das ist ja der Clou!'
Then everything must be proved.	Dann muß alles geprüft werden.
No caution is enough. No failure can be allowed.	Keine Kaution reicht aus. Kein Fehler kann zugelassen werden.
That's the brief.	So lautet der Brief.
A long process, almost an ordeal in itself.	Ein langer Prozeß, fast ein Urteil an sich.
Ah, things were easier when he was only a magistrate!	Ach, das Leben war leichter, als er nur im Magistrat war!
Justice takes long. So long, it is almost a crime.	Die Justiz braucht lange. So lange, es wird fast zum Krimi.
But 'life' is longer still. And death perhaps also.	Aber das Leben ist noch länger. Der Tod vielleicht auch.
If only this were the last instance!	Wäre dies nur die letzte Instanz!

Field 21: School Life, Teaching, Didactics

Area 1: Learning and Teaching

Your Task

Distinguish between the following pairs of ill-translated sentences, each of which contains one or more pairs of false friends – but also the occasional 'true friend' – from the realm of school and learning.

1. a) Der besorgte Direktor ließ den Referendar zu sich kommen.
   *b) Worried, the director sent for the reverend.

2. a) Auf der Lehrerkonferenz ging es um die Rolle des Assessors.
   *b) At the Teachers' Conference, the role of the assessor was at issue.

3. a) Ihre Noten ließen sich immer sehen.
   *b) Her notes were always something to be seen.

4. a) Er konnte sich kaum an die Lektüre erinnern.
   *b) He could hardly remember the lecture.

5. a) Er fand die einschlägigen Notizen nicht.
   *b) He could not find the relevant notices.

6. a) The primus smelt somewhat unpleasant.
   *b) Der Primus roch leicht unangenehm.

7. a) In Thomas Arnold's educational scheme the Sixth Form had a central role to play.
   *b) Im Erziehungskonzept Thomas Arnolds fiel der sechsten Klasse eine zentrale Rolle zu.

8. a) He consulted the Director of Studies.
   *b) Er konsultierte den Studiendirektor.

9. a) The best thing about the school was its eleven.
   *b) Das Beste an der Schule waren ihre Eleven

If a TL false friend is used frequently enough in the SL it can eventually become a 'true friend' by taking on that SL meaning in addition to its own.

MARK SHUTTLEWORTH & MOIRA COWIE, *Dictionary of Translation Studies.* Manchester 1997

Area 2: At School

Your Task

Read the passage below, paying especial attention to the key words of school life, fourteen of which are false friends. Then deal with the statements below.

Text

They had chosen St Phee's because pupil-teacher relations were so much better there than in the state sector. For example, at his old school, Harry had been a bit of a rebel. He had hated everything – especially the head's dictats. But now his new form-master said Harry was 'growing in wisdom'! He had produced good map work. He had even been made blackboard monitor. Colleagues too were 'most impressed'.

Harry used to be inarticulate: frankly, one had difficulty grasping his meaning. The censure from his old English teacher spoke volumes. But now the new form-master had written a most encouraging letter: Harry had 'the makings of a promising scholar'! And the house-master too spoke warmly of him.

And another telling example: Harry used to hate the gymnasium and the gym teachers. But now his attitude to sport had changed – and so had his physique.

Perhaps Harry would make a success of High School after all! There seemed to be no cloud on the horizon. If only it wasn't for the school fees. And if only one didn't have the shrinking suspicion that the new master was just *saying* these encouraging things. Was he serious?

Statements

In the light of the above passage, which of the following statements are true? The answers are to be found on page 153.

1. St. Phee's hat eine günstige Relation Lehrer-Schüler.
2. Harry wurde nach Ansicht des neuen Klassenlehrers zum erfolgversprechenden Schüler.
3. Auch dessen Kollegen seien ‚beeindruckt'.
4. Die Zensur von seinem alten Englischlehrer sprach Bände.
5. Früher hasste Harry das Gymnasium sowie die Gymnasiallehrer.
6. An der neuen Schule war er bald besser in Physik.
7. Er legte schöne Arbeitsmappen vor.
8. Er war für das schwarze Brett zuständig.
9. Vorher war er ein Rebell gewesen.
10. An der neuen Schule lobte ihn auch der Hausmeister.
11. Früher waren seine Meinungen kaum zu verstehen.
12. Er hatte auch die Diktate des Rektors gehasst.
13. Jetzt wuchs sein Wissen.
14. Harry könnte vielleicht an der Hochschule Erfolg haben.
15. Aber: Der Lehrer von St Phee's war vielleicht nicht seriös, oder?

Field 22: University and Student Life

Area 1: University Studies

Your Task

In each of the sentences below, the sense is disturbed by at least one grave misuse of word concerning university study and courses. Replace the offending terms by correct alternatives. The answers are to be found on page 154.

*1. He had been Dean of Faculty for six long years. Now he could look forward to a sabbatical year, absolved of all duties – no more committees and commissions, no more listening to dull referents at duller meetings of the Convent or Senate.

*2. Promotion was the first step, then habilitation, then, as his dear old mentor used to say, the 'sky's the limit'. Research, conferences, publications, renown, guest professorships. Happy hunting grounds!

*3. It was a 'sandwich course': in order to gain your academic grade you had to absolve a practical in business abroad.

*4. How much better British university libraries were! Student-friendly opening times, fully computerized catalogues, easy CD-ROM research facilities, no waiting 24 hours for books from the magazine.

*5. A study was still a good investment. Students could look forward to starting salaries at least 50% higher than their contemporaries.

*6. Romanticism and university were at times incompatible. Byron said of Cambridge 'the place is the devil'; Shelley was chased from his Oxford college in 1811 for his religious views.

*7. Key parts of life in the German student fraternity are the fencing or mensuration and the (in)famous commerce or drinking sessions.

*8. Sue had really starred in her finals. Not just a First – an exam with predicate! Great stuff and surely the herald of greater things to come!

*9. Among the most famous colleges in German academic history were those held by Hegel on Philosophy of History five times over between 1822/23 and 1830/31.

*10. He hadn't met Miss Right yet, but one thing was sure: she must have studied, must be an academic. If she was promoted, even better.

Überhaupt ist das Englische die Vorratskammer, in welcher wir unsre veralteten Wörter und auch den ursprünglichen Sinn der noch gebräuchlichen aufbewahrt wiederfinden.

ARTHUR SCHOPENHAUER, ‚Über Sprache und Worte', *Paralipomena,* 1851

Area 2: The University Hierarchy

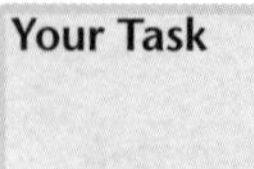

In the table of university officers and staff below, all but two words underlined are false friends from the field of university life. Translate each word in its context, assembling your version from the options beneath. The correct answers are to be found on page 155.

Universitätspräsident
Prof. Dr. Burghard Fest

Prorektor Forschung
Prof. Dr. habil. Dr. Dr. h.c. Benno Foerder

Prorektorin Bildung
Prof. Dr. habil. Irmgard Kusch

Kanzler
Dr. Paul Rachlitz

Abteilungsleiter
Dr. Ing. Roland Rabowsky

Dekan
Prof. Dr. habil. Eberhard Stuhr

Akademischer Oberrat
PD Dr. habil. Friedhelm Zähm

St. Dir. im Hochschuldienst
Dr. Waltraud Klaerig

Akademischer Mitarbeiter
Florian Suchsland

Lektorin für Französisch
Dr. Amélie Chuchard

Lektor für Amerikanisch
Howard ('Howdy') Kahn M.A., Ph.D.

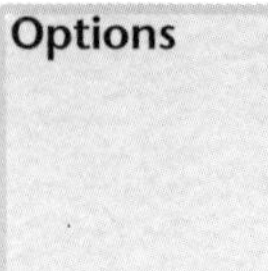

Academic Affairs – Administrative Head – Building – Chair – Chancellor – Deacon – Dean (of Faculty) – Departmental – Director – Director of Studies – Head (of) – Head of Dept. – Junior Lecturer – Language Assistant – Leader – Lector – Lectrice – Lecturer – President – Reader – Rector – Sectional Head – Senior Lecturer – Treasurer – Vice-Chancellor – Vice-Vice-Chancellor – Vice-Rector

Field 23: Thought, Logic and Mental Processes

Area 1: Thinking

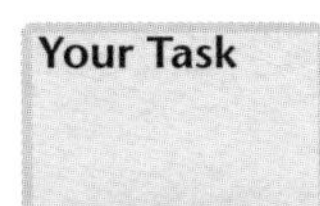

Distinguish between the following pairs of ill-translated sentences, each of which contains one or more pairs of false friends – and some the occasional true friend – from the realm of logic and argument. For the answers see page 155.

1. a) Do you owe much to your doctoral supervisor? Oh, yes. I owe him several fine points and pointers.
   *b) Hast du deinem Doktorvater viel zu verdanken? O ja, ich verdanke ihm etliche feine Pointen.

2. a) The crux of the matter was that the expedition was pretty dangerous.
   *b) Die Expedition war recht gefährlich. Das war die Crux.

3. a) It was hard to construe the sense. Was it all conjecture and hypothesis?
   *b) Es war schwer, den Sinn zu konstruieren. War alles bloß Konjektur und Hypothese?

4. a) His ingenuity was beyond doubt. But it seemed too simple.
   *b) Seine Ingenuität stand außer Frage. Es erschien zu einfach-simpel.

5. a) It was all a question of the ratio.
   *b) Es war alles eine Frage der Ratio.

6. a) The consequence was that her life had been useless.
   *b) Die Konsequenz war: Ihr Leben war nutzlos gewesen.

7. a) Life consists more in journeying hopefully than in arriving safely.
   *b) Das Leben besteht hoffentlich eher aus Reisen als aus sicherer Ankunft.

8. a) Does the sign determine consciousness or vice versa?
   *b) Bestimmt das Sein das Bewußtsein oder umgekehrt?

Most talk of meaning requires tacit reference to a home language in much the way that talk of truth involves tacit reference to one's own system of the world, the best that one can muster at the time.

WILLARD V. O. QUINE, *Word and Object*. Cambridge, Ma. 1960

Area 2: Up for Debate

Your Task

Complete the crossword below, which is made up of fourteen pairs of false friends from the field of discussion, argument and persuasion. The clues are the words underlined. Correct answers are to be found on page 156.

Crossword

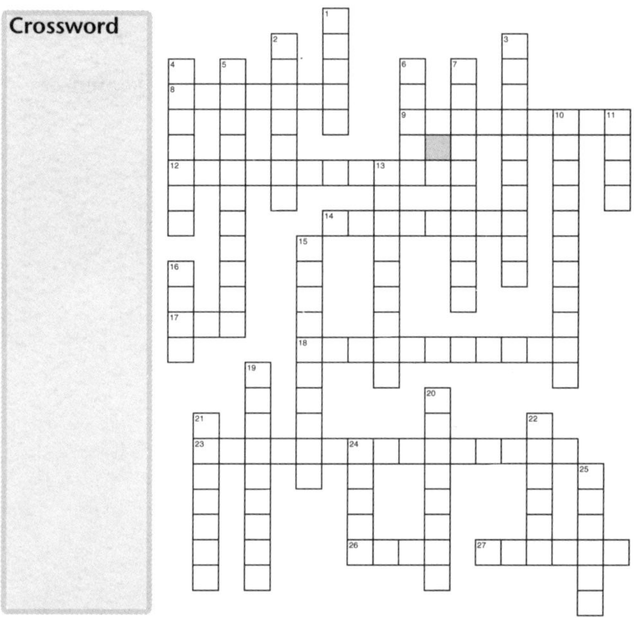

Clues

Across 8. eventuell 9. ein Versehen 12. inkonsequent 14. hinreichend 17. probieren 18. prinzipiell 23. irrelevant 26. auch 27. überblicken

Down 1. raten 2. Bedeutung 3. daraus resultierend 4. Meinung 5. hauptsächlich 6. Untersuchung 7. schließlich 10. Übersicht 11. auf die Probe stellen 13. also 15. konsequent 16. einstufen 19. extra 20. übersehen 21. eine adäquate Übersetzung 22. das Moment 24. zusätzlich 25. der Augenblick

Field 24: Time, Past Time, History

Area 1: The Passage of Time

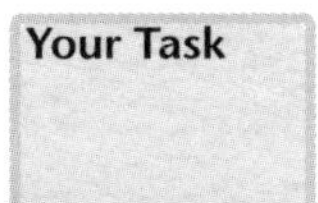

The twenty-four pairs of words below all derive from the field of time and time's passage, only six of them, however, being genuine equivalents. Find the true friends and then distinguish between the false. The correct answers are to be found on page 157.

Word Pairs

der Äon – the aeon
aktualisieren – to actualize
aktuell – actual
alltäglich – all-day
am anderen Tag – the other day
die Ära – the era
die Anciennität – the ancientness
dalli, dalli – to dilly-dally
das Datum – the datum
epochemachend – epoch-making
die Fete – the fête
halb zehn – half ten
in kurzem – in short
momentan (adv.) – momentarily
das Moratorium – the moratorium
nun – noon
die Partie – the party
die Phase – the phase
punktuell – punctual
der Termin – the term
das Uhrglas – the hour-glass
das Ultimatum – the ultimatum
der Ultimo – ultimo
weilen – to while away

> *As with borrowings, there are many fixed calques which, after a period of time, become an integral part of the language. These too, like borrowings, may have undergone a semantic change, turning them into* faux amis.

Jean-Paul Vinay & Jean Darbelnet, *Comparative Stylistics of French and English: A Methodology for Translation.* Amsterdam 1995

Area 2: The Historical Sense

Your Task

Read the passage below, paying especial attention to the key words concerning the historical sense, all but six of which are false friends. Then consider the statements beneath.

Text

Armine Wallenhain, geb. Alterius, Witwe des Mittelalterkenners, war Habituée des Geschichtsvereins. Da traf man ja auf Gleichgesinnte. Auf Prof. Dr. Altenhoff etwa, passionierter Verfechter der Antike und der Historik, seines Zeichens Pharaonen- und Mumienforscher. Auf Pastor Lämmerzahl, dessen Pfarrhaus seit 550 Jahren stand – das Jubiläum hatten sie unlängst *sehr* würdig, nicht mit einem Fest, sondern mit einem Vortrag begangen. Auf die Gebrüder Lorbeer, die beide mit Vergangenem handelten, Lothar als Buchantiquar, Louis als Antiquitätenhändler. Auf das Ehepaar Sensenschmidt, das es unwiderstehlich in die Kathedralen zog, um andächtig vor mittelalterlichen Epitaphen zu stehen. Was war es, das jede Exkursion des Vereins zu einer Freude machte? Das gemeinsame Altern? Humbug. Die gemeinsame Vergangenheit? Mumpitz. Das *memento mori?* Eher. Alle waren sie sich nämlich der Aktualität des Ephemeren bewußt. Auf den Wällen der keltischen Fliehburg, am Limes mit seinen Palisaden – überall war ja gestorben worden. Überall hatte sich der Mensch aufgebäumt, um dann kläglich zu *scheitern* und zu *verenden.* Weiland Waldemar, seines Zeichens Mediävist und Thanatologe, hatte es auf das Wort gebracht. „Wir schauen, bauen, werden zerhauen." *Videmus, aedificamus, caedimur.* Sie hatte es auf seinen Grabstein meißeln lassen. Mitten im Leben sind wir von Vergeblichkeit umgeben. *Das* erlöste.

Statements

In the light of the above passage, which of the following statements are definitely true? Correct answers are to be found on page 158.

1. Armine had stood on Celtic walls and by the palisades of the Roman Limes.
2. Her late husband, Waldemar, had been a mediaevalist.
3. Lothar Lorbeer was an antiquary.
4. Prof. Altenhoff was an expert on the pharaohs and mummies.
5. He was an advocate of the antique and the historic.
6. The Sensenschmidts revered middle-aged epitaphs.
7. The Rev. Lämmerzahl had had a jubilee to celebrate.
8. But he had not done so with a feast.
9. Louis Lorbeer dealt in antiquity.
10. Waldemar had researched into middle age and thanatology.
11. It was not altering that brought them together.
12. What united them was the actuality of the ephemeral and the eternal *memento mori.*

Area 3: Terms with a History

Your Task

Study the quotations below, paying especial attention to the eleven words underlined, each of which was once (usually well before the time of the quotation) closely linked in meaning to a German word. Then select the correct translation for each from the options beneath, noting that one true friend is involved. For the answers see page 159.

Sentences

1. WARWICK: I, then in London, keeper of the King,
Mustered my soldiers, gathered flocks of friends,
Marched towards Saint Albans to intercept the Queen [...]
WILLIAM SHAKESPEARE, *Henry VI, Part III*, II, i

2. Thus the clergy for a thousand years have been the scholars of the nation. RALPH WALDO EMERSON, 1856

3. The honest dealer is always undone, and the knave gets the advantage. JONATHAN SWIFT, *Gulliver's Travels*, I, vi, 1726

4. Ywayne and Gawayne [...] war knightes of the tabyl rownde (= were knights of the round table). *Ywain and Gawain*, c. 1350

5. Then weapon-clang, and martial call, / Resounded through the funeral hall. WALTER SCOTT, *The Lady of the Lake*, 1810

6. Each soldier will have with him three good flints.
DUKE OF WELLINGTON, 'Despatch IV, 49', 1808

7. It has been said, that the name and office of Regent are unknown to our Law and Constitution. *Edinburgh Review* XXIII, 1811

8. You shall be every day at the king's levee and I at the queen's.
JOHN DRYDEN, *Marriage à la Mode*, 1672

9. This was a dede (= deed) of queint list. *Seuyn Sag.* (W.), C 14th

10. The lady was in a gown [...] lined and faced with sables.
LADY M. W. MONTAGU, *Letter to Countess Mar*, 30 January 1717

11. The Egyptian conjurers, that are said to have turned their rods into serpents. THOMAS HOBBES, *Leviathan*, 1651

Options

Feuerstein – Flinte – Gelehrte – Knabe – Knecht – Konjurant – Levee – Lever – List – Liste – mustern – Prinzregent – Regent – Ritter – Säbel – Scholar – Schurke/Spitzbube – versammeln – Waffe(n) – Wappen – Zauberer – Zobel

Translation Theory IV: The Didactics of False Friends

The Need The high risks involved in an ignorance of 'false friends' make them an essential part in any fully-fledged curriculum of English or Translation Studies. Leading figures such as Koller, Kußmaul and Baker have duly called for more didactic attention to be accorded them. But what form should a didactics of 'false friends' take?

Thesis The thesis (and practice) of the present volume is that 'false friends' should be taught in a manner fully commensurate in scope, form and methodology to the problem they pose.

The Inadequate The mere listing of 'false friends' in dictionaries devoted to them is as potentially useful as the works concerned are detailed, differentiated and rich in example and context. As contributions to the didactics of the subject, however, they are at best quarries. As one student reviewer (of a work on Franco-German *faux amis*) pertinently, if cruelly, wrote, an alphabetical listing might seem to be useful for looking up, but the nature of false friends is that one does not suspect them to be false and hence does not look up – *‚Dumm gelaufen'.*

The several works which offer a listing of 'false' word-pairs followed by revision exercises on them have recognized the problem without really providing its solution. The exercises offered are often only of the substitution kind.

The Promising A far more promising line is that of Parkes and Cornell (1993). They offer a varied and creative series of exercises that do indeed engage the difficulties encountered. There too, however, the assumption and approach is 'teach first, test later'. *Erst kommt das Dozieren, dann kommt die Kontrolle.*

Approach The different approach of the present volume is to conflate the processes of learning and teaching. First comes the struggle with the material, then comes the clarifying elucidation. The student-reader becomes the discoverer and then his or her own instructor. This is not *Kuschelpädagogik,* but it is not *Frontalunterricht* either.

Piaget This 'new' approach is, like many 'new' things, not so young. It is based on the educational principles of Jean Piaget – notably as expressed in the section 'L'enseignement des sciences' in *Où va l'éducation?* (1972). The central tenet here is that 'comprendre, c'est inventer, ou reconstruire par réinvention', a tenet to which Piaget adds: 'et il faudra bien se plier à de telles nécessités si l'on veut, dans l'avenir, façonner des individus capables de production ou de création et non pas seulement de répétition'.

Merits

For a didactics of 'false friends' the approach has several merits. It
- enables the reader to activate all the prior knowledge he or she has;
- confronts the learner/self-instructor with the very *Irritationen* which false friends cause;
- prompts and demands differentiation;
- contextualizes;
- offers memorable – 'rememberable' – learning situations;
- offers the pleasures of discovery and *réinvention*.

University Teaching

The didactics of university teaching are, alas, in their infancy – some 800 years after the first European *universitates* emerged. The many individual examples of brilliant university teaching have yet to coalesce into a coherent didactics. The relatively small number of teachers at university level deprives such a didactics, perhaps, of an adequate audience.

Language Teaching

In addition, foreign language teaching at German universities is, alas, not all that it was. A rising number of students is often confronted with a diminishing, often dramatically diminishing, number of courses and staff. All too often, the assumption concerning university language teaching is *les serviteurs feront ça pour nous.*

Keynotes

In such a situation, it seems all the more urgent to devote time and reflection to the content and philosophy of central areas of *Sprachpraxis*.

The key elements in a didactics of 'false friends' should, the present volume argues, be as follows:
- a scope and quantity suited to the target audience concerned;
- the active development of differentiation skills;
- ongoing exposure to the reality of language – in which the 'false' come surrounded by and jostling with a crowd of the 'true';
- the constant contextualization of the language material involved;
- content which is mnemotechnic;
- a structure which goes beyond the alphabetical without sacrificing easy consultability;
- the development of an improved terminology and conceptual frame;
- the systematic study of areas and groups of 'false friends';
- a concern for the theory and history of both material and subject.

It was on the basis of such considerations that the present volume was conceived.

Field 25: Language and Slang

Area 1: Qualities of Language

Your Task

Study the statements below, paying especial attention to the fourteen words underlined, all but three of which are false friends from the area of language quality. Then select fitting translations from among those listed below. Correct answers are to be found on page 159.

Statements

1. Im Anfang war das Wort – am Ende die Phrase. STANISLAW LEC
2. Die Katzen halten keinen für eloquent, der nicht miauen kann. MARIE V. EBNER-ESCHENBACH
3. Metaphern ... diese dichten Zäune aus Wörtern. MARTIN WALSER
4. Eine Sentenz ist eine Anmaßung oder eine Vorsicht. [...] Die wirkliche Leidenschaft des Lebens spricht nicht in Sentenzen. FR. NIETZSCHE
5. Prägnanz: genaue, kurze und treffende Ausdrucksweise
6. Das Erlebnis unaufhebbarer Unzulänglichkeit wird dreifach beantwortet: mit Pathos, mit Ironie, mit Humor. LUDWIG MARCUSE
7. Du überwindest die Sprachbarriere nur, wenn du den Mut zum Versuchen hast. JULIE REDNER
8. In Abgrenzung zum Indikativ drückt der Konjunktiv [...] eine Relativierung des durch die Proposition des betreffenden Satzes zum Ausdruck gebrachten Sachverhaltes aus. NORBERT FRIES
9. Vokabel: einzelnes Wort, besonders aus einer fremden Sprache
10. Vokale sind normalerweise stimmhaft (Ausnahme: Flüstern). BERND POMPINO-MARSCHALL
11. Terminus: aus Inhaltsseite und Ausdrucksseite bestehender Fachausdruck eines Fachgebiets. BURKHARD SCHAEDER
12. Beiwort: In Schulbüchern Sammelbezeichnung für Adjektiv und Adverb.
13. Postmoderne: Vor lauter Parolen fehlt die Devise. ERNST MANDELBAUM

Options

byword – conjunctive – device – eloquent – empty phrase – epithet – impassioned tone – language barrier – maxim – metaphor – motto – parole – pathos – phrase – pithiness – pregnancy – sentence – slogan – subjunctive – term – terminus – verbal hurdle – verbal image – vocabulary – vocals – vowels – well-spoken – word

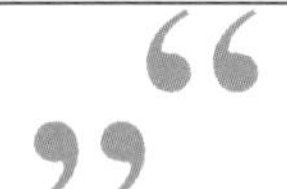

Fremdwörter sind die Gastarbeiter der Sprache.

WOLFRAM WEIDNER

Area 2: Echt tu Matsch

Your Task

Read the dialogue below, paying especial attention to the words underlined, eight of which are false friends from the area of modern slang, and trying to find translations for them as appropriate. Correct answers are to be found on page 160.

Dialogue

– Hi, Flori, Alter, du siehst vielleicht gestreßt aus.
– Ja, so kann man's auch formulieren.
– Na, hat es endlich auch dich erwischt, die Hektik der Leistungskurse? Hab' ich dir doch gesagt: Boxen sind besser als Pauken. Der Walkman ist die Oberstufe des freischwebenden Geistes.
– Red' doch nicht so'n Blödsinn. Ich bin gestreßt vor lauter Mangel an Streß.
– Das kenn' ich. Die Schule ist eine Leere fürs Leben. Echt wahr. *True for you too.* Woher kommen heute die schlechten Vibrations? Von den vielen Nullen in Mathe? Von den entfremdeten Arbeitsverhältnissen in GK?
– Weit gefehlt. Das ist ja der Hammer. Ich komme gerade – nein, ich wache gerade von unserem Leistungskurs Deutsch auf.
– Na ja, besser Schule als gar kein Schlaf. Aber jetzt mal ernsthaft. Das gibt's doch nicht. In Deutsch bist du total stark. Literatur törnt dich an. Da checkst du alles. Letztes Jahr hast du auch noch die irren Kleist-Auslegungen gerafft.
– Das war einmal. Seit Anfang dieses Schuljahres liege ich mit dem neuen Deutschlehrer im Dauerclinch. Der Mann nervt mich total.
– Tja, als Gott Lehrer schuf, hatten sie seine Hausaufgaben auch nicht so ganz richtig erklärt. Wieso diesmal der Trouble?
– Der Mann realisiert einfach nicht, daß die sprichwörtliche Würze in der Kürze liegt. Ach Hanjo, warum muß das Interpretieren von Kurzgeschichten immer so lange dauern? Da pennt alles.
– Das gab's bereits bei Goethe: ‚Über allen Bänken ist Ruh, auch vom Katheder spürest du kaum einen Hauch …'.
– Und dann hat er die Unverfrorenheit, die allgemeinen Dämmerzustände uns zum Vorwurf zu machen. ‚Früher waren die Teens anders. Damals lasen wir Chomsky, ihr lest nur noch die Charts. Damals lasen wir Foucault, ihr lest nur noch die Fanzines. Wir schrieben Flugblätter, ihr schreibt höchstens SMS. Bla, bla.'
– Und du bist ja der Bücherwurm in Person! Au weia! Heavy. Echt tu matsch. Ja, Flori, Schule ist, wenn man trotzdem hingeht. Kopf hoch! Kopf hoch und Walkman drauf!

Field 26: Current Idioms

Area 1: Interhuman Affairs

Your Task

Of the eighteen pairs of common idioms below, all of which have to do with human interaction, nine pairs are false friends and nine are true. Find the true friends and then distinguish between the false. The correct answers are to be found on page 160.

Idiom Pairs

sich die Finger verbrennen
to get one's fingers burned

jdm ein Bein stellen
to give s.o. a leg-up

(bei jdm.) auf den Busch klopfen
to beat about the bush

sich auf französisch empfehlen
to take French leave

mit Glacéhandschuhen behandeln
to handle with kid gloves

aus der Hüfte schießen
to shoot from the hip

Konsequenzen ziehen
to take the consequences

eine Lanze brechen für jdn
break a lance with s.o.

an der Nase herumführen
to lead by the nose

jdn auf etwas festnageln
to nail s.o down to sth

ganz Ohr sein
to be all ears

jdn zur Räson rufen
to call s. o. to reason

in den Schatten stellen
to put in the shade

ich pfeif dir was
put that in your pipe and smoke it

ins Schlepptau nehmen
to take in tow

Staub aufwirbeln
to raise the wind

aufs Tapet bringen
to carpet

ein Waschlappen sein
to be a wet blanket

We must think things not words, or at least we must constantly translate our words into the facts for which they stand, if we are to keep the real and true.

Oliver Wendell Holmes, address to New York State Bar Association, 1889

Area 2: The Path of Life

Distinguish between the following pairs of ill-translated sentences, all of which contain one or more sets of false friends from the field of idioms concerning our path through life. Note that also the occasional true friend is present. For the correct answers see page 161.

Your Task

Sentences

1. a) Er war über den Berg und kam bald zu Potte.
   *b) He was over the hill and soon went to pot.
2. a) Er war eindeutig ein blutiger Laie. Was nun?
   *b) He was clearly a bloody liar. What now?
3. a) Über den Daumen gepeilt sollte die Schottland-Exkursion etwa Euro 450,- kosten.
   *b) As a rule of thumb the excursion to Scotland was likely to cost Euro 450,–.
4. a) Wo war der rote Faden?
   *b) Where was the red tape?
5. a) Bereits zwei Wochen vor den Klausuren waren sie am Rande.
   *b) Two weeks before the written exams they already were on edge.
6. a) Nicht die Bohne!
   *b) Not a bean!
7. a) Es war wohl der letzte Strohhalm.
   *b) It was probably the last straw.
8. a) Die Luft war zum Schneiden. Plötzlich fiel ein Schuß. Der Schurke biß ins Gras.
   *b) You could have cut the air with a knife. All of a sudden, a shot fell. The rogue bit the carpet.
9. a) Er war einst Hahn im Korb gewesen, aber jetzt war er vor die Hunde gegangen. Alles auf tönernen Füßen!
   *b) He had once been cock of the walk, but now he had gone to the dogs. Feet of clay!
10. a) Es war klar wie Kloßbrühe. Sie waren auf hoher See.
    *b) It was as clear as mud. They were all at sea.

Field 27: *Homo Ludens*

Area 1: Free Time Activities

Your Task

This exercise contains eleven pairs of false friends from the world of free time activities. Discover them by translating the sentences below, as in the example. Correct answers are to be found on page 162.

Example

Von Beruf Dreher war er in seiner Freizeit begeisterter **Turner**.
*A **turner** by profession, he was a keen gymnast in his spare time.*

Sentences

1. Ursprünglich wollten wir den beiden ein riesengroßes Puzzle schenken, aber jetzt haben wir ein Buch mit tollen Denkspielen gekauft.

2. Sie planschte kurz am Ufer, fasste dann Mut und stürzte sich von einem Felsen in den See.

3. Er trat auf die Bühne und fing gleich an, zu steppen.

4. Nein, schwimmen könne sie nicht. Nicht richtig. Aber paddeln könne sie. Ihr Bruder könne immer noch nur planschen.

5. Sie ging direkt vom Meer in die Spielbörse am Strand und latschte in Schwimmflossen und Schwimmmaske zum Flipper.

6. Nachdem sie zwei Stunden lang erfolgreich gepuzzelt hatten, rätselten sie lange über das Setzen der letzten Teile.

7. Immer wieder vermochten Beckhams butterweiche, wohlplatzierte Flanken die Schwächen des Gegners am rechten Flügel bloßzulegen.

8. Ja, die Armeeangehörigen waren verdammt gut beim Military.

9. Wie bringen wir die Pferde am besten von den Boxen in den Pferdetransporter?

10. Damals war das Tanzen im Dancing das höchste der Gefühle.

11. Nachdem man ein paar Minuten mit ihm gerungen hatte, wollte man ihm am liebsten den Hals umdrehen.

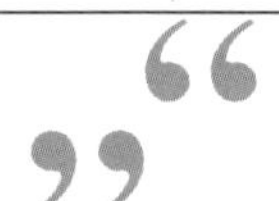

A word is its own little solar system of meaning.

TED HUGHES

Area 2: This Sporting Life

Your Task

Fill in the gaps in the sentences below, choosing the appropriate word from the list beneath. Of the thirty words in brackets only nine have 'true friends' in English. Correct answers are to be found on page 163.

Sentences

1. 'You're simply not in good *(Kondition)* _____. In fact, you're getting almost as fat as a Sumo *(Ringer)* _____. It's high time you began to *(sich trimmen)* _____.'
2. Typical Old Trafford! The spectators were huddled together in the *(Tribüne)* _____ watching the rain stream down onto the pitch.
3. He liked to *(turnen)* _____ at a young age – when still 3 he could do a good *(Handstand)* _____ – and later he turned into a capable *(Catcher)* _____.
4. Everyone looked forward to the *(Revanche)* _____. Time to *(sich rächen)* _____! Time to book a place in the *(Finale)* _____. And what a game it turned out to be – a real cliff-hanger with a gripping, dramatic, breath-taking *(Schlußakt)* _____.
5. He proved a most useful member of the cricket team, not because he could bat, but because he was an excellent *(Fänger)* _____.
6. She was prominent in several field events, her best disciplines being *(Diskus)* _____ and *(Speerwerfen)* _____. Later she became a representative, a kind of *(Volkstribun)* _____, for all athletes.
7. He's damaged his ankle. He finds it difficult to *(drehen)* _____.
8. 'We must be careful on Saturday: I've heard that our opponents will have two *(hineingeschmuggelte Stars)* _____ in their team. It seems they're determined to win the *(Liga)* _____ by whatever means.
9. 'Sorry. In my *(Zustand)* _____ I'd be a fool to go jogging with anyone, let alone with you and your *(Stoppuhr)* _____.'
10. Every Saturday he would *(Schlange stehen)* _____ for hours, *(Queue)* _____ in hand, just to get a game of snooker.
11. That's life. At first you play with *(Knicker)* _____, then with a *(Fußball)* _____, then it's *(Rugby)* _____ and *(Krickett)* _____, then just *(Langlauf)* _____ or *(Golf)* _____ until, at the end, all you can manage is *(Minigolf)* _____ or a *(Robber)* _____ at whist. Or not even that.

Options

all-in wrestler / American football / catcher / condition / crazy golf / cricket / croquet / cross-country skiing / cue / disc / discus / final / finale / football / golf / grandstand / do gymnastics / handstand / javelin / keep fit / knickers / league / long-distance running / marbles / queue / return match / revenge / ringer / robber / rubber / rugby / shape / soccer ball / somersault / spear / stop-watch / table / take revenge / tribune / trim / turn / wrestler

Field 28: Literature and Theatre

Area 1: Genres and Ages

Your Task

Study the statements below, paying especial attention to the fourteen words underlined, all but two of which are false friends from the area of literary genres and periods. Then select fitting translations from among those below. Correct answers are to be found on page 164.

Statements

1. Das Schreiben eines Romans ist ein umgekehrter Striptease, und alle Romanciers sind diskrete Exhibitionisten. MARIO VARGAS LLOSA
2. Wo die Sprache versagt, beginnt der Vers. RUDOLF LEONHARD
3. Wenn schon die Poesie überhaupt ein Rätsel ist, so ist die Lyrik das Rätsel der Rätsel. CARL SPITTELER
4. Das Epos steht der Musik näher als jede andere Dichtungsart. TH. MANN
5. Im Schwank macht sich der Überlegene über die Dummheit oder Unbeholfenheit des Unterlegenen lustig. HANS GERD RÖTZER
6. Die Novelle beschäftigt sich mehr mit dem Werden, der Roman mit dem Gewordenen. HEINRICH LAUBE
7. Unter Klassikern verstehen Verleger einen Schriftsteller, der tantiemenfrei geworden ist. ROBERT LEMBKE
8. Die Gattungsbezeichnung Posse begegnet zuerst im 17. Jahrhundert für die kurzen derb-komischen Nachspiele der Wanderbühne. JÜRGEN KÜHNEL
9. Pamphlet: Form publizistischer Angriffsliteratur. HELMUT WEIDHASE
10. Der Novellist, wie er weniger Personen auf die Leinwand zu bringen hat, [...] hat auch weniger Farben auf der Palette. FRIEDRICH SPIELHAGEN
11. Sagen, Volkslieder, Überlieferungen [...] sind noch trübe Weisen und daher den Vorstellungen trüber Völker eigen. G. W. F. HEGEL
12. Die ganze Fragwürdigkeit solcher Bezeichnungen wie Klassik und Romantik [...] wird an der Dichtung Jean Pauls deutlich, ähnlich wie an der Dichtung Hölderlins. WOLFDIETRICH RASCH

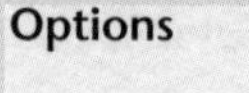

Options

burlesque / classic / Classical Age / epos / epic / farce / lampoon / lines of verse / lyric / lyric verse / novel / novelist / novella / pamphlet / polemic / posse / Roman / romancer / Romantic / Romanticism / saga / sage / swank / verses / writer of novellas

In a world full of audio-visual marvels, may words matter to you and be full of magic.

GODFREY SMITH, 'Letter to a new grandchild', *Sunday Times,* 5 July 1987

Area 2: Anglo-American Theatre

Your Task

Fill in the gaps in the sentences below, choosing the appropriate word from the list beneath. Of the words in brackets only two have 'true friends' in English. Correct answers are to be found on page 165.

Sentences

1. The *(Rampe)* _____ allowing close contact between the cast and the *(Publikum)* _____ – which often stood in the pit rather than *(Platz nehmen)* _____ in the *(Ränge)* _____ – became a key feature of Shakespearean theatre and theatricals.
2. Together with classical *(Fabeln/Handlungen)* _____, the *(Chor)* _____ is revived in wartime and post-war theatre – in Sartre's *Les Mouches* (1943), in T. S. Eliot's *(Versdramen)* _____ and in Arthur Miller's *The Crucible* (1953).
3. Sir Laurence Olivier, one of the great *(Mimen)* _____ of post-war Britain, was also a gifted *(Imitator)* _____.
4. One of the great traditions of London theatre is the RADA Theatre Club, where *(Karten)* _____, even in the *(Parkett)* _____, cost next-to-nothing, and the student actors give their all as they reach out for career and fame.
5. Thora Hird, famous for her *(Chargen)* _____ in TV comedies, began her English stage career as a *(Statistin)* _____ at a tender age.
6. In British theatres, three bells are sounded before the performance and at the end of each *(Pause)* _____ to summon the audience in to their seats and *(Logen)* _____.
7. Among the scandal-ridden plays whose first performance ended not with *(Akkoladen)* _____ but with a *(Spektakel)* _____ are Samuel Beckett's *Waiting for Godot* (1952/4) and Howard Brenton's *Romans in Britain* (1980).
8. Existentialist theatre is marked by few *(Requisiten)* _____ – the bareness of the stage mirroring the bleakness of the world-picture.
9. The *(Theaterdame)* _____, played traditionally by a man, is one of the key parts in the British *(Weihnachtsspiel)* _____ ('panto').
10. Few modern dramatists have used *(imposantes Schauspiel)* _____ on the stage more effectively than Peter Shaffer.
11. The idea of a theatrical *(Probe)* _____ is first found just before Shakespeare's day and of course features in *A Midsummer Night's Dream* (*c.* 1596).

Options

accolade / actor / applause / apron stage / audience / aunt / box / cards / character part / charge / choir / chorus / circle / Dame / fable / imitator / interval / lodge / mime / mimic / mute / pageantry / pantomime / parquet / pause / plot / poetic drama / probe / prop / public / ramp / rehearsal / requisites / rung / spectacle / stalls / statist / take a seat / take place / tickets / uproar / verse drama / walk-on part

Area 3: The Literary World

Your Task

This exercise contains ten pairs of false friends from the literary world. Discover them by translating the sentences below, as in the example. Correct answers are to be found on page 166.

Example

*Among the writings of Harold Pinter are several film **scripts**.*
Zu den **Schriften** von Harold Pinter gehören auch einige Drehbücher.

Sentences

1. In his lectures of 1808 S. T. Coleridge makes a distinction essential to British Romanticism – between fantasy and imagination.

2. The frank sexuality in D. H. Lawrence's *The Rainbow* (1915) met with the censure of critics and also fell foul of censorship.

3. T. S. Eliot's literary criticism – from *The Sacred Wood* (1920) on – makes him perhaps the finest critic among English-language poets.

4. A first edition copy of Robert Lowell's *Life Studies* (1959) is a rare and valuable thing. Its ironic autobiographical style is now seen as the exemplar for much post-war American verse.

5. Characteristic of the novels of Joyce Cary (1888–1957) is the close character study of artistic figures by means of first-person narrative.

6. The blood-boltered *Revenger's Tragedy* (1608), ascribed to Cyril Tourneur, is the epitome of Jacobean revenge tragedy, notable more for its intricate plot than for its subtle handling of character.

7. The Gospels of St. Matthew and St. Mark are the two great recensions of the essential Bible story. Only in the writings of George Eliot does the term mean 'book-review'.

8. Salman Rushdie, now a leading novelist and commentator, worked first as a publicist, writing the advertising copy he ably satirizes in the *The Moor's Last Sigh* (1995).

9. There is still something about possessing your own copy signed in your presence by the author, instead of just the class-marked book taken from a library shelf.

10. One of the great pleasures in working with George Orwell's *Collected Essays, Journalism and Letters* (1968) is the magnificent index compiled by Sonia Orwell – a register of all that was happening in British literature between the Wars.

Field 29: The Arts and the Art World

Area 1: Music

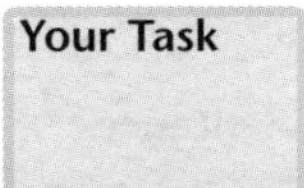

The sixteen pairs of words below all derive from the field of music and musical instruments, only three of them, however, being genuine equivalents. Find the true friends and then distinguish between the false. The correct answers are to be found on page 167.

Word Pairs

der Akkord
the accord

der Bügel
the bugle

das Kornett
the cornet

dudeln
to doodle

das Fagott
the faggot

die Hoboe
the hobo

die Lieder
the lieder

die Melodie
the melody

die Opera
the opera

die Pfeife
the fife

das Plektron
the plectrum

der Takt
the tact

das Tamtam
the tom-tom

das Tamburin
the tambourine

der Ton
the tone

überspielen
to overplay

Eine Bedeutung eines Wortes ist eine Art seiner Verwendung. Denn sie ist das, was wir erlernen, wenn das Wort zuerst unserer Sprache einverleibt wird.
Wenn sich die Sprachspiele ändern, ändern sich die Begriffe, und mit den Begriffen die Bedeutungen der Wörter.

LUDWIG WITTGENSTEIN, *Über Gewißheit* (1969), §§ 61 & 65

Area 2: Anglo-American Art

Your Task

In each of the sentences below, the sense is disturbed by at least one grave misuse of word concerning art. Replace the offending terms by correct alternatives. The answers are to be found on page 168.

Sentences

*1. In American art, with its strong Puritan background, a famous absence is the act – an absence played on by Raphaelle Peale (1774–1825) in his ironic and suggestive towel-covered non-act, 'After the Bath' (1823).

*2. Willem de Kooning (1904–97) and Robert Rauschenberg (1925–) are two of the leading lithographs in modern-day American art, creatively using the medium for their abstract Expressionist visions.

*3. Few painters have a more distinctive art than Howard Hodgkin (1930–): his pastose canvases, all brushstrokes, dabs, and colourful coloration, highlight the very elements of art and the creative process.

*4. Perhaps the most-viewed plastic in all of Britain is Anthony Gormley's magnificent, monolithic 'Angel of the North' (1996) – its rusting steel a cryptic comment on the achievement of industrialism.

*5. Turner's oil-paintings 'The Fighting Temeraire' (1839) and 'Hannibal Crossing the Alps' (1830) are remarkable depictions of military action swallowed by landscape. As so often in his oeuvre, it is not the craft of man and machine that is admired but that of Nature.

*6. In the post-impressionist work of Mark Gertler (1891–1939) the motif of the circus artist, evocatively characterized, plays a key part.

*7. In the work of the leading photograph Jane Bown (1929–), the artistic medium, the whole photo apparatus – objective, blend, blitz and all – is central.

*8. James Gillray (1757–1815) and George Cruikshank (1792–1878) are the leading caricaturists of their day. They enlarge the scope of pictorial satire and personalize it, thus forming the artistic bridge between the general social comment of William Hogarth (1697–1764) and the newspaper caricaturists of our own day.

Field 30: Religious Practices

Area 1: The Religious Life

Distinguish between the following pairs of ill-translated sentences, each of which contains one or more pairs of false friends from the realm of church affairs. For the correct answers see page 168.

1. a) Ja, sie hatte ein sinnvolles Leben geführt.
   *b) Yes, she had led a sinful life.
2. a) Das Vatikanum stimmte viele Gläubige nachdenklich.
   *b) The Vatican gave many believers food for thought.
3. a) Er ließ es sein: Das Sekret des Superintendenten wollte er nicht stören.
   *b) He let things be: he did not want to disturb the superintendent's secret.
4. a) Das enggedruckte Brevier war kaum zu lesen.
   *b) The closely-printed brevier was hardly legible.
5. a) Sie gingen beide ins Vikariat.
   *b) The two of them went into the vicarage.
6. a) Was war das Beste an der Konfession? Die Erlösung, die sie versprach.
   *b) What was the best thing about the confession? The deliverance it promised.
7. a) Der Eremit hielt sich fast nur in der Klause auf.
   *b) The hermit stuck closely to the clause.
8. a) Die Kasualien konnten teuer ausfallen.
   *b) The casuals could be dear.

Durch Worte und Begriffe werden wir nie hinter die Wand der Relationen, etwa in irgendeinen fabelhaften Urgrund der Dinge gelangen, und selbst in den reinen Formen der Sinnlichkeit und des Verstandes, in Raum, Zeit und Kausalität gewinnen wir nichts, was einer veritas aeterna *ähnlich sähe.*

Friedrich Nietzsche, *Die Philosophie im tragischen Zeitalter der Griechen* (1903)

Area 2: The Church-Goer

Your Task

Read the passage below, paying especial attention to the key words from the world of the Church and liturgy, seventeen of which are false friends. Then consider the statements beneath.

Text

Johann zog es in Kirchen. In Kirchen, nicht in die Kirche. Dafür hatte er zu viel Schleiermacher gelesen. Und Camus. Und Deschner. Nichtsdestotrotz betrat er gerne die stillen, leeren Räume, musterte kundig Kanzel und Altarraum, stand kurz vor der Statue des Patrons, ging in die Querschiffe, in die Seitenkapellen, in die Sakristei.

Fand eine Messe statt, oder wurde nur in einer Ecke still gebetet, so zog er sich rasch zurück. Dem Christen wich er generell aus. Nichts war ihm unangenehmer als ein junger, mit verklärtem Blick herbeieilender Vikar. Das Christentum hatte ja zu viel Unheil angerichtet. Dessen Moral war ihm suspekt, Gottesdienste und Liturgie waren ihm zu pathetisch, die Kollekte hielt er für anrüchig.

Aber nichtsdestotrotz: In den stillen Räumen wehte ein Geist. Ein Geist fern aller Unrast, aller Geschäftigkeit. Er spürte ihn ganz besonders auch in Klöstern. Und dieses Geistliche zog ihn noch an. Etwas Sakrales, Nichtprofanes. In den Schriften der Evangelisten war es auch vorhanden, ebenfalls in den Upanischaden, den Veden.

Aber was hatten sie nur daraus gemacht, die Eiferer, die Bigotten, die Popen und Ajatollahs! So bereitwillig er die Gotteshäuser betrat, so gerne verließ er sie auch. War nicht die Natur – die ‚Schöpfung' – Tempel genug? Jedenfalls: Er war lieber unter dem Sternenhimmel, dem Firmament. Wie hieß es doch bei Camus? *J'aime la nuit et le ciel, plus que les dieux des hommes.*

Statements

In the light of the above passage, which of the following statements are definitely true? Correct answers are to be found on page 169.

1. Christendom, in Johann's opinion, did much harm.
2. Johann disliked the Church's moral and asceticism.
3. Nevertheless, he liked going to the kirk – far from all unrest.
4. He looked at the chancel, at the patrons, at the side-chapels.
5. And he was especially fond of cloisters.
6. But he disliked any mess and any betting in churches.
7. He found the liturgy pathetic. Especially the collect.
8. Church buildings, however, had something sacred, non-profane.
9. What appealed to him above all was the ghostly, a ghost present also in the writings of the Evangelists and the Upanishads.
10. Popes, ayatollahs and bigots had played old Harry with religion.
11. Johann avoided meeting Christ. He found vicars insufferable.
12. Nature was temple enough.

Revision Exercises I (Fields 1–6)

Exercise 1

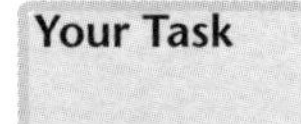

Translate the headlines and sentences below, each of which contains at least one 'false friend' from those covered in the first six Fields. Correct answers are to be found on page 171.

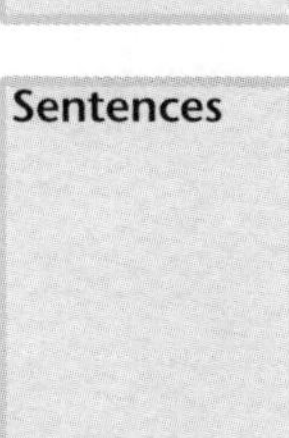

1. Gute Lehre muß irritieren. *SäZ*, 14. 02. 03
2. Psychologen beraten über psychisch kranke Kinder. *DNN*, 15. 04. 03
3. Mein Lenkrad flattert. *Bild*, 02. 01. 03
4. „Brandsimulator" macht erstmals Station im Kreis. *SäZ*, 04. 12. 02
5. Schöpfung bewahren. *DW*, 27. 11. 02
6. Mit neuen Rezepten gegen das Altern. *FAZ*, 16. 11. 02
7. Die Ölpest wird zur Chefsache *taz*, 09. 12. 02
8. Es fällt immer eine erste Schneeflocke, was für ein Gewimmel nachher kommen mag. WILHELM RAABE

Exercise 2

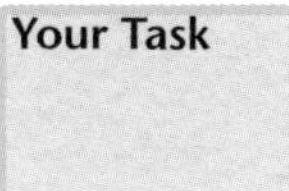

Translate the passage below, the opening of Ödön von Horváth's short story 'Geschichte einer kleinen Liebe' which contains several 'false friends' and several 'true' from those covered in the first six Fields. A correct translation is to be found on page 171.

Still wirds im Herbst, unheimlich still.

Es ist alles beim alten geblieben, nichts scheint sich verändert zu haben. Weder das Moor noch das Ackerland, weder die Tannen dort auf den Hügeln noch der See. Nur, daß der Sommer vorbei. Ende Oktober. Und bereits spät am Nachmittag.

In der Ferne heult ein Hund und die Erde duftet nach aufgeweichtem Laub. Es hat lange geregnet während den letzten Wochen, nun wird es bald schneien. Fort ist die Sonne und die Dämmerung schlürft über den harten Boden, es raschelt in den Stoppeln, als schliche wer umher. Und mit den Nebeln kommt die Vergangenheit. Ich sehe Euch wieder, Ihr Berge, Bäume, Straßen – wir sehen uns alle wieder! [. . .]

Revision Exercises II (Fields 7–12)

Exercise 1

Your Task

Translate the sentences below, each of which contains at least one 'false friend' from those covered in Fields 7–12. Correct answers are to be found on page 171.

Sentences

1. Kindlich sein heißt zur Kindheit hinaufsteigen, kindisch sein zur Kindheit herabsteigen. Aus den *Fliegenden Blättern*
2. Die Laster der Großen nennt man Allüren. FRIEDL BEUTELROCK
3. Wer sagt, was er tut, ist eitel. Wer tut, was er sagt, ist gut. MARTIN WALSER
4. Ich glaub ich hab ein Faible für Idioten. LASSIE SINGERS
5. Ein Mensch ist faul, wenn er sich lieber ärgert als aufzustehen. THOMAS NIEDERREUTHER
6. Genialität ist zeitlos gewordene Gegenwart. HANS LOHBERGER
7. Kraft ist die Materie der Stoffe. NOVALIS
8. Alle Worte scharwenzeln um die Wahrheit herum; sie ist keusch. WILHELM BUSCH
9. Der Spott endet, wo Verständnis beginnt. EBNER-ESCHENBACH
10. Die Dummheiten beider Geschlechter bleiben streng getrennt. ANNEMARIE WEBER
11. Eine eitle Frau braucht einen Spiegel. Ein eitler Mann ist sein eigener Spiegel. FRANÇOISE SAGAN
12. Plunder ist alles, was seine Brauchbarkeit eingebüßt hat. OLIVER HERFORD

Exercise 2

Your Task

Translate the newspaper headlines and passage below, each of which contains at least one 'false friend' from those covered in Fields 7–12. Correct answers are to be found on page 172.

Headlines

1. Das neue Preissystem ist besonders für Senioren attraktiv. DB
2. Schalke blamiert sich gegen Wisla Krakau. *SäZ*, 11. 12. 02
3. In den letzten Monaten hatte viel darauf hingewiesen, daß Gore auf Rache und Revanche aus war. *DNN*, 17. 12. 02
4. Handyverbot in Theatern. *SäZ*, 19. 02. 02
5. London – Weltstadt der skurrilen Verkehrsmittel. *WeKu*, 02. 01. 03
6. Auch klügste Köpfe kennen das: Statt genialer Geistesblitze tröpfeln lahme Ideen, weil die Denkzentrale nur mit halber Kraft arbeitet. Das können Sie ändern. *JfdF*, 26/2002

Revision Exercises III (Fields 13–18)

Exercise 1

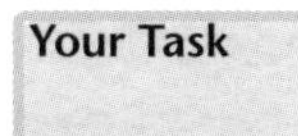

Translate the aphorisms and headlines below, each of which contains at least one 'false friend' from those covered in Fields 13–18. Correct answers are to be found on page 172.

1. Die Zeitschriften sind [...] die Pißecken der Literatur, aber alle Annoncen sind dort angeschlagen. Heinrich Heine
2. Das Risiko ist die Bugwelle des Erfolges. Carl Améry
3. Eine Konferenz ist eine Sitzung, bei der viele hineingehen und wenig herauskommt. Werner Finck
4. Prospekt: illustrierte Vortäuschung von Informationen. H. Nahr
5. Slogan ist das Wort, das die Konkurrenz schlägt. Karl Korn
6. Technik: das sind auch die aufgespeicherten Resultate der langen Kämpfe gegen die Feinde der Menschen. Insofern ist sie zu preisen. Ludwig Marcuse
7. Die Löhne sind das Maß der Würde, welches die Gesellschaft einer Arbeit verleiht. Johnnie Tillmon
8. ‚Aller Anfang ist schwer', sagte der Volontär und schrieb zuerst einen Leitartikel. Markus Ronner
9. Stipendium: Trinkgeld für Wissensdurstige. Wolfram Weidner
10. Die Bürger honorieren Ehrlichkeit, auch unbequeme Ehrlichkeit. Erwin Staudt

1. Unternehmen nehmen Reklamationen ernst. *FAZ*, 18. 01. 02
2. Tarifkonflikt spitzt sich zu. *SäZ*, 19. 12. 02
3. Konjunkturklima in Europa verschlechtert sich. *FAZ*, 01. 04. 03
4. Keine Zweifel an der Bonität des Staates. *DNN*, 17. 12. 02
5. Sparen – vor allem bei Personalkosten. Stadtrat verabschiedet Haushalt für 2003. *SäZ*, 25. 11. 02
6. Der damalige Verkäufer ließ die Waggons von seinem Bruder nach Nürnberg expeditieren. *DW*, 16. 12. 02
7. Reklameverbot für Tabak erregt die Werbebranche. *DW*, 04. 12. 02
8. Rentner, Angestellte, Beamte am spendabelsten. *DNN*, 17. 12. 02
9. Kopfstand im Modehaus. Dafür gab's 20 Euro Rabatt. *Bild*, 30. 12. 02
10. Messe sucht nach neuen Konzepten. *MoPo*, 12. 02. 03
11. Sie wollen controllen statt kontrollieren? *FAZ*, 13. 07. 02
12. Pessimisten übernehmen wieder das Ruder. *FAZ*, 01. 11. 02
13. Mittelstand beklagt Kreditkonditionen *FAZ*, 27. 11. 02
14. United Airlines steht vor sicherem Konkurs *taz*, 09. 12. 02

Revision Exercises IV (Fields 19–24)

Exercise 1

Your Task

Translate the headlines and sentences below, each of which contains at least one 'false friend' from those covered in Fields 19–24. Correct answers are to be found on page 173.

Sentences

1. Mörder ist einer, der tötet, und der schwächer ist als die Polizei. HELMAR NAHR
2. Die Frau kontrolliert ihren Sex, weil sie für Sex all das bekommt, was ihr noch wichtiger ist als Sex. ESTHER VILAR
3. Alle unsere Irrtümer übertragen wir auf unsere Kinder, in denen sie unaustilgbare Spuren hinterlassen. MARIA MONTESSORI
4. Solch ein friedliches Land –! Da tragen die Polizisten noch Säbel. KURT TUCHOLSKY
5. In Österreich resigniert man schon so lange und so erfolgreich, daß daraus Zerfallsenergie entsteht. ERICH SOKOL
6. Die Deutschen haben, wenn sie über auswärtige Politik sprechen, kaum eine andere Ressource als Moral. HERFRIED MÜNKLER
7. Auch Schritte der Vorsicht hinterlassen Spuren. STANISLAV LEC
8. Die Resignation rührt aus der Erkenntnis, daß es den Hafen gar nicht gibt und ein Ankommen erst recht nicht, sondern immer wieder ein Beginnen mit neuen Entwürfen, neuen Menschen, neuen Utopien und Kapitulationen. JUDITH HERMANN

Newspaper Texts

1. Handy-Aktien feiern ein furioses Comeback. *DW*, 04. 12. 02
2. Schlechte Noten für die Wirtschaftsförderung. *SäZ*, 11. 12. 02
3. 47 Prozent der Männer betrügen mindestens einmal ihre Frau. *La*, 51/2002
4. Vielen Schulen in Deutschland sieht man die Finanzmisere der Kommunen an. *FAZ*, 03. 04. 03
5. Ob die Kliniken Revision gegen das Urteil einlegen wollen, ist noch offen. *WeKu*, 31. 12. 02
6. Wichtige Teile des Konzepts wurden nicht umgesetzt. PETER HARTZ, VW-Manager
7. Koch wirft Rot-Grün „Betrug am Wähler" vor. *DW*, 25. 11. 02
8. Bahn spurt wieder. *SäZ*, 11. 12. 02
9. Gegen den Wind von der Basis. *FAZ*, 01. 04. 03
10. Die Kommunen sehen sich ebenfalls nicht in der Lage, mehr für ihr Personal auszugeben. *FAZ*, 04. 01. 03

Revision Exercises V (Fields 25–30)

Your Task

Translate the sentences below, each of which contains at least one 'false friend' from those covered in Fields 25–30. Correct answers are to be found on page 173.

Sentences

1. Die Moral, die gut genug war für unsere Väter, ist nicht gut genug für unsere Kinder. MARIE VON EBNER-ESCHENBACH
2. Die Novelle ist ein Gleichnis, der Roman ein Beispiel, das Drama ein Urteil. OTTO STÖẞL
3. Das Christentum ist die Religion der tiefsten Beunruhigung. GERHART HAUPTMANN
4. Wer mit mir reden will, der darf nicht bloß seine eigene Meinung hören wollen. WILHELM RAABE
5. Die Zeit der Not ruft Apostel und nicht Doktoren auf die Kanzel. ENRIKA VON HANDEL-MAZZETTI
6. Lyrik ist gemalte Poesie. HANS LOHBERGER
7. Die kommende Romantik ist [. . .] ein Stück Eis, in dem eine Flamme brennt. WASSILY KANDINSKY
8. Die Lektüre ist das Zusammenwirken des Lesers mit dem Gelesenen. PÉGUY
9. Sie tanzte im Takt. Jedoch mit dem falschen Partner. HANS L. DAVI
10. Die Phrase ist die Muttersprache der Politik. KARLHEINZ DESCHNER
11. Ich weiß, daß ich eine Art handwerklicher Romancier bin. Ein Novellist bin ich ganz gewiß nicht. ROBERT WALSER
12. Die Phantasie ist ein ewiger Frühling. FRIEDRICH SCHILLER
13. Die Zensur ist die jüngere von zwei schändlichen Schwestern, die ältere heißt Inquisition. JOHANN NESTROY
14. Die Kritik erscheint wie Ate: Sie verfolgt die Autoren, aber hinkend. J. W. V. GOETHE
15. Die Melodie ist die Sprache des Herzens. PARMET
16. Pathos ist Faulheit der Logik. HANS KASPER
17. ‚Würde' ist ein Konjunktiv. HANNS-HERMANN KERSTEN
18. Am grünen Tisch verloren sie den roten Faden. JOSEPH BISIG
19. Zu Lebzeiten eines Autors werden seine Bücher rezensiert; nach dem Tode er selbst. Die Schlußrezension fällt meist etwas günstiger aus. HANNS-HERMANN KERSTEN
20. Unerfüllbare Wünsche werden als ‚fromme' bezeichnet. Man scheint anzunehmen, daß nur die profanen in Erfüllung gehen. M. V. EBNER-ESCHENBACH

Revision of Revisions

Exercise 1

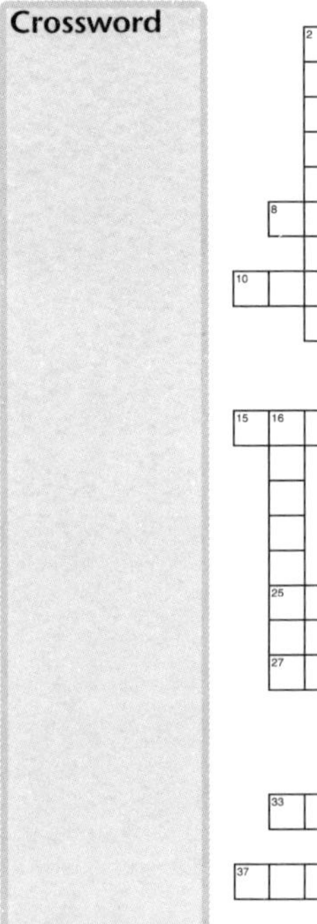

Your Task

Complete the crossword below, which is made up of some forty 'classic' 'false friends' covered in this volume. The correct answers are to be found on page 174.

Crossword

Clues

Across 2. resignieren (6,8) 4. konsequent (10) 6. Unternehmer (12) 8. Puzzle (6) 10. Föhre (4) 11. Dom (9) 13. bekommen (3) 14. Reklamation (9) 15. Moor (3) 18. City (4,6) 20. & 24. trimmen (4,3) 21. Allee (6) 23. Mist (6) 24. *see* 20 25. Ruder (3) 26. sinnvoll (10) 27. bewahren (4) 30. Gymnasium (7,6) 33. Prozeß (5) 34. massiv (Holz) (5) 35. Note (4) 37. Christ (9) 38. Lust (8)

Down 1. sensibel (9) 2. genial (9) 3. Kontrollen (6) 5. aktuell (7) 7. Marine (4) 9. Rezept (vom Arzt) (12) 11. engagiert (9) 12. human (6) 16. übersehen (8) 17. sympathisch (8) 18. Stuhl (5) 19. Lektüre (7) 22. peinlich (12) 28. eventuell (7) 29. Exemplar (4) 31. Kartoffelchips (6) 32. Übersicht (6) 36. wandern (4)

Exercise 2

Your Task

Translate the following texts, from both literature and the press, noting that each contains at least two – and at times more – false friends from among those encountered in all the foregoing Fields.

Sentences

1. Noch ein Gremium: Senioren im Kreis bilden den Konvent. *SäZ*, 27. 11. 02
2. Silvester-Fete: Die Rezepte. *JfdF*, 26/2002
3. Durch die Aktionen in der Hauptstadt Wroclaw wurde das Thema nun landesweit aktuell. *SäZ*, 02. 12. 02
4. Dichtung: ein Text im Smoking; engagierte Dichtung: ein Text im Smoking mit roter Fliege. SCHLOSSER
5. Geniale Naturen verfolgen kein Ziel – sie werden vom Ziel verfolgt. ANITA DANIEL
6. Einen nie auf die Probe gestellte Frau denkt stets von sich zu gut, und von dem Sieg zu leicht. JEAN PAUL
7. Phantasie ist der Goldglanz, der über dem Dasein liegt, und es über das Grau des Alltags erhebt. WLADIMIR LINDENBERG
8. Auch die aktuelle Konjunkturkrise setze dem Unternehmen nicht so stark zu wie anderen Branchen. *DW*, 16. 12. 02
9. Ministerin fordert spätere Rente für Akademiker. *Bild*, 18. 12. 02
10. Wer sich nach Konjunkturprognosen richtet, ist schlecht beraten. *DZ*, 24. 11. 02
11. Spender aus dem Stall. *DZ*, 31. 10. 02
12. Urlaub auf Rezept – Blaumacher schaden ihren Chefs. *DZ*, 31. 10. 02
13. Statt auf der Kanzel landen viele Vikare der Evangelischen Kirche im Aus. *DZ*, 29. 05. 02
14. Die Kraft der Seele offenbart sich in der Höhe des Zieles. ELSE HASSE
15. Die Liebe lebt vom Wunder, nicht vom Recht. CHRISTINE BUSTA

Exercise 3

Your Task

Translate the following passages into German, paying especial attention to the one or more 'false friends' that each contains. Correct translations are to be found on page 175.

Sentences

1. A mere scholar, who knows nothing but books, must be ignorant even of them. WILLIAM HAZLITT
2. I cannot see that lectures can do so much good as reading the books from which the lectures are taken. SAMUEL JOHNSON
3. Eventually, the novel will be just an academic exercise, written by academics to be used in classroom in order to test the ingenuity of students. GORE VIDAL
4. Believe a woman or an epitaph, / Or any other thing that's false, before /You trust in critics who themselves are sore. LORD BYRON
5. Proper words in proper places make the true definition of style. JONATHAN SWIFT
6. The expansion of knowledge implies that each book ... contains a progressively smaller fraction of all that is known. ALVIN TOFFLER
7. The only important thing in a book is the meaning it has for you. SOMERSET MAUGHAM
8. The impulse to write a novel comes from a momentary unified vision of life. ANGUS WILSON
9. You think it horrible that lust and rage / Should dance attention upon my old age; / They were not such a plague when I was young; / What else have I to spur me into song? W. B. YEATS
10. Adjectives are the betrayers of poetry, the poet's chief enemies. SAUNDERS LEWIS
11. The poet is really engaged in recreating the familiar, he's not committed to introducing the unfamiliar. PHILIP LARKIN
12. Some reviews give pain. That is regrettable, but no author has any right to whine. E. M. FORSTER
13. For rhyme the rudder is of verses, / With which like ships they steer their courses. SAMUEL BUTLER I
14. In language there is a spice of spelling. GEOFFREY GRIGSON
15. Literature in many of its branches is no other than the shadow of a good talk. R. L. STEVENSON
16. It is so dull and gruesome how we die. ROBERT LOWELL
17. I write a book for no other reason than to add three or four hundred acres to my magnificent estate. JACK LONDON
18. Yes, for the last two weeks I have written scarcely anything. I have been idle; I have failed. KATHERINE MANSFIELD

Answers

Um auch momentanen Verwechslungen vorzubeugen, werden im Antwortteil englische Vokabeln durchweg normal, *deutsche Vokabeln* hingegen kursiv gesetzt.

Field 1: The World of Matter

Page 9: The Physical World

Solutions

The solutions to this exercise are: A4, B8, C10, D9, E17, F13, G15, H19, I5, J16, K20, L3, M14, N11, O18, P6, Q7, R2, S12, T1

The details of the false friends involved are as follows:

blank	shiny, shining, bright; *(Augen)* bright, feverish; *(Schwert)* uncovered, naked; *(Entsetzen)* sheer
blank	leer, unbeschrieben; *(Formular)* nicht ausgefüllt
blasen	to blow; (*Blasinstrumente*) blow, sound, play
to blaze	*(auf)flammen, brennen, lodern*
blenden	to dazzle; to blind; to put out s. o.'s eyes
to blend	*(ver)mengen, (ver)mischen, Mischung zusammenstellen*
blubbern	(*Wasser*) to bubble; (*Mensch*) to gabble
to blubber	*heulen, weinen, flennen, schluchzen*
breit	broad, wide; (*Dialekt*) broad
bright	*hell, glänzend; (Wetter) heiter; (Mensch) aufgeweckt, intelligent; fröhlich*
luftig	airy; (*Kleidung*) cool; (*Mensch*) happy-go-lucky
lofty	*hochragend; hochfliegend, erhaben, edel*
massiv	(*Holz, Struktur*) solid; (*Angriff*) heavy; (*Vorwürfe*) grave
massive	*wuchtig, klobig; schwer, massig*
plombieren	(*Zahn*) to fill; (*Gefäß, Wagen*) to seal
to plumb	*ausloten, sondieren; als Klempner arbeiten*
quellen	(*Wasser, Tränen*) to well up; (*Fluß*) to spring
to quell	*bezwingen; (Aufstand, Gefühle) unterdrücken*
ranken	(*Pflanzen*) to climb, creep, run
to rank	*rangieren; einstufen, einreihen, einordnen*
stickig	suffocating, stifling; (*Luft*) stuffy, close
sticky	*klebrig*

Page 10: States, Qualities and Quantities

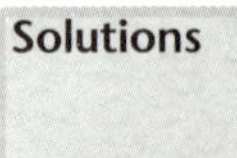

Solutions

The solutions to this exercise are: 1. a) fire b) smoke 2. pinch 3. a) bronze b) gift 4. a) damp b) rottenness 5. a) qualms (*or*: scruples) b) poison 6. steam 7. (fire) brands 8. prise 9. a) glance b) shone c) sheen 10. a) notch b) tuft 11. foulness 12. a) lime b) kerb 13. a) chalk b) crystal 14. a) lava b) fossil 15. bushel

True Friends

The true friends involved in the exercise are thus 'bronze', 'crystal', 'fossil' and 'lava'. The details of the false friends involved are as follows:

False Friends

der Brand	the fire, blaze; (*Großbrand*) conflagration
the brand	*die Brandfackel, brennendes Holzscheit*
das Büschel	(*Haare, Gras*) tuft; (*Blätter, Blüten*) cluster
the bushel	*der Scheffel* (8 bushels = 2,909 *Hektoliter*)
der Dampf	(*Wasser~*) the steam; (*Dämpfe*) vapours
the damp	*die Feuchtigkeit*
die Fäulnis	the rottenness; decay; (*stinkend*) putrefaction
the foulness	*die Schmutzigkeit, der Schmutz; die Gemeinheit*
das Gift	the poison; (*Schlangen~*) venom
the gift	*das Geschenk; das Präsent*
der Glanz	the brightness; (*funkelnd*) lustre; (*Politur*) shine
the glance	*der flüchtige Blick*
der Kalk	the lime; (*im Körper*) calcium
the chalk	*die Kreide; die Zeichen~*
die Kerbe	the notch, nick
the kerb	*der Randstein, die Straßenkante*; (~ drill) *Verkehrserziehung für Fußgänger*
die Prise	(*Salz, Schnupftabak*) pinch
the prise	*die Hebelwirkung, -kraft*
der Qualm	(thick/dense) smoke
the qualm	*der Skrupel, der Zweifel*
der Schein	(*Sonnen~, Lampen~*) shine; (*Schimmer*) gleam
the sheen	*der Glanz* (*besonders von Stoffen*)

Page 11: Man-Made Substances and States

Solutions

The solutions to this crossword are: 1. split 2. factory 3. gum 4. decoction 5. crushed stone 6. glue 7. suds 8. rubber 9. putty 10. shavings 11. lacquer 12. lime 13. fabric 14. span 15. the kit 16. pap 17. paintwork 18. cardboard
Key Phrase: touched by human hand

The details of the false friends involved are as follows:

False Friends

die Fabrik	the factory, (*altm.*) mill
the fabric	*der Stoff, das Gewebe; das Gefüge, Gebilde*
das Gummi	(*Radiergummi*) eraser, rubber
the gum	*Klebstoff, Gummilösung; Kaugummi*; (gums) *Zahnfleisch*
der Kitt	putty; filler; cement
the kit	*die Ausrüstung; der Baukasten*
der Lack	(*Öl~*) paint; (*Firnis*) varnish; (*Nagel~*) lacquer; (*am Auto*) paintwork

the lacquer	*der Farblack, der Lackfirnis*
der Leim	the glue; *(Vogel~)* bird-lime
the lime	*der Kalk*
die Pappe	cardboard
the pap	*der (Kinder)Brei, Papp*
der Span	chip, chipping, shaving, splinter
the span	*die Spanne; (Brücke) Stützweite; (Brückenbogen) Spannweite*
der Splitt	loose gravel, crushed stone, chippings
the split	*der Riß, der Spalt, der Sprung*
der Sud	the decoction, brew
the suds	*die Seifenlauge, das Seifenwasser*

Field 2: Geography and Topography

Page 12: General Topography

False Friends

The details of the false friends involved in this exercise are as follows:

der Acker	the ploughed field, arable land
the acre	*der „Morgen" (Flächenmaß)*
der Anger	meadow, pasture; *(Dorf~)* common, village green, greensward
the anger	*der Zorn, die Wut*
die Brücke	the bridge; *(schwimmende)* pontoon bridge
the brook *(poet.)*	*der Bach, das Bächlein*
der Damm	*(zur Insel)* causeway; *(Bahn-, Ufer-)* embankment
the dam	*der Staudamm, das Stauwehr, die Talsperre*
das Fell	*(größere Tiere)* hide; *(kleinere Tiere)* skin; *(rohes von Pelztieren)* pelt
the fell	*der kahle, felsige Berg; (selten) Tierfell*
frisches Wasser	cool water
freshwater	*Süßwasser*
das Grummet	the second hay harvest
the grummet	*(Naut.) der Tauring; (altm.) der Kajütenjunge*
der Herbst	BrE the autumn, AmE the fall
the harvest	*die Ernte; Erntezeit; der Ertrag*
die Heide	the heath, the heathland
the hide	*der Hochsitz, das Jägerversteck; das Fell*
der Mist	the manure, dung; *(Tierkot)* droppings
the mist	*der (feine) Nebel, Dunst*
das Moor	the fen, bog, swamp
the moor	*das Hochmoor, die Bergheide; Öd~, Heideland*
die Rille	small furrow; *(Saat~)* drill; *(Indus.)* groove
the rill	*das Bächlein, das Rinnsal*

die Schleuse — (*am Kanal*) the lock
the sluice — *das kleine Schleusentor; künstlicher Wasserkanal; (altm.) der Schleusenkanal*
der Schlick — the slime, mud
the slick — *der Ölteppich*
der See — the lake, the mere, ScE loch
the sea — *das Meer, die See; der Ozean, das Weltmeer*
der Strom — the river; current
the stream — *der Bach, das Rinnsal*
der Torf — the peat
the turf — *die Rasensode; oberste Rasenfläche*

Language Lineage: Acre

The word 'acre' is a good example of meaning deviation from a common source. It derives from L 'acer', from OFris 'ekker' and OHG 'achar'. Originally, around 975, it meant 'a piece of tilled or arable land'. In this sense it is still found in place or road names, such as 'Long Acre' in central London. As early as 1000, however, it took on its present sense of an 'amount of land' – at first the amount that a yoke of oxen could plough in one day. Under Edward I and Edward III, this amount was given legal status as 32 furrows of plough, each 1 furlong in length. A modern acre is of any shape amounting to 4,840 square yards. It is striking that *Acker* in earlier times also meant an amount of land – varying widely in size across the German-speaking areas.

Page 13: The Whole Wide World

True Friends

The eight true friends involved in this exercise are 'Adriatic', 'archipelago', 'cliff', 'cosmopolitan', 'insular', 'Ivory Coast', 'Scandinavia' and 'Walloon'. Details of the false friends involved are as follows:

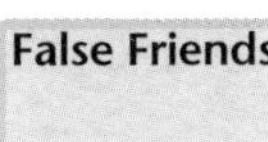

der Afrikaner — the African
the Afrikaner — *der Afrika(a)nder, Weiße(r) aus Südafrika*
ausländisch — foreign; external; (Bot.) exotic
outlandish — *fremdartig, seltsam, exotisch*
der Berg — hill; mountain
the berg — *der Eisberg*
der Bure — the Boer
the boor — *der Flegel, der 'Bauer'*
die Förde — fiord, fjord
the ford — *die Furt*
der/die Germane — the Teuton
the German — *der/die Deutsche*
der Golf — gulf; bay

the golf	*das Golfspiel*
der/die Ire/in	the Irishman, ~woman
the ire	*der Zorn*
der Isländer	the Icelander
the islander	*der/die Inselbewohner(in)*
die Klamm	ravine, AmE canyon, ScE glen
the clam	*die Venusmuschel*
die Reede	the roads, the roadstead
the reeds	*das Schilf, das Riedgras*
der Romane	the Latin, member of the Romance peoples/races
the Roman	*der/die Römer(in)*
der/die Schwede/in	the Swede
the suede	*das Wild-, Veloursleder*
der Strudel	the whirlpool, eddy; (*großer*) maelstrom
the strudel	*der Apfelstrudel*

X Page 14: The British Countryside

True Friends

The three true friends involved in this exercise are 'fen'(*Venn*), 'flatlands' and 'hinterland'. The false friends involved are:

False Friends

die Alm	the Alpine pasture
the alms (*pl.*)	*die Almosen*
das Loch	the hole
the loch	ScE *der See; die Bucht*
die Marschen (*pl.*)	the marshes, marshland
the marches (*pl.*)	*die Marken, das Grenzgebiet*
das Meer	the sea; the ocean
the mere	*der kleine See, Weiher*
das Tor	the gate; gateway; (*Stadt~*) town/city gate
the tor	*der Felsturm*
der Wald	wood, (*groß*) forest; (*~stück*) woodland
the Weald	*wellige Hügellandschaft in Kent, Sussex*
der Wald	wood, (*groß*) forest; (*~stück*) woodland
the wold	(*hügeliges*) *Heideland, Ödland*

Language Lineage: Weald

The term 'Weald' is an excellent example of meaning shift under the impact of social forces. The word is linked etymologically to OFris and OHG 'wald' and originally, from 893, meant a 'wooded district' – a meaning in which it is still found in George Meredith and Tennyson. The Weald, a tract of rolling country in Sussex, Kent and Surrey lying between the North and South Downs, was indeed once wooded. The trees, however, were cut down by the itinerant iron industry, which needed them for charcoal – a prime example of pre-industrial landscape change. The term 'wold' is of similar origin.

Field 3: Flora and Fauna

Page 15: The Animal World I

Sentences

Correct translations revealing the false friends would be:
1. The *bustard* lay motionless in the **trap**. A martyrdom.
2. Still no *trace*. He gave his horse the **spurs**. On, on.
3. While the lord was *grouse*-shooting in the highland glens, the lady preferred to feed the **moor-hens** on the castle pond.
4. That barking monster is not a dog but a **hound**!
5. All kinds of birds came to the bird-bath: *great tits*, finches, **coaltits** and robin redbreasts.
6. The *mastiff* had a vigorous sniff at every **dog**, however small.
7. Disturbed by their **natter(ing)** the *adder* slipped quietly away.
8. What began as a schoolboys' **prank** ended tragically in the lion's *paws*.
9. His education left him in the **lurch** as early as the 8,000 Euro question. Did it belong to the family of *amphibians* or to that of the reptiles?
10. The *keeper* dropped the **halter** in despair. The horse could not be broken in.
11. Whether *foal* or **filly**, the offspring of the renowned race-horse was always in demand.

Page 16: The Animal World II

True Friends

The four true friends involved in this exercise are 'falcon', 'hamster', 'lark' and 'weasel'. The details of the false friends involved are as follows:

False Friends

der Esel	the ass, donkey; (*männlicher*) he-ass, jackass
the easel	*die Staffelei*
der Gaul	the old nag, farm-horse; (*alter* ~) old jade
the Gaul	*der/die Gallier(in)*
die Grille	the cricket
the grille	*das (Tür-), (Fenster-), (Schalter-)Gitter; die Kühlerhaube*
der Igel	the hedgehog
the eagle	*der Adler*
die Libelle	the dragonfly; (*Wasserwaage*) spirit level
the libel	schriftliche Verleumdung
das Maultier	the mule
the muleteer	*der Maultiertreiber*
die Mücke	the gnat, midge; mosquito
the muck	*Mist, Dung; Kot, Dreck; Blödsinn, Schund*

die Schnecke	the snail
the snake	*die Schlange*
der Stier	the bull; (*junger* ~) bullock
the steer	*der junge Ochse; AmE. männliches Schlachtvieh*

Page 17: Flora

Solutions

The solutions to this exercise are: A. 3 B. 10 C. 14 D. 18 E. 21 F. 27 G. 1 H. 16 I. 24 J. 25 K. 5 L. 6 M. 8 N. 22 O. 4 P. 2 Q. 7 R. 30 S. 23 T. 12 U. 13 V. 28 W. 9 X. 11 Y. 15 Z. 17 AA. 26 BB. 29 CC. 20 DD. 19

The details of the false friends involved are as follows:

False Friends

der Baum	the tree
the beam	der Balken, Tragbalken; der Lichtstrahl
das Beet	the bed, patch; (*Blumen*~) flower-bed
the beet	*die Runkelrübe; der Mangold; die Bete*
das Blatt	the leaf; the page
the blade	*der Halm*
die Blume	the flower; (*Wein*) aroma, bouquet; (*Bier*) froth
the bloom	*die einzelne Blume in voller Blüte; die Blüte*
das Bukett	bouquet, (*altm.*) nosegay
the bucket	*der Eimer, der Kübel*
die Ferne	the distance; the remoteness
the fern	*das Farnkraut*
die Föhre	the pine (tree), Scotch fir
the fir	*die Tanne, die Fichte*
der Klee	clover, trefoil; (~*Blatt*) clover-leaf
the clay	*der Lehm; der Ton*
die Knolle	the tuber, corm, bulb
the knoll	*der kleine Hügel*
das Korn	(*Getreide~, Sand~*) grain; (*Roggen*) rye;
the corn	EnglE *Weizen*; ScE, IrE *Hafer*; AmE *Mais*; (*Pferdefutter*) Hafer; ~ on the cob *Mais am Kolben*
die Ragwurz	ophrys, insect orchis
the ragwort	*Kreuzkraut, insbes. Jakobskreuzkraut*
die Rüster	the elm (tree)
the rooster	*der (Haus-)Hahn*
die Schote	(*Erbse*) the pod; husk, shell
the shoot	*die Sprosse; der Schößling*
der Splint	sap wood; splint pin, cotter
the splint	(*Med.*) *die Schiene*
der Trunk	the drink; the draught
the trunk	*der Baumstamm*; AmE *Kofferraum*

der Fox	the fox-terrier
the fox	*der Fuchs*
der Milan	the kite
Milan	*Mailand*
die Otter	the (true) viper
the otter	*der Otter*
die Rinde	(*Baum*) the bark
the rind	*die Käserinde, die Speckschwarte*

Language Lineage: Beam, Knoll
The word 'beam', derived from OE 'béam', OFris 'bâm' and OHG, MHG 'boum' did indeed mean 'tree' around 826. This meaning is still found in some tree types, such as 'hornbeam' *Hain-, Weißbuche*. As early as 978, however, the sense of 'a large piece of squared timber, long in proportion to its breadth and thickness' became dominant. Likewise, 'knoll' is connected to a MHD word meaning *Erdscholle, Klumpen,* but the two terms have since largely gone their separate ways, although 'knoll' has briefly meant 'turnip' *weiße Rübe* and 'lump, large piece'.

Field 4: The Human Being and Health

Page 18: The Human Body

The nine true friends involved in this exercise are 'aorta', 'deltoid', 'head of humerus', 'kneecap', 'nerve fibre', 'papillary muscle', 'pore', 'rib' and 'wart'. The details of the false friends involved are as follows:

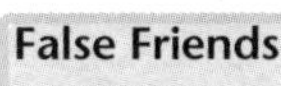

False Friends

die Achsel	the shoulder; *(~höhle)* armpit
the axle	*die (Rad) Achse*
die Backe	cheek; (*Hinter~*) buttock
the back	*der Rücken*; (~bone) *das Rückgrat*
der/die Ballen	ball(s) of the feet
the balls	*die Hoden, 'Eier'*
der Buckel	the hump, humpback, hunchback; (*schlechte Haltung*) the stoop
the buckle	*die Schnalle, Spange*
der Gaumen	the palate, roof of the mouth
the gums (*pl.*)	*das Zahnfleisch*
der Grind	the scab, the crust (of/on a wound)
the grind	*die Schinderei, Plackerei; Strapaze*
das Gut	the good (thing); property; treasure; estate
the gut	*die Eingeweide, Gedärme; der Darm;* (guts) *Mumm*
die Haare (pl.)	the hair (*sing.*)

	hairs	einzelne Haare; Schamhaare, Härchen
	der Körper	the body
	the corpse	*der Leichnam, die Leiche*
	die Koteletten	the sideboards, sideburns
	the cutlets	*die Koteletts, Rippchen*
	die Lunge	the lungs (*pl.)*
	the lunge	*der Sprung vorwärts; (Sport) Ausfall*
	der Nacken	the nape (of the neck)
	the neck	*der Hals*
	der/die Pickel	the spot(s); (*Mitesser*) blackhead(s)
	pickles (*pl.*)	*Eingepökeltes*
	das Pony	the fringe, AmE the bangs
	the ponytail	der Pferdeschwanz
	der Rist	(*des Fußes*) the instep; (*der Hand*) back of the hand
	the wrist	*das Handgelenk*
	der Rumpf	the trunk, torso
	the rump	*der Steiß, Hinterteil*
	der Spleen	the craze, fad
	the spleen	*die Milz; üble Laune; Melancholie*
	der Teint	the complexion
	the tint	*der (Haar-) Farbton, die Tönung*
	die Wimper	the eyelash
	the whimper	*das Wimmern, Winseln*

Page 19: Health and Medicine

True Friends The three true friends involved in this exercise are 'dialysis', 'indisposed', 'intensive care unit'. The details of the false friends involved are as follows:

False Friends	*ambulant*	(~ *behandelt werden*) to be treated/receive treatment as an out-patient
	ambling	*schlendernd; im Paßgang gehend/reitend*
	die Ambulanz	the outpatient(s') dept.; *Mil.* ambulance
	the ambulance	*der Kranken- Sanitätswagen, das Krankenauto*
	die Angina	the sore throat, tonsillitis
	the angina	*Herzschmerzen, Angina pectoris*
	die Indikation	medical grounds for; (*medizinische* ~) on medical grounds
	the indication	*der Hinweis; das Anzeichen*
	der/die Kranke	the patient, sick person, invalid
	the crank	*der komische Kauz; die Verschrobenheit*
	kränklich	sickly, ailing, poorly
	cranky	*launenhaft, wunderlich, verschroben*

das Lazarett	military hospital/infirmary, field hospital
the lazaret(to)	*das Isolier- od. Aussätzigenspital*
liften	to face-lift, give a face-lift to s. o.
to lift	*hochheben, emporheben; 'klauen'*
die Präservative	the contraceptives; condoms
the preservatives	*die Konservierungsmittel*
das Rezept	(*Arzt-*) prescription; (*Koch-*) recipe
the receipt	*der Kassenbon, -beleg, die Quittung*
der Samariter	medical orderly
the Samaritan	*Mitglied der brit. Organisation gegen Selbstmord;* (the Good ~) *der barmherzige Samariter*
das Sekret	the secretion, the oozing liquid
the secret	*das Geheimnis;* (~ to success) *der 'Schlüssel'*
die Station	(*Kranken-*) the ward; (*Krebs~*) cancer ward
station	*der Bahnhof;* (bus ~) *Busbahnhof; die Polizeiwache*

Language Lineage: Crank

The words 'crank' and Ger, Du *krank* are both linked to a literal sense group present in OE 'cranc' and ME 'crank' and meaning 'something bent together or crooked'. OE 'cring-an' meant to 'fall in battle', lying crooked on the field. From 1572 the word 'crank' meant 'crooked path'; in the C 16th it also briefly meant a 'rogue who feigned sickness'. The present dominant meaning of a 'person with a mental twist' is of American origin, from 1833. The famous vegetarian restaurant in London took the ironic name *Cranks*.

Page 20: Medicine and Pain

True Friends

The nine true friends involved in this exercise are 'acupuncture', 'Black Death', 'gastric', 'migraine', 'placebo', 'quack', rickets', 'tuberculosis' and 'yellow fever'. The details of the false friends involved are as follows:

die Absence	(fit of) absent-mindedness; epileptic vertigo
the absence	*die Abwesenheit*
fatal	disastrous; awkward, embarrassing
fatal	*mit tödlichem Ausgang; unheil- verhängnisvoll,*
das Fieber	(*hohes ~*) high temperature; (*gelbes*) yellow fever
the fever	(yellow) *gelbes Fieber; Fieberhitze, Erregung*
das (Uni)Klinikum	the (university) teaching hospital
the clinic	*die Klinik*
die Pein	torment, torture; agony
the pain	*der Schmerz; die Nervensäge*
die Pest	the plague, pestilence
the pest	*die Nervensäge, der lästige Mensch; die Plage*

	die Plage	the nuisance, bother
	the plague	*die Pest, Seuche*
	psychisch	psychological
	psychic	*seelisch/geistig krank; übersinnlich; spiritistisch*
	rumoren	to rumble, to 'make a noise'
	to rumour	*Gerüchte verbreiten*; (It was r~ed) *Man munkelte*
	die Schnake	the mosquito
	the snake	*die Schlange*; (~ in the grass) *geheimer Feind*
	der Stich	(*Sonnen-*) sun-stroke; (*Mücken-*) bite; (*Wespen-*) sting
	stitch	(*Med.*) *das Seitenstechen*; (sewing) *der Stich*; (knitting, crochet-work) *die Masche*
	virulent	rife
	virulent	*giftig, bösartig, sehr ansteckend*
Further False Friends	*das Attest*	the doctor's certificate, medical certificate
	to attest	*bestätigen, bescheinigen*

Field 5: Eating and Drinking

X

Page 21: Market Day

True Friends

The four true friends involved in this exercise are 'cherry tomatoes', 'mange-tout', 'yoghurt' and 'zucchini'. The details of the false friends involved are as follows:

False Friends	*das Apfelmus*	apple purée
	the apple mousse	*das Apfelmousse*
	das Aroma	the flavour
	the aroma	*der Duft, die Würze, (bei Wein) die Blume*
	die Backpflaume	the prune
	the baked plum	*die gebackene Zwetschge*
	der Berliner	BrE doughnut AmE donut
	the Berliner	*der Einwohner Berlins*
	das Biskuit	sponge cake; (*~teig*) sponge; (*~boden*) flan
	the biscuit	*der Keks, das Plätzchen*
	der Broiler OD	the grilled chicken
	the broiler	*der Bratrost; die Grillvorrichtung; der glühend heiße Tag*
	der Gries, Grieß	(*Weizen~, Grießbrei*) semolina; (*von Getreide*) groats
	the grease	*das Fett, Schmalz; das Schmierfett, die Schmiere*
	die Gurke	the cucumber
	the gherkin	*die Essig-, Senf-, Pfeffer-, Spreewaldgurke*
	der Kakao	the cocoa
	the cacao	*der Kakaobaum; ~bohnen Pl.*

der Keks	BrE biscuit, AmE cookie
the cakes (*pl.*)	*die Kuchen* (*pl.*)
die Limone	the lime
the lemon	*die Zitrone*
die Marmelade	(*Konfitüre*) jam
the marmalade	*die Marmelade aus Zitrusfrüchten*
das Mehl	the flour; (*gröberes ~*) meal
the meal	*das Mahl, Essen; gröberes Mehl*
der Porree	the leek
the porridge	*der Haferbrei, die ~grütze, das Porridge*
die Printe	gingerbread; oblong spiced biscuit
the print	*der Druck; der Stich; die Druckschrift*
der Puffer	potato-cake; (*Eisenbahn*) BrE buffer, AmE bumper
the puffer	*der Paffer; der Marktschreier; Preistreiber bei Auktionen*
die Rosine	the raisin; (*ohne Kerne*) sultana
the resin	*das Harz*
der Salat	the lettuce
the salad	*der fertige Salat*
die Sellerie	(*Knollen-*) celeriac; (*Stangen-*) (stick) celery
the celery	*Stangensellerie*
das Toastbrot	sliced bread; (*~ Hawaii usw.*) toasted rarebit
the toast	*die geröstete Brotscheibe(n); der Trinkspruch*

Pages 22–23: On the Menu

The five true friends involved in this exercise are 'ketchup', 'to poach', 'portion', 'ratatouille' and 'rosemary'. The details of the false friends involved are as follows:

True Friends

das dt. Beefsteak	the fried minced meat patty, rissole, Vienna steak
the beefsteak	*gutes Stück vom Rind*
die Butterbohnen	runner beans cooked in butter
butter beans	*weiße Bohnenkerne*
die Chips	(*Kartoffel~, Mais~*) BrE the crisps, AmE chips
the chips	*die Pommes (frites)*
die Creme	custard (cream); (*Schuh~*) shoe polish/cream
the cream	*die Sahne, der Rahm*
die Dorade	the bream
the dorado	*goldfarbener südamerik. Fisch*
gratinieren	to cook *au gratin*
to grate	*reiben, raspeln*
köstlich	delicious, tasty
costly	*teuer; kostbar*

	die Krabbe	(*klein*) shrimp; (*groß*) prawn
	the crab	*der Taschenkrebs*
	das Menü	the set meal, dish of the day
	the menu	*die Speisekarte*
	das Nougat	the noisette
	the nougat	*(etwa) türkischer Honig*
	die Pastete	(*Leber- usw.*) the pâté; (*gedeckt*) the pie, patty; (*Königinpastetchen*) vol-au-vent
	the pastry	*das Blätterteigstückchen*
	die (Käse)Platte	the platter
	the plate	*der Teller*
	paniert	fried in bread-crumbs, 'breaded'
	panned	*in der Pfanne gebraten*
	der Pudding	the blancmange
	the pudding	*der süße Auflauf; Nachtisch*
	raffiniert	sophisticated
	refined	*kultiviert, vornehm*
	scharf	spicy
	sharp	*sauer*
	der Schellfisch	(*Fisch*) the haddock
	the shellfish	*die Meeresfrüchte* (*pl.*)
	die Scholle	the plaice; (*Erd~*) the clod, lump
	the sole	*die Seezunge, Meeres~; die Fußsohle*
	der Speck	(*Schweine~*) bacon; (*Wal~*) blubber
	the speck	*der Fleck; das Stückchen; die faule Stelle* (*Obst*)
	die Torte	the gateau, layer cake; flan
	the tart	*der (ungedeckte) Obstkuchen*

Page 24: In the Glass

True Friends

The eight true friends involved in this exercise are 'abstinence', 'alcohol', 'burgundy', 'fendant', 'narcotics', 'rum', 'spirits' and 'vine stock'. The details of the false friends involved are as follows:

False Friends		
	die Alkoholika	the alcoholic drinks
	the alcoholics	*die Alkoholiker*
	das Bier	beer; ale; stout
	the bier	*die (Toten)Bahre*
	die Bowle	a cold drink made of fruit/herbs, hock/ champagne and soda water, AmE bowl
	the bowl	*die Schüssel;* AmE *die Bowle*
	das Bukett	the bouquet
	the bucket	*der Eimer*
	das Diner	dinner, dinner party
	the diner	*der Speisewagen; das Restaurant;* (motorway ~) *Autobahnraststätte; der Tischgast*

das Etikett	the label	
the etiquette	*die Etikette, das Zeremoniell, die Anstandsregeln*	
die Flasche	the bottle	
the flask	*der Flacon, die kleine, flache Flasche*; (hip ~) *der Flachmann*; (thermos ~) *die Thermosflasche*	
der Gusto	the taste, liking	
the gusto	*das Vergnügen*, (with ~) *mit großer Freude*	
der Likör	liqueur	
liquor	alkoholisches Getränk, Alkohol	
die Pinte	SwD, OsD the pub; AuD 1 to 2 litres; (*Steinkrug*) earthenware mug; (*Metallkrug*) tin jug	
the pint	*brit., amerik. Maß (BrE 0,57, AmE 0,47 Liter)*	
pur	(*Whisky*) neat	
pure	*rein, sauber; unschuldig; völlig, bloß, pur*	
der Sekt	sparkling wine; champagne, 'fizz', 'champus'	
the sect	*die Sekte*	
der Wein	the wine	
the vine	*die Rebe, der Rebstock*	
fasten	to fast	**Further False Friends**
to fasten	*befestigen, festmachen, -binden*	
die Speisen	food; dishes	
the spices	*die Gewürze*	

Language Lineage: Gusto

'Gusto' and *Gusto* are a typical false friend pair derived from the European language stock – L 'gustus', Fr 'goût', Italian and Spanish. The earliest recorded meaning in English was indeed an 'individual or particular liking', as in the current German. The senses 'flavour' and 'aesthetic appreciation' also surfaced briefly. Prevalent from 1656, however, and especially common from the early C 19th was 'keen relish or enjoyment' – a meaning found already in Pepys and then in Walter Scott, George Eliot etc.

Field 6: Human Perception and Action

Page 25: Perceiving

Solutions

The solutions to this exercise are: A. 7 B. 17 C. 6 D. 16 E. 13 F. 15 G. 5 H. 14 I. 8 J. 4 K. 19 L. 18 M. 20 N. 1 O. 12 P. 3 Q. 9 R. 11 S. 2 T. 10

The details of the false friends involved are as follows:

behalten	to keep, retain; remember	**False Friends**
to behold	*erblicken, anschauen*; (Behold!) *Siehe da!*	
bewahren	to preserve, keep	

	to beware (of)	*sich hüten vor, sich in acht nehmen*
	glotzen	to stare, goggle; (*mit offenem Mund*) to gape
	to gloat	*sich hämisch freuen;* (~ over) *sich weiden an*
	irritieren	confuse, puzzle, intrigue; annoy, exasperate
	irritate	*verärgern*
	der Klang	the sound, tone; (*Glocken*) peal, ring; (*Gläser*) chink, clink; (*Geld*) chinking
	the clang	*das metallische Geklirr*
	klingen	to sound, ring; (*Ohren*) tingle
	to cling (to)	*sich klammern an*
	riechen	to smell
	to reek	*übel riechen*
	schmecken	to taste; sample
	to smack (of)	*einen Beigeschmack von etwas haben*
	tasten	to feel
	to taste	*schmecken; kosten, probieren; erleben*
	unsichtbar	invisible
	unsightly	*häßlich, unansehnlich*

Page 26: Doing, Overdoing, Outdoing

Solutions

The solutions to this exercise are: 1. present 2. outplay 3. manage 4. overcome 5. overworked 6. overlooking 7. go over 8. failed to hear 9. overhearing 10. neglected 11. played to the finish 12. 'overslept' 13. sleep on 14. revising 15. overheated 16. perish 17. come out 18. lost 19. forgo 20. go ahead 21. undergo 22. underlay 23. overwound 24. overreached 25. overshadowed 26. overseeing
The details of the false friends involved are as follows:

False Friends	*auskommen (ohne)*	to manage/do/get along (without)
	to come out	*sich outen;* (book) *erscheinen;* (flower) *blühen*
	ausspielen	to play to a finish/to the end
	to outplay	*besiegen, besser spielen als; 'vorführen'*
	überarbeiten	to revise, work over, re-work
	to overwork	*sich überanstrengen; mit Arbeit überlasten*
	übergehen (tr.)	to neglect, overlook, pass over in silence, ignore
	to go over	*wiederholen*
	überhören	to fail to hear, to not hear
	to overhear	*zufällig (mit an)hören*
	überreichen	to present; to hand over; (*schriftlich*) to submit
	to overreach (o. s)	*sich überfordern, sich übernehmen*
	überschlafen	to sleep on sth.
	to oversleep	*(sich) verschlafen*
	übersehen	to overlook, miss, fail to notice
	to oversee	*überwachen, beaufsichtigen*
	überwinden	to overcome, overpower, conquer, subdue, defeat

to over-wind	*überdrehen*
untergehen	to perish, go under; (*Schiff, Pläne*) to founder
to undergo	*sich unterziehen; durchmachen, erleben*
unterliegen	to be defeated by, to lose to
to underlie	*zugrunde liegen*
vor(aus)gehen	to go ahead of, go in front of
to forgo	*verzichten auf, aufgeben, Abstand nehmen von*

Page 27: Essential Actions

False Friends

The details of the false friends involved in the exercise are as follows:

bilden	to form; to constitute; (*gestalten*) to shape
to build	*(er)bauen, errichten, aufbauen*
flattern	to flutter, flit; beat/flap the wings; shake, wobble
to flatter	*schmeicheln; Komplimente machen*
flüstern	to whisper, speak under one's breath
to fluster	*verwirren, nervös machen, durcheinanderbringen*
frohlocken	to rejoice, exult, shout for joy
to frolic	*tollen, spaßen, vergnügt kapriolen*
graben	to dig; (*Brunnen, Schacht*) to sink
to grab	hastig ergreifen, an sich reißen; 'kapieren'
gründen	to found, establish; start, open, set up
to ground	*ein Startverbot erteilen; (Phil.) begründen*
handeln	to act; to proceed, take action; to trade with
to handle	*behandeln; anfassen, berühren; handhaben*
hemmen	to obstruct, impede, block
to hem	*säumen, umnähen*; (~ in) *einschließen; hüsteln*
huschen	to scurry, flit, 'zoom'
to hush	*besänftigen*; (~ up) *vertuschen*
hüsteln	to cough slightly, to hem
to hustle	*drängen; anrempeln*
jammern	to wail, moan; (~ *über*) to bewail, bemoan
to jabber	*quasseln*
lugen	to peep, peer, look out
to lug	*schleppen, zerren*
robben	to crawl, creep
to rob	*rauben, stehlen; berauben*
stemmen	(*abstützen*) prop, support; (*Gewichte*) lift; (*sich* ~) press against, resist, oppose
to stem	*eindämmen;* (~ o.s. against) *ankämpfen gegen, sich entgegenstemmen*
sticken	to embroider
to stick	*kleben; ankleben, haften*
weinen	to cry
to whine	*winseln, wimmern, greinen*

Field 7: Clothing and Accessories

Page 30: Special Attire

True Friends

The one true friend involved in this exercise is 'blouson jacket'. The details of the false friends involved are as follows:

False Friends

der Bouton	the button-shaped earring
the button	*der Knopf*
der Cut(away)	the morning coat, cutaway coat
the cut	*der Schnitt*
der Dress	sports clothing, outfit, kit
the dress	*das Kleid*
der Frack	the tail-coat, dress coat (~ *und Fliege*) bow-tie and tails
the frock	*das Kleid; der Gehrock*
die Gala	festive dress, gala dress; (*in* ~) in full/gala dress
the gala	*die Festlichkeit, die Feier*
die Gaze	(*textile*) gauze; (*feine*) gossamer
the gaze	*der starre, feste Blick*
die Hose	the (pair of) trousers
the hose	*langer Strumpf, Strümpfe; die Kniehose*
der Mantel	the coat, overcoat, trench-coat
the mantle	*der ärmellose Umhang, Cape*
der Morgenmantel	the dressing gown
the morning coat	*der Cut(away)*
der Morgenrock	the dressing gown
the morning dress	*der Konferenzanzug, der Stresemann; (Frau) das Hauskleid*
der Pulli	the pullover, sweater, jersey
the pulley	*der Flaschenzug*
der Pullunder	the sleeveless sweater, the tank-top
the pullunder	*der Unterziehpullover*
der Schal	the scarf
the shawl	*das Kopf-, Schultertuch*
der Smoking	BrE the dinner jacket, 'DJ'; AmE the tuxedo
the smoking	*das Rauchen*
die Weste	the waistcoat
the vest	BrE *das Unterhemd;* AmE *die Weste*
der Zylinder	the top hat
the cylinder	(*Math.*) *der Zylinder, die Walze*

Page 31: Fashion and Accessories

True Friends

The four true friends involved in this exercise are 'blazer', 'brooch', 'ear-rings' and 'T-shirt'

False Friends

das Armband	the bracelet; bangle
the armband	*die Armbinde*
die Brieftasche	BrE the wallet, AmE the pocket book
the briefcase	*die Aktentasche, -mappe*
der Button	the badge
the button	*der Knopf; die Taste*
das Collier, Kollier	the necklace
the collier	*der Kohlenarbeiter, Bergmann; das Kohlenschiff*
fleckig	spotted, spotty, speckled, stained
flecked, fleckered	*gesprenkelt*
die Fliege	the bow-tie
the fly	*der Hosenlatz*
geflickt	repaired, mended, patched
flicked	*weggeschnipst*
gescheckt	mottled; (*Pferd*) dappled
checked	*kariert*
der Gürtel	the belt
the girdle	*der Hüfthalter;* (*Med.*) *Knochengürtel*
juckend	itchy, itching
yucky	*ekelhaft, widrig*
die Konfektion	the ready-made clothing, off-the-peg clothing
the confectionery	*die Süßwaren*
das Kostüm	(women's) suit
the costume	*das Masken-, Bühnenkostüm*
die Krawatte	the tie, AmE necktie
the cravat	*das (in das Hemd hineingebundene) Halstuch*
die Mode	the fashion
the mode	*die Art, Weise, Form; der Modus*
das Muster	the pattern; (*Strick-*) knitting pattern
the muster	*das Antreten zum Appell; das Aufgebot*
der Slip	(*Frauen-*) the panties; (*Männer-*) the pants
the slip	*der Unterrock; der Flüchtigkeitsfehler*
der Slipper	the slip-on shoe, casual shoe
the slipper	*der Hausschuh, die Pantoffel*

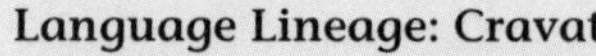

Language Lineage: Cravat

Both 'cravat' and *Krawatte* are derived from the Serbo-Croatian 'Khrvat', the original neckwear being first sported by Croatian mercenaries in the C 17th and then coming into vogue in France. Whereas the German *Krawatte*, however, follows the original Croatian style of long flowing bands around the neck, the English 'cravat' took on the meaning of a 'linen or silk handkerchief passed around the neck', a type of 'comforter'. Often worn outside the shirt in C 18th and 19th, it now tends to be tucked in. The first use in this sense is in Butler's *Hudibras* (1663).

Field 8: Human Nature and Characteristics

Page 32: Basic Character

False Friends

The details of the false friends involved here are as follows:

das Faible	the soft spot, the liking
the foible	*die Schwäche, schwache Seite; Marotte*
die Genialität	the brilliance, brilliancy
the geniality	*die herzliche Freundlichkeit*
das Genie	the genius
the genie	*der Wasser-, Erd-, Luft-, Feuer-, Flaschengeist; der Kobold*
die Lust	the desire, liking, wish; enjoyment
the lust	*die Wollust*
der Mut	the courage, mettle, spirit
the mood	*die Laune*
das Selbstbewußtsein	the self-confidence, self-assurance
the self-consciousness	*die Befangenheit, Gehemmtheit*
der Spleen	the fad, whim, craze, crotchet
the spleen	*die Milz; der Ärger, üble Laune*
die Sympathie	the liking, state of being liked
the sympathy	*das Mitleid, -gefühl, die Teilnahme*
der Trost	the comfort, consolation, solace,
the trust	*das Vertrauen, Zutrauen*
die Vorsicht	the care, precaution
the foresight	*die Voraussicht; Vor-, Fürsorge*

Language Lineage: Spleen
'Spleen', deriving from the OF 'esplen' and L 'splen' is an ancient word, which meant first the abdominal organ, the *Milz*, but soon also the several – often contrasting – emotions or characteristics connected with it. As early as 1390 one finds in Gower that 'The Splen is to Malencholie Assigned'. In Shakespeare's age, and notably in his dramas, it can mean 'merriment and gaiety' *(Love's Labours Lost)*, 'hot temper' *(Romeo and Juliet)*, 'violent ill nature' *(Richard III)* and also 'impulse, whim' (Venus and Adonis). Between 1664 and 1838 it came to mean at times 'dejection, depression'. It is such subsequent meanings that have been taken over into French and German, whereas in English the organ (and ill-temper) remain dominant.

Page 33: Essential Characteristics

Solutions

The solutions to this crossword are: 1. clumsy 2. jolly 3. neat 4. petty (-minded) 5. severe 6. vain 7. impetuous 8. bold 9. of genius 10. indolent 11. sprightly 12. splendid 13. swift 14. brusque 15. content 16. well-behaved 17. large 18. unscrupulous 19. clean 20. graceful 21. chaste 22. slender 23. over-excited
Key phrase: '...content of their character'
The details of the false friends involved in this exercise are as follows:

False Friends

adrett	neat, smart, well-groomed; (*Kleid*) smart, neat
adroit	*geschickt, gewandt*
brav	well-behaved, good; (*anständig*) honest, upright
brave	*tapfer, mutig*
brüsk	brusque
brisk	*flink, flott, rasch, energisch*
eitel	vain, conceited
idle	*untätig, unbeschäftigt, müßig*
exaltiert	over-excited, wrought-up, overwrought, agitated
exalted	*gehoben, hoch; gepriesen*
famos	splendid, magnificent
famous	*berühmt, bekannt*
faul	lazy, idle, indolent
foul	*widerlich; unanständig; unehrlich*
genial	brilliant, of genius
genial	*sehr freundlich, jovial*
glücklich	happy, content
lucky	*Glück habend*
graziös	graceful
gracious	*gnädig, huldvoll; anmutig*
groß	large, big; tall
gross	*grob, rüde; derb, vulgär; unanständig; 'krass'*
heftig	impetuous; violent; fierce

hefty	*stämmig, kräftig gebaut*
keusch	chaste, virginal, pure
coy	*schüchtern, scheu; spröde; geziert*
kleinlich	petty(-minded), small-minded; ungenerous
cleanly	*reinlich, sauber, gepflegt*
kühn	bold, fearless, intrepid
keen	*eifrig, begeistert; (~* on*) scharf/erpicht auf*
lustig	jolly, merry, jovial
lusty	*kräftig, rüstig, stark, gesund*
plump	clumsy, awkward
plump	*mollig, pummelig, 'vollschlank'*
rasch	swift, quick
rash	*vorschnell, voreilig, unüberlegt*
rüstig	sprightly, lively, active
rusty	*rostig, verrostet; aus der Übung*
skrupellos	unscrupulous, without scruple
scrupulous	*gewissenhaft, skrupelhaft*
schmal	slender, slim
small	*klein, unbedeutend*
sauber	clean; tidy
sober	*nüchtern*
streng	strict, severe
strong	*stark, kräftig*

Page 34: Positive Characteristics

True Friends

The true friends involved in this exercise are 'background', 'cultivated', 'feminine', 'humanist', 'manly', 'sensitive', 'well-situated'

False Friends

adäquat	suitable, fitting; appropriate
adequate	*hinreichend*
apart	stylish, distinctive, striking
apart	*getrennt;* (a thing ~) *etwas ganz Anderes*
engagiert	committed, involved, busy
engaged	*verlobt*
initiativ	showing/full of initiative
the initiative	*die Initiative*
integer	of integrity, upright
integrated	*einbezogen, eingegliedert, integriert*
musisch	(*Mensch*) appreciative of the fine arts
musical	*musikalisch*
mutig	courageous, brave
moody	*launisch, launenhaft, wetterwendisch*
die Phantasie	the imagination
the fantasy	*die ungezügelte Einbildungskraft; das Hirngespinst; die sexuelle Phantasie*

repräsentieren	to be presentable, to uphold appearances
to represent	*vertreten*
selbstbewußt	self-confident, self-assured
self-conscious	*befangen, gehemmt*
sensibel	sensitive
sensible	*vernünftig, verständig*
souverän	confident, self-confident, self-assured
sovereign	*vorzüglich; äußerst, höchst*
sympathisch	likeable, pleasant, agreeable, nice
sympathetic	*mitfühlend, verständnisvoll, einfühlsam*
temperamentvoll	vivacious, high-spirited, ebullient, bubbly
temperamental	*sehr eigen; reizbar, launisch, leicht erregbar*

Page 35: Problematic Characteristics

The two true friends involved in this exercise are 'choleric' and 'lethargic'. The details of the false friends involved are as follows:

True Friends

False Friends

amusisch	inartistic, without aesthetic sensibilities
amusing	*amüsant, unterhaltsam*
bäurisch	rustic, churlish
boorish	*ungehobelt, flegelhaft, philisterhaft*
frivol	dirty, smutty, risqué; flippant
frivolous	*leichtfertig*
grimmig	grim
grimy	*schmutzig, verrußt*
launisch	moody
loony	*'bescheuert', 'behämmert'*
ordinär	vulgar, coarse, low
ordinary	*gewöhnlich*
skurril	bizarre, ludicrous
scurrilous	*unflätig, schlüpfrig*
der Schurke	the rogue, scoundrel
the shirker	*der Drückeberger*
stupide	dull, monotonous, tedious
stupid	*blöd, dumm, doof*
süffisant	self-satisfied
sufficient	*ausreichend*
unverschämt	(*Verhalten*) disgraceful; (*dreist*) impertinent
unashamed	*schamlos, unverhohlen*
unsympathisch	not likeable
unsympathetic	*ohne Mitgefühl*
verwildert	wild, unruly; degenerate
bewildered	*verwirrt, verdutzt, verblüfft*
der Windbeutel	the loose liver
the windbag	*der Schwätzer, der Maulheld*

Page 36: The Kaleidoscope of Character

Solutions

The solutions to this exercise are: A. 5 B. 10 C. 7 D. 2 E. 16 F. 13 G. 20 H. 18 I. 23 J. 1 K. 8 L. 21 M. 3 N. 30 O. 25 P. 4 Q. 24 (*or* 15) R. 6 S. 11 T. 26 U. 12 V. 28 W. 14 X. 9 Y. 29 Z. 19 AA. 15 (*or* 24) BB. 27 CC. 17 DD. 22

The details of the false friends involved are as follows:

False Friends

artig	well-behaved
arty	*mit künstlerischen Prätentionen bzw. Allüren*
devot	submissive, humble
devout	*fromm, frömmig*
feist	fat, corpulent, stout
feisty	*kämpferisch*
fröhlich	content, happy, cheerful, AmE chipper
frolicsome	*vergnügt kapriolend, ausgelassen tollend*
gelenkig	agile, lithe, lissom
lanky	*schlaksig, schlank, hochaufgeschossen*
gentil	genteel, well-bred
gentile	*nichtjüdisch, christlich;* (rare) *heidnisch*
human	humane; (*leutselig*) affable
human	*menschlich; allzumenschlich, fehlbar*
kindlich	childlike, like a child; innocent
kindly	*gütig, freundlich, liebenswürdig*
mondän	fashionable, society, high society
mundane	*alltäglich; weltlich*
offiziös	semi-official
officious	*diensteifrig, dienstbeflissen, wichtigtuerisch*
pünktlich	punctual
punctilious	*penibel, exakt, peinlich genau, pedantisch*
rank	slender, slim
rank	*übelriechend, ranzig; üppig wachsend;* (a ~ rank outsider) *ein krasser Außenseiter*
schlicht	plain, simple, modest, unpretentious
slight	*schmächtig, dünn; unbedeutend*
urban	urbane, 'towny'
urban	*städtisch*
virtuos	virtuoso
virtuous	*tugendhaft, rechtschaffen*

Page 37: Character Mix

True Friends

The true friends involved in this exercise are 'apathetic', 'good-hearted', 'phlegmatic'. The details of the false friends are as follows:

False Friends

akkurat	meticulous, painstaking, precise
accurate	*genau; richtig zutreffend*
'blau'	drunk, 'tight', 'soused'
'blue'	*traurig, schwermütig, melancholisch*
bleich	pale, pallid, wan; (*verblasst*) faded
bleak	*düster, öde; ungeschützt windig gelegen*
deftig	(*Humor*) earthy
deft	*gewandt, geschickt*
desinteressiert	uninterested, indifferent, incurious
disinterested	*uneigennützig; unparteiisch*
die Galanterie	courtesy
the gallantry	*die Tapferkeit*
herzig	sweet, lovely, charming
hearty	*herzlich, warm;* (meal) *herzhaft, kräftig, zünftig*
der Knacks	the character defect, the 'screw loose'
the knack	*der Kunstgriff, der Dreh*
konzentriert	(adv.) with concentration
concentrated	*geballt, stark*
kräftig	strong, sturdy, robust, brawny, hefty, AmE husky
crafty	*listig, schlau, verschlagen*
penetrant	intrusive
penetrating	*durchbohrend*
proper	clean, neat
proper	*anständig, korrekt, schicklich*
rüde	coarse, rough
rude	*unhöflich; ungehobelt, grob;* (health) *unverwüstlich*
tatterig	tottery, unsteady on one's feet
tatty	*zerlumpt*

Further False Friends

blauäugig	naive, starry-eyed; (literal) blue-eyed
blue-eyed	*(wortwörtlich)* blue-eyed; ~ boy *Liebling*
routiniert	experienced, sure-footed
routine	*Routine-*

Field 9: Inter-Human Relationships

Page 38: Human Interaction

True Friends

The two true friends involved in this exercise are 'the mistress' and 'the grass widower'. The details of the false friends are as follows:

False Friends

sich arrangieren	to come to an agreement/arrangement; (*mit Gläubigern*) to compound with
to arrange oneself	*seine Kleidung zurechtrücken*
das As	the ace

the ass	*der Esel, Dummkopf;* AmE *Arsch*
belügen	to lie to s. o.
to belie	*Lügen strafen; (selten) Lügen erzählen über*
der 'Bonze'	the functionary, the 'bigwig'
the bonze	*buddhistischer Priester in Japan od. China*
der Bubi	the sunny-boy
the booby	*der 'Dummbatz'*
der Crack	the ace, the expert, skilful player etc.
the crack	*der Krach, Knall; die Fuge; der Versuch;* (drug) *'Crack'*
der Depp	idiot, 'twit'
the dep. (= deputy)	*der Stellvertreter*
der Flirt	the flirtation
the flirt	*Mensch, der gerne flirtet*
der Gaffer	the gaper, gawper
the gaffer	*das Väterchen; der Oberbeleuchtungsexperte*
herzen	(*umarmen*) embrace, hug; (*kosen*) caress, fondle
to hearten	*aufmuntern, ermutigen*
herumpoppen	to sleep around
to pop around	*schnell bei jdm. vorbeischauen*
die Koryphäe	eminent authority in a field, distinguished expert
the coryphaeus	*der Leiter eines Chors*
das Kraut	(*Kohl*) the cabbage; (*Pflanze*) plant
the kraut	(*pej.*) *der/die Deutsche*
nagen	to gnaw
to nag	*nörgeln, keifen*
necken	to tease
to neck	*schmusen*
die Nutte	the 'tart', prostitute, AmE hooker
the nutter	*der/die Behämmerte, Bescheuerte*
der Pimpf	little rascal/ruffian; member of Hitler *Jungvolk*
the pimp	*der Zuhälter*
der Puff	the brothel, whore-house
the pouf, poof, puff	(offensive) *der Schwule*
eine Runde schlafen	to have/take 'forty winks', to take a short snooze, to take a nap
to sleep around	*'herumbumsen'*
der/die Senior(in)	the senior citizen;
the senior	*der/die Ältere, Dienstältere*
der Spanner	the peeping Tom, the voyeur
the spanner	*der Schraubenschlüssel*
wanken	to totter, stagger, reel, sway; waver, falter
to wank	(*vulg.*) *'wichsen', 'sich einen runterholen'*

Page 39: Relating to Relations

Then two true friends involved here are 'faux pas' and 'indiscretions'. The details of the false friends involved are as follows:

True Friends

False Friends

die Allüren	airs, mannerisms, 'airs and graces'
the allure	*die Anziehungskraft*
die Bagage	the *hoi polloi*, the riff-raff, the rabble
the baggage	*das Gepäck; das schnippische Mädel*
die Base	the female cousin
the base	*der Unterteil, das Fundament, der Sockel; der Stützpunkt*
belabern	to blah-blah to/at s. o.
belabour	*plagen, 'bearbeiten'; durchprügeln*
beraten	to advise, counsel; to discuss, deliberate
berate	*ausschelten, auszanken*
der beste Mann	the best of the men
the best man	*der Brautführer, Trauzeuge*
der Bimbo	(offensive) the 'nignog'
the 'bimbo'	*die 'Tussi'*
die Blamage	the embarrassment, disgrace, shame
the blame	*der Tadel*
sich blamieren	to make a fool of oneself
to blame	*tadeln, jdm. die Schuld geben*
familiär	family
familiar	*vertraut, bekannt, geläufig, gewohnt*
insensibel	insensitive
insensible	*bewußtlos (meist bei Rausch); unempfindlich*
peinlich	embarrassing, awkward
painful	*schmerzhaft*
die Partie	(*Mensch*) the match; (*Spiel*) game, match; (*Schlitten~ usw.*) excursion
the party	(*Mensch*) *'Individuum'; die Partei; die Fete*
der Pate	the god-father
the pate	*der Schädel, die 'Birne'*
scharf auf	keen on, hot on
sharp on	*bissig gegenüber*
der Spott	the mockery, derision, disdain
the spot	*der Fleck; der Pickel*
schwindeln	to tell lies, tell 'fibs'
to swindle	*betrügen, mogeln*
der Tratsch	the gossip
the trash	*der Müll; der Unsinn, 'Quatsch'*
der Vetter	the cousin
the fetters	*die Fesseln, Fußfesseln*

Field 10: House, Home and Hearth

Page 40: Domestic Architecture

True Friends

The true friends involved in this exercise are 'balcony', 'balustrade', 'majolica', 'mausoleum', 'panel' and 'veranda(h)': The details of the false friends involved are as follows:

False Friends

das Areal	(*Bau~*) the site; (*eines Hauses*) the grounds
the area	*die Umgebung, die Gegend; das Viertel*
der (Vogel)Bauer	the cage, aviary
the bower	*die Gartenlaube, das schattige Plätzchen*
das Büro	the office
the bureau	*das Secrétaire, Schreibpult mit Schubläden*
der Flur	(*Parterre*) the hall; (*1. Stock*) the landing
the floor	*der Boden*
die Gabel	the fork
the gable	*das Giebel*
das Geländer	the banister
the landing	*der Flur im ersten Stock*
die Halle	(*Vor-*) vestibule; (*Säulen-*) portico; (*Hotel*) lounge
the hall(way)	*der Hausflur*
das Kanapee	the settee, sofa
the canopy	*der Baldachin*
das Klosett	water-closet, W. C.
the closet	*der (eingebaute) Vorratsschrank; die kl. Kammer*
die Kommode	the chest of drawers
the commode	*der Nachtstuhl*
das Lokal	the pub; eating place
the locale	*der Ort, der Schauplatz*
die Mansarde	the attic, loft, garret
the mansard	*das Mansardendach*
die Markise	the canopy, blind, window awning
the marquee	*das große Festzelt; AmE Markise*
der Ofen	the stove
the oven	*der Herd; das Backrohr*
die Office	the pantry (*meist im Hotel*)
the office	*das Büro*
der Plunder	the junk, bric-à-brac, rubbish
the plunder	*die (Kriegs-)Beute*
der Stuhl	the chair
the stool	*der Hocker*
die Tapete	the wall-paper
the tapestry	*der Wandteppich, der Gobelin*
der Wäscheständer	the clothes-horse
the washstand	*das Waschbecken*

Language Lineage: Plunder
The term 'plunder' is a product of the Thirty Years War and became common in Britain during the Civil War from 1642. It is derived from Du 'plunder' (meaning 'household goods') and from Du 'plunderen' and late MHG *plündern* (meaning literally to carry off such goods as booty). The British noun 'plunder', however, never took on either the Dutch or the German meanings, although in American it can mean 'household goods', as in Fenimore Cooper's *The Prairie* (1827): 'You seem to have but little plunder, stranger, for one who is so far abroad'.

Page 41: The Household

Sentences

Correct translations revealing the false friends would be:
1. His **jealousy** pictured what was happening behind the *blinds*.
2. In the garden shed were all kinds of tools – spades, rakes, *brooms*, hoes, a **besom** for autumn leaves, *scissors*, **shears** and a lawn-mower.
3. The hall of mirrors, the illustrious guests, the many *chandeliers* – everything gave the evening a **lustre** of its own.
4. Even the ivy-*clad/covered* wall was **bedecked** with pennants.
5. It was an almost abandoned area – bomb-sites, **demolished** houses and buildings, derelict industrial plant, a *vandalised* petrol station.
6. The *pot-warmers* were under the table-cloths and dishcloths in the drawer by the **stove**.
7. Only with a magic **wand** could you conquer such walls.
8. Whatever you looked for, there it was in the sole kitchen cupboard – tins and **cans**, *trays* and **tablets**, the coffee *pot* . . .
9. You can't behave in the *lounge* as in a Wild West **saloon**!
10. The apartment was fully *air-conditioned*. Nevertheless, it took them days to become **acclimatised** to the heats of the American South.
11. In one room in the long uninhabited *wing* they found many papers, sermons, edifying **tracts** and some occasional verse.
12. The Post Office was in a small, cosy corner **store**, in whose bay windows hung yellowing *lace curtains*.

Further False Friends

die Armatur	(*Bad, Spüle*) fittings; (*Magnet*) armature
the armature	*die Rüstung, die Panzerung*
das Whirlpool	the jacuzzi
the whirlpool	*der Strudel*

Field 11: The Built Environment

Page 42: Cities

False Friends

The details of the false friends involved in this exercise are as follows:

die Allee	the avenue, AmE boulevard
the alley	*die Gasse, das Gäßchen*
die City	the city centre, AmE downtown
the city	*die Großstadt*
der Dom	the cathedral
the dome	*die Kuppel, das Kuppeldach*
das Gasthaus	the restaurant; (*mit Unterkunft*) inn, hotel
the guest-house	*die Pension; das Gästehaus*
die Kanalisation	the sewerage system
the canalization	*die Kanalisierung*
das Kastell	the citadel
the castle	*die Burg, Burganlage*
die Messe	the trade fair; (*Kirche*) the mass, Mass
the mess	*das Offizierskasino; die Schiffsmesse*
der Palas	knights' hall, great hall of mediaeval castle
the palace	*das Schloß, der Palast*
die Passage	the mall, the concourse
the passage	*die schmale Gasse*
die Pension	the quest house
the pension	*die Rente*
das Pflaster	the cobblestones, cobbles
the plaster	*der Gips; der (Ver)Putz*
der Platz	the square
the place	*der Ort; die Stelle*
das Rathaus	the town hall
the council house	*das Haus im sozialen Wohnungsbau*
die Residenzstadt	the town with a royal court
town of residence	*der Wohnort*
sanieren	to clear, reconstruct, refurbish
to sanitize	*‚verbürgerlichen'*
das Warenhaus	the department/dept. store
the warehouse	*das Lagerhaus, das Lager*
die Warte	the watch-tower
the wart	*die Warze*

Page 43: Downtown

True Friends

The one true friend involved in this exercise is 'smithy'. The details of the remaining false friends are as follows:

False Friends

die Baracke	the hut, ramshackle building
the barracks	*die Kaserne*
der Blitz	the lightning
the blitz (or: Blitz)	*dt. Bombenangriffe auf britische Städte (insbes. London sowie die Industrie- u. Hafenstädte) im Zweiten Weltkrieg*
die Busstation	the bus-stop
the bus-station	*der Busbahnhof*
die Empore	the gallery
the emporium	*das Kauf-, Warenhaus, 'Laden'*
der/das Gully	the drain (at side of street)
the gully	*die schmale Schlucht*
die Hochstraße	the fly-over
the High Street	*die Hauptstraße, Einkaufsstraße*
das Kaff	the god-forsaken place, AmE hick-town
the 'caff'	*(coll., pej.) das Café*
das Kittchen	the clink
the kitchen	*die Küche*
das Lager	the storehouse
the lager	*das leichte Bier*
das Lokal	the pub; eating place
the local	*die Stammkneipe, das Ortsgasthaus*
die Mensa	the students' canteen/refectory
Mensa	*amerik.-engl. Verein für Hochbegabte*
das Stadium	the stage, phase
the stadium	*der Stadion*
der Stall	the stable; cow-shed; pigsty
the stalls	*(Theater) das Parkett*
die Stadthalle	the municipal hall
the town hall	*das Rathaus*
das Tollhaus	the madhouse, (*coll.*) the 'loony bin'
the toll-house	*das Maut-, Zollhaus*

Further False Friends

das Kasino	the officers' club/mess; (*Spielbank*) casino
the casino	*die Spielbank*
die Trafik (Austr.)	the tobacconist's
the traffic	*der Verkehr; der Handel*

Field 12 The Media and Communications

Page 44: On the Air

Solutions

The solutions to this exercise are: A 11, B 16, C 6, D 13, E 15, F 3, G 12, H 9, I 17, J 14, K 1, L 5, M 2, N 8, O 4, P 7, Q 18, R 10
The details of the false friends involved are as follows:

False Friends

die Antenne	the aerial
the antenna	*der Fühler, das Fühlhorn; die – meist vorläufige – Antenne draußen*
das Fernsehspiel	the TV drama
the screenplay	*das Drehbuch*
der Gaffer	the lighting expert on a film set
the gaffer	*der Glotzende*
das Handy	the mobile, mobile phone, cell phone
the handy	*das leicht Zugängliche*
der Moderator	the presenter, (*rare*) moderator
the Moderator	*der Vorsteher der* Church of Scotland
das Erste Programm	Channel One
the first programme	*die erste Sendung*
der Recorder	the cassette recorder
the recorder	*die Blockflöte; der Protokollführer*
der Sender	the broadcasting station
the sender	*der Absender*
der Spot	the commercial, ad; party political broadcast
the spot	*der Fleck; der Pickel; der Ort*

Page 45: Communication

Solutions

The solutions to this exercise are: 1. funked 2. denied 3. talk 4. a) wire b) send out 5. debate 6. demented 7. winked 8. broadcast 9. parley 10. sent out 11. sound out 12. waved.
The details of the false friends involved are as follows:

False Friends

dementiert	denied
demented	*wahnsinnig, verrückt*
funken	to wire; (SOS) to send out
to funk	*'Schiss kriegen'*
parlieren	to talk, discuss
to parley	*unterhandeln; sich besprechen mit*
senden	to broadcast, to transmit
to send	*schicken, verschicken, versenden*
winken	to wave; (*her-*) to beckon
to wink (at)	*zuzwinkern, zublinzeln*

Page 45: The Press

The three true friends involved in this exercise are: 'the feature', 'the guest column' and the 'leading article'. The details of the false friends are as follows:

Solutions

False Friends

das Comic — the comic strip
the comic — *das Kinder-, Witzblatt*
das Exemplar — the copy, the edition
the example — *das Beispiel*
das Impressum — the imprint
the impression — *der Eindruck; die Auflage*
die Karikatur — (*Zeitung*) the cartoon
the caricature — *das Spott-, Zerrbild, (Literatur, Kunst) die Karikatur*
das Magazin — the colour supplement
the magazine — *die Illustrierte, die Zeitschrift*
die Rezension — the book review; (*Theater*) theatrical review
the recension — *die Textversion (meistens der Bibel)*
die Rubrik — the article; the column
the rubric — *(selten) Anweisungen, bes. Prüfungsanweisungen*

Further False Friends

die Glosse — the light commentary; (*Wissenschaft*) the gloss
the gloss — *der Glanz, der äußere Schein; der Anstrich; die Randbemerkung*

Field 13: The World of Work

Page 48: Essential Professions

Solutions

The solutions to this crossword are: 1. personnel manager 2. mechanic 3. staff doctor 4. partner 5. physicist 6. computer technician 7. auditor 8. financier 9. wholesaler 10. ticket collector 11. commission agent 12. laboratory assistant 13. entrepreneur 14. producer 15. window-dresser 16. design engineer 17. caretaker 18. boss
Key Phrase: '[. . .] life stifles and dies'
The details of the false friends involved in this exercise are as follows:

False Friends

der Administrator — the computer technician
the administrator — *der/die Verwalter(in)*
der Chef — the head, boss
the chef — *der Küchenchef, Koch*
der Controller — the auditor
the c/Controller — *der Leiter (z.B. der BBC)*
der Dekorateur — the window-dresser, interior decorator
the decorator — *der Tapezierer u. Anstreicher*

	der Grossist	the wholesaler
	the grocer	*der/die Kolonialwarenhändler*
	der Hausmeister	the caretaker, janitor
	the house-master	*der Hausleiter in einem brit. Internat*
	der Kommissionär	the trading agent
	the commissionaire	*der (livrierte) Portier*
	der Kompagnon	the partner, associate
	the companion	*der Lebens-, Reisegefährte*
	der Konstrukteur	the design engineer
	the constructor	*(selten) der Erbauer*
	der Laborant	the laboratory/'lab' assistant
	the labourer	*der ungelernte Arbeiter*
	der Personalchef	the personnel/human resources manager
	the personal chef	*der Leibkoch*
	der Personalarzt	the staff doctor
	the personal doctor	*der Leibarzt*
	der Physiker	the physicist
	the physician	*AmE der Arzt, die Ärztin*
	der Unternehmer	the entrepreneur, businessman
	the undertaker	*der Leichenbestatter*

Page 47: Puzzling Professions

Solutions

The solutions to this exercise are: A. 14 B. 7 C. 8 D. 9 E. 3 F. 2 G. 12 H. 10 I. 24 J. 18 K. 19 L. 1 M. 17 N. 20 O. 22 P. 6 Q. 23 R. 11 S. 16 T. 21 U. 15 V. 5 W. 13 X. 4

The details of the false friends involved are as follows:

False Friends		
	der Akquisiteur	the commercial traveller, representative
	the acquisitor	*der Käufer*
	der Aktuar	clerk of court, registrar
	the actuary	*der Versicherungs(risiko)experte*
	der Börsianer	stock-jobber, Stock Market player
	the bursar	*der Schatzmeister, bes. von einem College*
	der Dealer	the drug peddler
	the dealer	*der Händler*
	der Expedient	the forwarding clerk
	the expedient	*das Hilfsmittel, der Notbehelf*
	der Hausmann	the husband who does the housework, (*selten*) househusband
	the houseman	*der/die junge Assistenzarzt/ärztin*
	der Knacker	the miser, skinflint; 'old fogey'
	the knacker	*der Schinder*

der Malermeister	the house painter
the master painter	*der begabte Maler*
der Pikkolo	the apprentice waiter
the piccolo	*die Pikkoloflöte*
der Prokurist	chief clerk, confidential clerk
the procurator	*der Bevollmächtigte, der Sachwalter; der Anwalt; der Königliche Anwalt des brit. Schatzamtes;* (ScE.) ~ fiscal *der Staatsanwalt*
der Propagandist	the representative of a firm
the propagandist	*der Verfasser/Vertreiber von Propaganda*
der Volontär	trainee journalist
the volunteer	*der/die Freiwillige*

Page 50: Office Work

Solutions

The solutions to this exercise are: 1. a) type b) key c) del-key 2. a) pile b) forms 3. a) staples b) envelopes c) re-fills d) photocopier 4. a) prospectus b) prospect 5. a) direction b) complaint c) packing / packaging material 6. a) advertisement b) advertise c) ad 7. a) board b) minutes 8. a) insert b) overleaf 9. a) brand b) label 10. a) get b) items c) staple

The details of the false friends involved are as follows:

die Annonce	the advertisement
the announcement	*the Ankündigung*
bekommen	to get, receive
to become	*werden*
die Direktion	the board (or directors), the management
the direction	*die Richtung*
das Etikett	the label
the etiquette	*die Etikette*
die Expedition	the forwarding department
the expedition	*die (Forschungs-)Reise*
das Formular	the form
the formula	*die Formel*
das Kuvert	the envelope
the cover	*die Decke, der Deckel, die Hülle, der Einband*
die Mine	the re-fill
the mine	*das Bergwerk; die (Land-, See-)Mine*
die Marke	the brand
the mark	*das Kennzeichen, das Merkmal*
der Posten	the item
the post	*die Post; die Stelle*
der Prospekt	the prospectus
the prospect	*die Aussicht*

das Protokoll	the minutes, the transcript
the protocol	*die Etikette*
die Reklamation	the complaint
the reclamation	*die Trockenlegung von Land; die Zurückforderung (von Geld)*
die Rückseite	the back, reverse; (s. ~) see overleaf
the backside	*der Hintern, die Hinterbacken*
der Stapel	the pile, heap
the staple	*die Heftklammer*
stapeln	to pile (up)
to staple	*(zusammen)heften*
die Taste	the key
the taste	*der Geschmack*
tippen	to type
to tip	*jdm. ein Trinkgeld geben; kippen; setzen auf*

Further False Friends

der Animateur	the entertainer, hostess
the animator	*der/die Trickzeichner(in)*
der Krämer	the shopkeeper
the crammer	*der/die Pauker(in), Nachhilfelehrer(in)*
der Kontrolleur	inspector; guard
the controller	*der Leiter*
reklamieren	to complain about
to reclaim	*trockenlegen; zurückfordern*

Field 14: Business, Industry, Commerce

Page 51: Big Business

True Friends

The four true friends involved in this exercise are: 'ambitions', 'consortia', 'integration' and 'presence'. The details of the false friends involved are as follows:

False Friends

die Branche	the sector (of the economy) ; the business, line of business; (*Fachgebiet*) the field, area
the branch	*die Zweigstelle, Filiale; (Baum) der Ast*
expedieren	to ship, to dispatch, to send
to expedite	*beschleunigen, forcieren*
forcieren	to expedite, to speed up; (*das Tempo~*) to force the pace
to force	*zwingen, nötigen; erzwingen, durchsetzen*
konkurrieren	to compete (with s. o.); to rival sth.
to concur	*übereinstimmen mit jdm.; zusammentreffen*
das Kontingent	the quota, share, allotment; (*Milit.*) contingent
the contingent	*(Milit.) das Kontingent*
der Konkurs	the bankruptcy, insolvency, (~ *anmelden*) to file a petition in bankruptcy/to file for b~

the concourse	*die Passage, die überdachte Fußgängerzone; die Menschenmenge*
der Konzern	the group, combine, group of companies
the concern	*die Firma, das Unternehmen; die Sorge; die Angelegenheit*
der Mittelstand	the medium-sized firms
the middle class(es)	*das Bürgertum, der Mittelstand*
perfekt	(*Überrraschung*) complete, total; (*Vertrag*) concluded, (*~ machen*) to conclude; (*vollendet*) perfect
perfect	*vollkommen, vollendet, makellos*
die Quote	quota
the quote	*der Kostenvoranschlag; das Zitat*
rentabel	profitable, profit-making, remunerative, lucrative, paying, money-spinning
rentable	*(ver)mietbar*
das Sortiment	the marketing/product mix
the assortment	*das Sortieren; die Zusammenstellung, die Auswahl, (Pralinés) die Selection*

Page 52: Company Development

True Friends

The true friends involved in this exercise include 'conflict', 'firm', 'future-oriented' and 'patent'. The details of the false friends involved are as follows:

False Friends

der Akkord	the chord; (*~Arbeit*) piece work
the accord	*die Übereinstimmung*
die Aktion	(*Export~*) the campaign; (*~ der Woche*) the bargain (offer)
the action	*die Handlung*
die Aktiva	the assets
the actives	*die Aktivformen (gramm.)*
der Arbeitsplatz	the job
the work place	*die Arbeitsstätte*
aufstocken	to take on (staff)
to stock up	*sich eindecken*
die Bonität	the soundness, reliability, solvency
the bounty	*die Freigebigkeit; die Spende*
die Fabrik	the factory, (*altm.*) mill
the fabric	*der Stoff, das Gewebe; das Gefüge, Gebilde*
die Fabrikation	the manufacture
the fabrication	*das 'Märchen', die erfundene Geschichte, Lüge*
die Fusion	the merger

	the fusion	*die (Ver)schmelzung; (Kernphysik) Fusion*
	die Konkurrenz	the competition, the rivals, competitors
	the concurrence	*die Zustimmung, das Einverständnis; das zeitl. Zusammentreffen*
	die Misere	the plight, the calamitous situation
	the misery	*der Kummer, Jammer, die Trübsal; das Elend*
	die Passiva	the liabilities
	the passives	*die Passivformen (gramm.)*
	die Pleite	the bankruptcy
	the plight	*die Misere*
	die Rentabilität	the profitability, lucrativeness
	the rentability	*die (Ver)mietbarkeit*
	der Tarif	(*Gehalt*) the salary scale; (*Bus, Bahn*) fare; (*Gebühren*) tariff
	the tariff	*die Zollgebühr;* (import ~) *der Einfuhrzoll*
	die Technik	the technology
	the technique	*das Verfahren, die Methode*
	übernehmen	to take over
	to overtake	*überholen*
	das Unternehmen	the company
	the undertaking	*das Unterfangen; das Versprechen*
Further False Friends	*die Expertise*	the expert's report
	the expertise	*das Fach-, Expertenwissen*
	die Occasion	the bargain
	the occasion	*das Ereignis, die Veranstaltung; der Anlaß*

Field 15: Technology and the Natural Sciences

Page 53: Do-It-Yourself

Solutions

The solutions to this crossword are: 1. insulate 2. nut 3. bolt 4. adjustable spanner 5. stroke 6. drill 7. insulation 8. ruler 9. mallet 10. pave 11. flex 12. load 13. groove 14. plumb-line 15. corner (*or*: elbow) 16. tarpaulin 17. pivot 18. button 19. (framing) square Key Phrase: '[. . .] substitute for brains'
The details of the false friends involved in this exercise are as follows:

False Friends	*die Angel*	(*Tür*) the hinge; (*Drehzapfen*) the pivot
	the angle	*der Winkel; das Knie(stück); der Standpunkt*
	der Bohrer	the drill
	the borer	(*Insekt.*) *der Bohrer*
	der Engländer	the adjustable spanner; (*Nation*) the Englishman
	the Englander	(Little ~) C 19th *Gegner des Empires,* C 20th/21st *Euroskeptiker*

der (Holz)hammer	the mallet
the hammer	*der Hammer*
der Hub	(*Werkzeugmaschine*) the stroke, travel
the hub	*die (Rad)Nabe; der Mittel-, Angelpunkt*
isolieren	to insulate
to isolate	*absondern*
die Isolierung	the insulation
the isolation	*die Absonderung; (~* ward*) die Isolierstation*
das Kabel	(*Gerät*) lead, flex, cord; (*Verkabelung*) cable
the cable	*das dicke Leitungskabel*
der Knopf	the button
the knob	*der Griff, der Knauf*
die Last	the load, burden
the last	*der Leisten*
das Lineal	the ruler
the lineal	*das Geradlinige*
das Lot	the plumb-line
the lot	*das Los, Schicksal; alle*
die Mutter	(*Schraube*) the nut
the mutter	*das Gemurmel*
die Nut	the groove, (*~ und Feder*) tongue and groove
the nut	*die Mutter*
die Plane	the awning, tarpaulin
the plane	*der Hobel; das Flugzeug*
pflastern	to pave
to plaster	*(ver)gipsen, verputzen; (über)tünchen*
der Winkel	*(Geom.)* the angle; *(Ecke)* the corner, nook
the winkle	*die eßbare Strandschnecke*

Page 54: In the Lab

The only (occasional) 'true friend' involved here is 'to smelt'. The details of the remaining false friends are as follows:

True Friend

False Friends

einschmelzen	*intr.* to melt, melt away; *tr.* to melt down; (*Schmiedeeisen usw.*) *tr. to smelt*
to smelt	*(Erz usw.) verhütten, (ein)schmelzen*
das Glas	the glass; (*Behälter*) jar
the glaze	*die Glasur*
die Glut	the heat, the glow, glowing fire; (*Asche*) embers
the glut	*das Überangebot; die Fülle*
das Labor	the laboratory
the labor	(AmE) *die Arbeit*
das Petroleum	BrE paraffin; AmE kerosene
the petroleum	*das Erdöl*

	das Pond	gram(me) force, gram(me) weight
	the pound	*das Pfund*
	das Quant	the quantum
	the quant	(BrE*) zum Staken von Booten verwendete Stange*
	das Quantum	the quantity, amount
	the quantum	*das Quant*
	der Quark	*etwa* curds, curd cheese, cottage cheese; (*Unsinn*) rubbish, tripe
	the quark	*das Quark*
	der Rest	the remainder, residue; (*Lieferrückstand*) the balance; (*Speise*) the left-overs; (*Bodensatz*) the dregs; (*sterbliche Reste*) mortal remains
	the rest	*die Übrigen, das Übrige; die Ruhe; der Aufenthalt; (Drehbank) die Auflage*
Further False Friends	*das Aggregat*	the unit; (*Strom*) the generator
	the aggregate	*die Summe, die Gesamtzahl, -menge*
	die Fuge	the crack
	the fugue	*(Mus.) die Fuge*
	raffiniert	sophisticated; (*ausgeklügelt*) ingenious
	refined	*kultiviert, gebildet, fein; (~* sugar*) Feinzucker, Raffinade; (~* steel*) Raffinierstahl*

Field 16: Money, Economics and Finance

Page 55: The Public Purse

True Friends

The two true friends involved in this exercise are 'recession' and 'subvention' (though for the latter 'subsidy' is still more common).

Translations

Correct translations of the words underlined in the headlines would be: 1. budget items 2. the economy/trade cycle 3. wage sacrifice 4. livelihoods 5. donor 6. retail trade/commerce 7. discount(s) 8. founders of new businesses 9. charitable gifts 10. budget 11. recession 12. pension(s) 13. subsidies 14. allowances. The details of the false friends involved are as follows:

False Friends	*die Diät*	the allowance, remuneration
	the diet	*die Abmagerungskur*
	der Etat	the budget
	the estate	*der Grundbesitz; das Landgut; (*real ~*) die Immobilie*
	die Existenz	(*neu gegründete*) new business; livelihood
	the existence	*das Dasein, Leben*
	der Handel	commerce; (*Einzel~*) the retail trade; (*Außen-*) the (foreign) trade; (*Börse*) trading; (*IHK*) Chamber of Commerce

the handle	*der Griff, Stiel usw.*
der Haushalt	(*Person, Staat*) the budget; household, home
the household	*Haus u. Hausrat*
die Konjunktur	the economy, state of the economy, trade cycle
the conjuncture	*das Zusammentreffen von Umständen; die Lage*
der Lohn	the wage(s)
the loan	*das Darlehen*
der Rabatt	the discount, reduction
the rebate	*die Rückzahlung, -vergütung*
die Rente	the pension
the rent	*die Miete*
die Spende	the charitable gift, donation
the spending	*die Ausgaben; das Ausgeben*
der/die Spender(in)	the giver to charity, donor; (*Organ*) donor
the spender	*der/die Verschwender(in)*

Language Lineage: Conjuncture
Although both German and English words here come from the same source – L 'coniungere' (to 'join together') Fr 'conjoncture', mod L 'conjunctura' – and although they both originally had the astrological sense of an 'astronomical conjunction', the English 'conjuncture' never had any of the German economic meanings, but meant the 'meeting of persons' 1644, the 'act of joining together' 1665, and above all its present sense of the 'meeting of circumstances, juncture, crisis' first noted from 1629.

Page 56: You and Your Money

Solutions

The solutions to this exercise are: 1. grant 2. rent 3. rates 4. a) broke b) rebate c) borrow/loan 5. a) loan b) mortgage 6. stipend 7. a) profiting b) profiteering 8. a) discount b) instalments 9. a) pump b) capital 10. pension 11. a) ask b) offer c) crisis d) resources 12. a) spend b) save c) to spare d) give to charity 13. a) stand b) generous
The details of the false friends involved are as follows:

False Friends

bitten	to ask, request; invite; beg, implore, beseech
to bid	*bieten, ein Angebot machen*
blank	broke, bust, 'skint', 'strapped for cash'
blank	*leer; gedankenleer*
die Hypothek	the mortgage
the hypothec	(*selten*) *die Bürgschaft eines Gläubigers;* ScE *die Hypothek;* ScE the whole ~ *der ganze Krempel*
der Lohn	the wage(s)
the loan	*das Darlehen*
profitieren	profit
to profiteer	*Wucherprofite machen*

pumpen	to borrow, to cadge
to pump	*(Geld) hineinpumpen, kanalisieren*
der Rabatt	the discount, reduction
the rebate	*die Rückzahlung, -vergütung*
die Rate	the instalment
the rate(s)	*die (ehemalige britische) Gemeindesteuer*
die Rente	the pension, state pension, old-age pension
the rent	*die Miete*
sparen	(*Person*) to save; (*Firma, Behörde, Staat*) to make savings, to economize
to spare	*übrig*
spendabel	generous, open-handed, liberal with one's money
spendable	*zum Ausgeben*
spenden	to give to charity, to make a donation; (*Organ*) to give
to spend	*ausgeben; verbrauchen, aufwenden*
spendieren	(*eine Runde*) to stand, to 'shout'
to spend	*ausgeben; verbrauchen, aufwenden*
das Stipendium	the scholarship, bursary, grant
the stipend	*das Gehalt (bei Lehrern und Geistlichen)*

Page 57: Hey, Big Spender

Solutions

The solutions to this exercise are as follows: 1. a) foreign notes and coins b) exchange rate c) foreign currency/currencies 2. a) debentures b) gratuity c) recompense 3. (new) issue 4. commission 5. quoted 6. a) sorts b) stocks 7. a) effect b) income c) consumer spending d) inflation 8. fund 9. a) course b) note c) price 10. alimony 11. compensation 12. find 13. provisions 14. a) safe b) treasure
The details of the false friends involved are as follows:

False Friends

die Devisen	foreign currency/currencies
the device	*der Plan, die Erfindung; das Gerät, die böse Absicht*
die Effekten	the stocks, bonds
the effects	*die Auswirkungen*
die Emission	(*Börse*) the (new) issue
the emission	*die Schadstoffemission*
der Fund	the find
the fund	*der Fonds*
die Gratifikation	the gratuity, the bonus
the gratification	*die Genugtuung; die Befriedigung*
honorieren	to reward
to honour	*ehren, würdigen*
der Kurs	(*Devisen*) exchange rate; (*Aktien*) price

the course	*die Verfahrensweise; (Uni) die Veranstaltung, der Kurs; der Lauf, der Gang, die Bahn*
notieren	(*Aktien*) to quote
to note	*beobachten; niederschreiben*
die Obligation	the debenture, bond
the obligation	*die Verpflichtung*
die Provision	the commission
the provision	*die Vorkehrung*
die Rekompensation	the compensation
the recompense	*die Belohnung, die Entschädigung*
die Sorten	foreign notes and coins
the sorts	*die Arten*
der Tresor	the strong-room, AmE the vault; (*Geldschrank*) the safe
the treasure	*der Schatz; der Reichtum*

Further False Friends

das Depot	(*Bank*) the deposit box, strong room
the depot	*(Straßenbahn) der Betriebsbahnhof*

Field 17: Travel and Transport

Page 58: Means of Transport

True Friends

The eight true friends involved in this exercise are 'battery', 'compressor', 'coupé', 'grille', 'limousine'; 'minibus', 'pickup truck' and 'snowmobile'. The details of the false friends involved are as follows:

False Friends

der (Auto)skooter	the dodgem car
the scooter	*der Motor-, Kinderroller;* AmE *die Eisjacht*
der Bagger	the excavator, digger; dredger
the bagger	*die Abfüllmaschine*
das Benzin	the petrol, AmE gas
the benzine	*der Fleckentferner*
der Blinker	the indicator
the blinker	*die Scheuklappe*
der Caravan	the estate car, AmE station wagon
the caravan	*der Wohnwagen; die Karawane*
die Hupe	the horn, the claxon
the hoop	*der Reif, der Ring*
der Katalysator	the catalytic converter
the catalyst	*(Chemie) der Katalysator*
der Kipper	the tipper, AmE the dump truck
the kipper	*der Räucherhering*
der Oldtimer	(*vor 1917*) the veteran car, (*1917–30*) vintage car
the oldtimer	*bes.* AmE *altmodischer Mensch; altmodisches Ding*

das Profil	(*Reifen*) the tread
the profile	*(Kopf usw.) das Profil; die Kurzbiographie*
der Roller	the scooter, motor scooter; (*City~*) city scooter
the roller	*die Walze; der Walzwerkarbeiter; die Gartenwalze; bes.* AmE *die Sturzwelle*
das Tachometer	the speedometer
the tachometer	*der Rotationsmesser*
das Vehikel	the old jalop(p)y, the boneshaker
the vehicle	*das (Land-)Fahrzeug*

Page 59: Travel

True Friends

The three true friends involved in this exercise are 'rucksack', 'wanderlust' and 'yacht'. The details of the false friends involved are:

False Friends

das Boot	the boat; (*großes*) launch, long-boat; (*flaches*) punt; (*Falt~*) collapsible boat
the boot	*der Kofferraum; der Stiefel*
die Fähre	the ferry, ferry-boat; (*Raum~*) space-shuttle
the fare	*das Fahrgeld, der Fahrtarif*
die Kreuzung	the cross-roads, intersection; (*Züchtung*) cross-breeding, interbreeeding
the crossing	*die Überfahrt; (*level ~*) der Bahnübergang; (Kirche) die Vierung*
mittwochs	on Wednesdays
midweek	*Mitte der Woche (= dienstags, mittwochs und donnerstags)*
das Ruder	the oar; (*am ~*) at the helm
the rudder	*das Steuerruder*
schwanken	to reel, sway, totter, stagger
to swank	*stolzieren, protzen, ‚angeben'*
tanken	to fill up
to tank (along)	*entlangdüsen*
trampen	to hitch-hike, to thumb down a car
to tramp	*mühselig stapfen, marschieren; vagabundieren*
der/die Tramper(in)	the hitch-hiker
the tramp	*der Landstreicher; der Fußmarsch; das Trampschiff;* AmE *das Luder*
überholen	to overtake, pass; (*übertreffen*) to outstrip, outrun
to overhaul	*warten, gründlich überprüfen; (selten) einholen*
wandern	to hike, ramble, go hiking/rambling
to wander	*umherirren*

der blinde Passagier	the stowaway	**Further False Friends**
the blind passenger	*der blinde Fahrgast*	
die Lore	wagon, tub, large mine-car	
the lore	*die Kunde, Lehre; das überlieferte Wissen; das Märchengut*	

Field 18: Ships and Navigation

Page 60: Messing About in Boats

True Friends

The true friends involved here are 'buoy', 'jolly-boat', 'roads' and 'tackle' . The details of the false friends are as follows:

False Friends

die Back	the forecastle, fo'c's'le; (*Schüssel*) mess tin
the back	*der Rücken; der hintere Teil; die Lehne*
der Bug	the bow(s); (*Flugzeug*) nose
the bug	*die Wanze, das Insekt; der Bazillus*
der Ewer	sailing barge; wherry; lighter
the ewer	*die Wasserkanne, -krug*
der Fang	the catch
the fang	*der Gift-, Fangzahn*
das Floß	the raft, float; (*~brücke*) floating bridge
the floss	*der Außenfaden des Seidenkokons*; (dental ~) *Zahnseide*
das Galion/ Gallion	the cutwater, knee of the ship's head; (*~sfigur*) figurehead
the galleon	*die Galeone*
das Haar	the hair; single hair
the haar	*der (Meeres)Nebel*
der Hafen	the harbour; (*die ~stadt*) port
the haven	*der Zufluchtsort*
das Heck	the stern; the poop
the heck	*die Reuse;* (AmE) *die Hölle;* (What the ~!) *Was zum Teufel!*
die Reede	the roads
the reeds	*das Schilf, Schilfrohr, Riedgras*
das Schiff	the ship; boat
the skiff	*das Skiff, das leichte Ruderboot*
das Stag	the stay
the stag	*der Hirsch*
der Stern	the star
the stern	*das Heck, Achterschiff; hinterer Teil*

Page 61: Voyages

True Friends The three true friends involved here are 'dock', 'mole' and 'rail(ing)'. The details of the false friends involved are as follows:

False Friends

der Helm	the helmet; (*Sturz~*) crash helmet
the helm	*das (Steuer)Ruder, das Steuer;* (to be at the ~) *am Ruder sein, an der Macht sein, herrschen*
die Hülle	the cover, shell
the hull	(ship, aircraft) *der Rumpf;* (fruit) *die Hülse*
das Ruder	the oar; (*kurzes*) scull
the rudder	*das Steuerruder, das Steuer;* (aircraft) *Seitenruder;* (~less) *ohne Ruder, steuerlos*
der Seehund	the seal
the sea-dog	*der alte Seebär;* (rare) *gemeiner Seehund, Meerkalb*
der Seetang	the seaweed
the tang of the sea	*der würzige, salzige Geruch des Meeres*
die Wasserkraft	the hydraulic power, water power
the watercraft	*das Wasserfahrzeug*
die Werft	the shipyard, ship-building yard, dockyard
the wharf	*der Kai, der Anlegeplatz*
der Prahm	the barge, lighter, the pra(a)m
the pram	*der Kinderwagen*

Field 19: Politics and Politicking

Page 64: Politicking

True Friends The true friends involved in this exercise are 'entourage', 'opposition', 'premier' and 'state organs'. The details of the false friends involved are as follows:

False Friends

das Engagement	the commitment, involvement
the engagement	*die Verlobung*
engagiert	committed, involved; (*Literatur*) *engagé*
engaged	*verlobt*
die Intelligenz	the intelligentsia
the intelligence	*der Verstand; der Geheimdienst*
die Kontrolle	the supervision, overseeing; (*Waffen~*) arms inspection
the control	*die Beherrschung*
kontrollieren	watch over, supervise
to control	*beherrschen*
der Pair	(*Oberhaus*) the peer, Peer

the pair	*das Paar, das Pärchen; (zwecks Abstimmung) die Paarung von Abgeordneten*
plakatieren	to put up posters
to placate	*beschwichtigen, versöhnlich stimmen, besänftigen*
der Rapport	the (formal) report
the rapport	*die (meist einvernehmliche) Beziehung*
die Schikane(n)	the harassment
the chicane	*(Bridge) Blatt ohne Trümpfe*
das Transparent	the banner
the transparency	*das Farbdia(positiv); die Overheadfolie*

Page 65: Political Life

The true friends involved in this exercise are 'cabinet (minister)', 'campaign of lies', 'corruption', 'minister'. The details of the false friends involved are as follows:

True Friends

False Friends

die Außenpolitik	the foreign policy
the foreign politics	*die Politik im Ausland*
die Basis	(*Politik*) the grass roots
the basis	*die Grundlage*
beraten	to advise; to discuss
to berate	*heftig ausschelten*
besiegen	to defeat
to besiege	*belagern*
besuchen	to visit, seek out
to beseech	*anflehen, ersuchen*
betrügen	to deceive, to cheat
to betray	*verraten*
der/die Feind(in)	the enemy, foe
the fiend	*der Unhold*
die Fraktion	the parliamentary party (the 'PP')
the fraction	*der Bruchteil*
der/die Kanzler(in)	(*Bundes~*) the (Federal) Chancellor
the Chancellor	*der brit. Schatzkanzler (Finanzminister); der dt. Bundeskanzler*
kommunal	(*Pol.*) local, on local authority level
communal	*gemeinsam*
das Konzept	the blue-print, plan
the concept	*der Begriff, die Idee, die Vorstellung*
das Manifest	the manifesto
the manifest	*die Passagierliste; das Evidente*
der Parlamentär	the bearer of the flag of truce, go-between
the parliamentarian	*der/die Parlamentarier(in)*

	resignieren	become resigned, to give up/in, throw in the towel
	to resign	*zurücktreten*
	das Ressort	the department, portfolio
	the resort	*der Bade-, Ferien-, Ski- usw. ort;* (last ~) *die letzte Zuflucht*
	das Schmiergeld	the bribe, the back-hander
	the smear	*die Verleumdung; (Med.) der Abstrich*
	der/die Sprecher(in)	the spokesman, spokeswoman
	the Speaker	*Vorsitzende(r) im brit. Unterhaus, (etwa) der/die Bundestagspräsident(in)*
	das Ziel	the aim, objective, goal
	the zeal	*der Eifer*
	der Zivildienst	the community service, alternative service
	the Civil Service	*das Beamtentum*
Further False Friends	*das Mandat*	the seat
	the mandate	*der Wählerauftrag; das Votum*

Page 66: War and the Military

True Friends The true friends involved in this exercise are 'collateral damage', 'friendly fire' and 'patrols'. The details of the false friends are:

False Friends	*der Anschlag*	the attack
	the onslaught	*der heftige Angriff, Ansturm*
	belagert	besieged
	beleaguered	*in trostloser Lage*
	besetzen	to occupy
	to beset	*bedrängen, verfolgen, umgeben*
	besiegen	to defeat
	to besiege	*belagern*
	bombardieren	(*von Luft*) to bomb; (*von Land/See*) to bombard
	to bombard	*bombardieren (von Land/See)*
	die Generalität	the generals
	the generality	*die Mehrzahl, große Masse; (Pl.) Gemeinplätze*
	die Granate	the shell
	the grenade	*die Handgranate*
	kommandieren	to command
	to commandeer	*requirieren*
	das Kommando	the command
	the commando	*das Mitglied einer Kommandotruppe*
	der Leutnant	second lieutenant
	the lieutenant	*der Oberleutnant*

die Marine	the navy
the marine	*der Marineinfanterist*
der Militär	the soldier, military man
the military	*das Militär*
der Pionier	(*Milit.*) the sapper
the pioneer	*der Vorkämpfer, Bahnbrecher, Pionier*
der/die Private	the private individual
the private	*der einfache/gewöhnliche Soldat*
die Repressalien	the reprisals
the repression	*die Unterdrückung*
requirieren	to requisition
to require	*benötigen*
die Salve	the salvo
the salve	*die Salbe, insbes. Lippen~*
die Schlacht	the battle; (*~feld*) battle-field
the slaughter	*das Gemetzel, das Niedermetzeln*
der Söldner	the mercenary
the soldier	*der Soldat*
spuren	to obey orders, to toe the line
to spur (on)	*anspornen*
strafen	to punish
to strafe	*mit Bordwaffen beschießen*

Further False Friends

defilieren	to march past
to defile	*beschmutzen; schänden, entweihen*
hissen	to hoist, raise
to hiss	*auszischen, -pfeifen*

Language Lineage: Besiege
Despite their similarity in appearance and affinity in meaning, 'besiege' and *besiegen* are of different etymological origins. *Besiegen* has to do with MHD 'sige' and Ing. 'segh-' meaning *festhalten, einen im Kampf Unterlegenen gepackt halten.* 'Besiege', however, derives from OF 'asegie', late L 'assediare', ME 'bi-, by-, besege' meaning to 'sit down before (a castle, town etc.) with armed forces in order to capture it'. Its first recorded use is in 1297.

Field 20: Crime and the Law

Page 67: In the Law Courts

Solutions

The solutions to this exercise are: A. 13 B. 17 C. 11 D. 14 E. 9 F. 8 G. 16 H. 20 I. 5 J. 19 K. 15 L. 7 M. 1 N. 18 O. 4 P. 6 Q. 12 R. 2 S. 3 T. 10 The details of the false friends are as follows:

X

False Friends		
	der Advokat	lawyer, barrister; solicitor, ScE advocate
	the advocate	*Befürworter*; (ScE) *Advokat*
	die Injurie	the insult
	the injury	*die körperliche Verletzung, Wunde*
	(die) Jura	Law, Legal Studies
	the Jura	*der Kanton Jura*
	die Pacht	the lease
	the pact	*das Abkommen; die Übereinkunft*
	der Paragraph	the section, article of law
	the paragraph	*der Absatz*
	die Police	(insurance) policy
	the police	*die Polizei*
	das Quiproquo	the case of mistaken identity
	the quid pro quo	*das Quidproquo, die Gegenleistung; Vergütung*
	die Revision	the appeal, rehearing
	the revision	*die Wiederholung, Überarbeitung*
	visitieren	to search, 'frisk'
	to visit	*besuchen*
	das Zivilrecht	(the) civil law
	civil rights	*Bürgerrechte*

X

Page 68: Crime and Punishment

Solutions

The details of the false friends involved in this exercise are as follows. Note that in the text 'life' means *lebenslänglich*.

False Friends		
	das Arsen(ik)	arsenic
	the arson	*die Brandstiftung*
	der Brief	the letter
	the brief	*der Gerichtsauftrag; Schriftsatz, Mandat*
	der Clou	the (important) point
	the clue	*die Indiz, der Anhaltspunkt, der Fingerzeig, die Spur*
	die Evidenz	the clarity, manifestness
	the evidence	*das Beweismaterial, die Tatspuren; die Zeugenaussage*
	der Fall	the case; (*Theologie*) the Fall
	the fall/Fall	*der Sturz*; (Theology) *der (Sünden-)Fall*
	der Fehler	the error, mistake, *(Flüchtigkeits~)* slip
	the failure	*das Versagen, das Scheitern*
	geil	lewd, lecherous, randy; (*affen-*) 'brilliant', 'brill'
	guileful	*listig, tückisch*
	grausam	cruel
	gruesome	*grausig, grauenhaft*
	die Instanz	the authority; the stage of appeal, (*Gericht der zweiten I~*) court of appeal

the instance	*der Fall, das Beispiel*
die Justiz	the legal system, the Law
(the) justice	*die Gerechtigkeit; das Recht; der gerechte Lohn;* (of the peace, JP) *Friedensrichter*
die Kaution	(*Gericht*) bail; (*Wohnung*) deposit
the caution	*die Vorsicht; die (milde) Warnung*
der Krimi	the 'whodunit', detective story
the crime	*das Verbrechen; der Frevel, die Übeltat*
der Kriminale	the detective
the criminal	*der Verbrecher, der Straftäter*
der Magistrat	the town council, Town Council
the magistrate	*der Friedensrichter*
der/die Mörder(in)	the murderer/murderess
the murder	*der Mord, die Ermordung;* (blue m~) *zetermordio*
der Prozeß	the trial; (*Rechtsstreit*) law suit, litigation
the process	*das Verfahren; die Prozedur; der Vorgang*
prüfen	to test, to examine, to scrutinize
to prove	*beweisen, darlegen*
das Urteil	the sentence, judgement, verdict
the ordeal	*die Feuer-, Mut-, Nervenprobe; schwere Prüfung*

Further False Friends

der Arrest	the detention; (*zehn Tage* ~) ten days in the guard-house; (*Haus~*) house arrest
the arrest	*die Festnahme, Verhaftung*
die Indizien	the clues
the indices	*die Register*
die List	the cunning, the guile
the list	*die Liste*

Language Lineage: Brief

The term 'brief', derived from the ME 'bref' and L 'breve', is indeed connected with OFris 'brêf' and OHG 'briof' and has a similar meaning field denoting 'letter, dispatch, note'. Apart from a short period between 1400 and 1652, however, when it could mean 'letter', it has tended to be an official or legal word denoting a 'letter of authority', a 'letter of the Pope', a 'letter of credentials', a 'letter patent' and, above all, a 'summary of the facts of a legal case revealing the issues of law involved'.

alarmieren — to call sb. out
to alarm — beruhigen

Ingenuität — ingenuasense
the ingenuity — die Klugheit, der Einfallsreichtum

Field 21: School Life, Teaching and Didactics

Page 69: Learning and Teaching

False Friends

The details of the false friends involved in this exercise are as follows:

der Assessor	the assistant teacher
the assessor	*der Bewerter, der Beisitzer; der Steuereinschätzer*
der/die Direktor(in)	the headmaster, headmistress, 'head'
the director	*der/die Firmenchef(in)*
die Eleven	the pupils
the eleven	*die Elf, die Fußball-, Cricketmannschaft*
die Lehrerkonferenz	the staff meeting
the Teachers' Conference	*die Tagung der Lehrergewerkschaft*
die Lektüre	the reading matter/material
the lecture	*die Vorlesung*
die Notiz	the note
the notice	*der Aushang*
die Note	the grade, mark
the note	*die Notiz*
der Primus	the top boy, AmE the ace pupil
the primus, Primus	*der Spirituskocher; (altm.) der ältere/ älteste Bruder*
der/die Referendar(in)	the trainee teacher
the reverend	*der Geistliche*
sechste Klasse	second/2nd year
the Sixth Form	*die (Unter- u. Ober-) Prima*
der Studiendirektor	(*etwa*) the senior master
the Director of Studies	*akademischer Berater an brit. Universitäten*

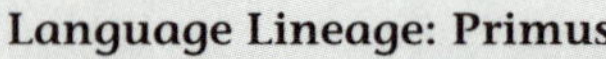

Language Lineage: Primus
This is a classic case of serendipity in false friend creation. The English term 'a primus' is simply a brand name (like 'a hoover') that has become a household expression. From 1904 it established itself as *the* term for a pressure cooker – or lamp – burning paraffin. When used in a British school context, 'primus' was otherwise an adjunct given to the oldest holder of a surname and denoting his seniority – 'Anscott primus'.

Page 70: At School

True Friends

The two true friends in this exercise are 'colleague' and 'rebel'. The details of the false friends involved are as follows:

False Friends

das Diktat	the dictation
the dictat	*die aufgezwungene Verpflichtung*
der/die Gymnasial-lehrer(in)	the grammar school teacher
the gym teacher	*der/die Sportlehrer(in)*
das Gymnasium	the grammar school
the gymnasium	*die Turn-, Sporthalle*
der Hausmeister	the caretaker, AmE facility manager
the house-master	*der Hausleiter in einem brit. Internat*
die Hochschule	the university, AmE. College
the high school	*das Gymnasium*
die Mappe	(*Sammel~*) the file, folder ; (*Akten~*) briefcase; (*Schul~)* school-bag, satchel
the map	*die Landkarte*
die Meinung	the opinion
the meaning	*die Bedeutung*
die Physik	physics
the physique	*der Körperbau*
die Relation Lehrer-Schüler	the pupil-teacher ratio
pupil-teacher relations	*die Beziehungen zwischen Lehrern und Schülern*
der Schüler	the pupil, schoolboy
the scholar	*der Stipendiat; der Gelehrte*
das schwarze Brett	the notice board, AmE bulletin board
the blackboard	*die Tafel*
seriös	to be taken seriously
serious	*ernst, ernsthaft*
das Wissen	the knowledge
the wisdom	*die Weisheit*
die Zensur	(*Schule*) mark, grade; (*Staat*) censorship
the censure	*der Tadel, die Rüge*

Further False Friends

das Konvikt	school boarding house; Catholic seminary
the convict	*der Zuchthäusler*
die Prima	the Sixth Form
the prime	*die besten Jahre*

Field 22: University and Student Life

Page 71: University Studies

True Friends

The true friends involved here are 'catalogue', 'College', 'Dean', 'exam', 'guest professor(ship)', 'habilitation' (a German loan-word in English), 'mentor', 'sabbatical year', 'salary' and 'Senate'. The details of the false friends involved are as follows:

False Friends

absolvieren	(*Studium*) to complete, finish; (*Praktikum*) to do
absolve	*lossprechen von*
der/die Akademiker(in)	the university graduate
the academic	*der/die Hochschullehrer(in), -dozent(in)*
der (akademische) Grad	the degree
the grade	*die Note;* (AmE) *die Klasse, Klassenstufe*
das Kolleg	the course of lectures
the college	*das College (Teil der engl. Hochschule)*
der Kommers	students' ceremonial drinking session
the commerce	*der Handel, ~sverkehr, die Kommerz*
die Kommission	(*an der Hochschule usw.*) committee; (*[inter]national*) commission
the commission	*die Provision; der Auftrag; die große Untersuchungskommission*
der Konvent	the assembly, university council
the convent	*das Nonnenkloster; die von Nonnen geleitete Schule*
das Magazin	*(Bibliothek)* stack room; *(Zeitung)* colour supplement
the magazine	*die Illustrierte*
die Mensur	students' duel
the mensuration	*das Messen, die Messung*
das Prädikat (*~sexamen*)	distinction, 'starred First'
predicate	*das Prädikat* (gramm.)
das Praktikum	*(BWL)* the placement, internship
the practical	*das Laborpraktikum*
die Promotion	the doctorate, doctoral degree; achievement of d~
the promotion	*die Beförderung*
promovieren	to gain/do a doctorate
to promote	*befördern; werben für*
der Referent	the speaker, holder of a presentation
the referent	*das Beziehungswort, Bezugsobjekt*
schassen	to send down, rusticate
to chase	*jagen, verfolgen*
das Studium	the studies
the study	*das Arbeitszimmer; das Studieren*

Page 72: The University Hierarchy

The details of the false friends involved are as follows:

False Friends

der/die Dekan(in)	the Dean; (*Studien~*) D~ for Academic Affairs
the Deacon	*der Diakon*
der/die Kanzler(in)	Administrative Head (and Treasurer)
the Chancellor	*Oberhaupt und Galionsfigur einer Universität*
der/die Leiter(in)	the Sectional Head; (*Kurs~*) course leader/holder
the leader	*(Kurs-)Leiter, (Gruppen-)Führer*
der/die Lektorin	the lector, (fem.) lectrice
the lecturer	*der/die Dozent(in);* (senior ~) *der/die Akad. Rat/Oberrat/rätin,* (junior ~) *der/die akad. Mitarbeiter(in)*
der/die Präsident(in)	(Uni-) BrE Vice-Chancellor, AmE President
the President	(politics, company) *Präsident*
der/die (Pro)-Rektor(in)	the (Vice-)Vice-Chancellor
the Rector	*der anglikan. Pfarrer;* ScE *Schuldirektor*
der/die Studiendirektor(in)	*etwa* the senior teacher/master/mistress (*~ im Hochschuldienst*) lecturer
the Director of Studies	*akad. Berater an engl. Universitäten*

Further False Friends

das Seminar	the seminar; the Institute, Department
the seminary	*das Priesterseminar*

Field 23: Thought, Logic and Mental Processes

Page 73: Thinking

True Friends

The true friends involved in this exercise are 'conjecture' and 'hypothesis'. The details of the false friends involved are as follows:

False Friends

die Crux	the 'catch', the problem, the difficulty
the crux	*der springende Punkt, die Hauptsache*
hoffentlich	I hope so, let us hope so, it is to be hoped etc.
hopefully	*hoffnungsvoll; (coll.) hoffentlich*
die Ingenuität	the ingenuousness
ingenuity	*die Erfindungsgabe*
die Konsequenz	the conclusion; consistency
the consequence	*die Folge, das Resultat, das Ergebnis*
konstruieren	to construct
to construe	*deuten*
die Pointe	the pointed formulation; (*Witz*) the punch line

	the point	*der Punkt; die Spitze*
	the pointer	*der Hinweis, Fingerzeig*
	die Ratio	the intellect, the mind
	the ratio	*die Relation, das Verhältnis*
	das Sein	being, existence
	the sign	*das Zeichen*
	simpel	simple-minded, simplistic
	simple	*einfach*
	stupide	(*Tätigkeit*) dull, monotonous, mindless; (*Mensch*) dull, slow-witted
	stupid	*blöd, dumm, doof*

X **Page 74: Up for Debate**

Solutions

The solutions to this crossword are: Across 8. perhaps 9. oversight 12. inconsistent 14. adequate 17. try 18. in principle 23. inconsequential 26. also 27. survey Down 1. guess 2. meaning 3. consequent 4. opinion 5. principally 6. probe 7. eventually 10. general idea 11. test 13. therefore 15. consistent 16. rate 19. specially 20. overlook 21. fitting 22. factor 24. extra 25. moment
The details of the false friends involved are as follows:

False Friends

adäquat	appropriate, fitting, suitable
adequate	*hinreichend, genügend*
also	therefore, so, hence, thus
also	*auch, ebenfalls*
eventuell	perhaps, possibly
eventually	*schließlich, endlich*
extra	specially, especially
extra	*zusätzlich*
inkonsequent	inconsistent, illogical
inconsequential	*irrelevant, belanglos, unerheblich*
konsequent	consistent, logical
consequent	*folgend, sich ergebend, resultierend*
die Meinung	the opinion
the meaning	*die Bedeutung, der Sinn*
das Moment	the factor, element, aspect
the moment	*der Augenblick, Zeitpunkt; die Tragweite*
prinzipiell	in principle
principally	*hauptsächlich, in erster Linie*
die Probe	the test, trial, experiment
the probe	*die Sondierung, Untersuchung*
probieren	to try, test, experiment with
to probe	*sondieren; einer Untersuchung unterziehen*
raten	to guess; to advise

to rate	*einstufen, einschätzen*
überblicken	to survey, have a clear view of
to overlook	*übersehen, nicht sehen*
die Übersicht	the general idea, overview, survey
the oversight	*das Versehen;* AmE *die Übersicht*

Field 24: Time, Past Time, History

Page 75: The Passage of Time

True Friends

The true friends involved here are 'aeon', 'epoch-making', 'era', 'moratorium', 'phase' and 'ultimatum'. The details of the false friends involved are as follows:

False Friends

aktualisieren	to up-date, to make topical
to actualize	*verwirklichen, realistisch behandeln*
aktuell	topical; current, up-to-date, present-day
actual	*wirklich, tatsächlich, eigentlich*
alltäglich	everyday, routine, humdrum
all-day	*ganztägig, Ganztags-*
am anderen Tag	the day after, the next day, the following day
the other day	*neulich, kürzlich*
die Anciennität	(*Dienstrang*) seniority
ancientness	*die Altertümlichkeit*
dalli, dalli	hurry up! get a move on! get your skates on!
to dilly-dally	*herumtrödeln; zaudern*
das Datum	(*Kalender~*) the date; (*Tatsache*) datum
the datum (pl. data)	*etwas Gegebenes; die Voraussetzung, Grundlage*
die Fete	the party
the fête	*das* (*meist karitative*) *Fest*
halb zehn	half (past) nine
half ten	*halb elf*
in kurzem	before long, shortly
in short	*kurzum*
momentan	at present, at the moment, for the time being
momentarily	*flüchtig, einen Augenblick lang*
nun	now, at present; well ...
noon	*Mittag(szeit)*
die Partie	the game, match; the excursion; (*Schlitten~*) ride
the party	*die Fete*
punktuell	at one point, ad hoc; isolated, individual
punctual	*pünktlich*
der Termin	the appointment, appointed day; (*Verlags-, Uni-*) deadline; (*Bauvorhaben*) target date

the term	*das Trimester; die Frist; die Laufzeit*
das Uhrglas	the watch glass
the hour-glass	*das Stundenglas, die Sanduhr*
der Ultimo	the last day (or end) of the month
ultimo	*vom letzten Monat, vorigen Monats*
(ver)weilen	to stay, linger, tarry
to while away	*sich die Zeit vertreiben*

Page 76: The Historical Sense

True Friends

The true friends involved here are 'ephemeral', 'gravestone', 'Limes', 'mediaevalist', 'mummy', 'palisade', 'pharaoh' and 'thanatology'. The details of the false friends involved are as follows:

False Friends

Aktualität	topicality, up-to-dateness
actuality	*die Wirklichkeit*
altern	to grow/become old(er), age, advance in years
alter	*leicht verändern, abändern, umändern*
die Antike	(classical) antiquity
the antique	*die Antiquität*
der (Buch)Antiquar	the second-hand bookseller/book-dealer
the antiquary	*der Altertümler, Altertumsforscher*
die Antiquität	the antique
antiquity	*das Altertum, die klassische Antike*
das Epitaph	memorial stone, memorial plaque
the epitaph	*der Grabspruch*
das Fest	the festival, celebration
the feast	*das Festessen, -gelage, -mahl; der Festtag*
die Historik	the academic study of history; the doctrine of historical method
the historic	*das Historische*
das Jubiläum	the anniversary
the jubilee	*das königliche Jubiläum*
das Mittelalter	the Middle Ages
middle age	*mittleres Alter*
mittelalterlich	mediaeval, medieval
middle-aged	*mittleren Alters*
der Wall	the rampart; earthwork
the wall	*die Mauer; die Wand*

Page 77: Terms with a History

The one (once) true friend involved in the exercise is 'list', which had the sense of *List, Tücke* between *c*900 and *c*1430. The details of the false friends involved are as follows:

True Friends

False Friends

die Flinte	the musket, flint-lock rifle
the flint	*der Feuerstein, Kiesel; Flint*
der Knabe	the boy, lad
the knave	*der Schuft, Schurke, Spitzbube*
der Knecht	servant; farm-labourer; slave, serf, bondsman
the knight	*der Ritter*
der Konjurant	the conspirator, plotter
the conjurer/or	*der Zauberer, Zauberkünstler, Taschenspieler*
die Levée	*levée en masse*
the levée	*das Lever*
mustern	to inspect, review
to muster	*versammeln, auftreiben; aufbieten*
der Regent	the ruler, sovereign; governor
the Regent	*der Prinzregent*
der Säbel	the sabre; (~*rasseln*) sabre-rattling
the sable	*der Zobel; das Zobelfell, -pelz*
der Scholar	the travelling student, itinerant student
the scholar	*der/die Gelehrte*
das Wappen	the coat of arms
the weapon	*die Waffe*

Field 25: Language and Slang

Page 80: Qualities of Language

The three true friends involved in this exercise are 'eloquent', 'language barrier' and 'metaphor'. The details of the false friends involved are as follows:

True Friends

das Beiwort	the epithet; (gramm.) the adjective/adverb
the byword	*das Sprichwort; der Inbegriff, das Musterbeispiel*
die Devise	the motto; (*Heraldik*) the device
the device	*der Plan, der Einfall; die Erfindung; die böse Absicht;* (heraldry) *die Devise*
der Konjunktiv	the subjunctive
conjunctive	*verbindend, Verbindungs-*
die Parole	the slogan, watch-word, pass-word, catch-word
the parole	*die bedingte Haftentlassung, Bewährung*
das Pathos	the impassioned tone
the pathos	*das Ergreifende; das Mitleid*

die Phrase	the catchphrase, cliché, hollow phrase
the phrase	*die Redensart, der Ausdruck; die Wortverbindung*
die Prägnanz	pithiness, sapidity, succinctness
the pregnancy	*die Schwangerschaft*
die Sentenz	the maxim, aphorism, sententia
the sentence	*der grammatikalische Satz; das Urteil*
der Terminus	the term
the terminus	*die Endstation*; (railway) *der Kopfbahnhof*
die Vokabel	the word, item of vocabulary
the vocabulary	*der Wortschatz; das Wortschatzheft*
der Vokal	the vowel
the vocal(s)	*der Liedtext*

Page 81: Echt tu Matsch

True Friends

The several true friends involved in this exercise are 'charts', 'fanzines', 'heavy', 'realize', 'stress', 'stressed (out)', 'trouble', 'turn on', 'vibrations' and 'walkman'. The details of the false friends involved are as follows:

False Friends

die Boxen	the loudspeakers, 'speakers'
the boxes	*die Kästen, Kisten, Schachteln*
checken	(*kapieren*) to 'get', 'suss'; (*abchecken*) to check
to check	*überprüfen, kontrollieren, abchecken*
der Clinch	the disagreement; (*im Clinch liegen mit*) to be at odds with/at loggerheads with
the clinch	*der feste Griff;* (boxing) *die Umklammerung*
die Hektik	the 'hassle', 'hass'
hectic	*hektisch*
nerven	to get on s. o.'s nerves, get on s. o.'s wick
to nerve	*stärken, ermutigen;* (~ oneself) *sich aufraffen*
pennen	to sleep, to 'kip'
to pen	*niederschreiben, verfassen*
die Teens	the teenagers
the teens	*die Jugendjahre (vom 13. bis zum 19. Lebensjahr)*

Field 26: Current Idioms

Page 82: Interhuman Affairs

True Friends

The nine true friends involved in this exercise are 'to get one's fingers burned', 'to take French leave', 'to handle with kid gloves', 'to shoot from the hip', 'to nail s.o down to sth.', 'to be all ears', 'to call s. o. to reason', 'to put in the shade' and 'to take in tow'. The details of the false friends involved are as follows:

False Friends

jdm ein Bein stellen	to trip s. o. up
to give s. o. a leg-up	*jdm unter die Arme greifen*
(bei jdm.) auf den Busch klopfen	to boast
to beat about the bush	*um den heißen Brei herumreden*
Konsequenzen ziehen	to draw one's conclusions
to take the consequences	*die Folgen tragen*
eine Lanze brechen/ einlegen für jdn	to champion/defend s. o.
break a lance with s.o.	*sich auseinandersetzen mit jdm.*
an der Nase herumführen	to lead up the garden path
to lead by the nose	*gängeln, bevormunden*
ich pfeif dir was	you can whistle for it
put that in your pipe and smoke it	*versuch, damit fertig zu werden*
Staub aufwirbeln	to cause a stir
to raise the wind	*Geld auftreiben*
aufs Tapet bringen	to bring up, to table, to discuss
to carpet	*jdm eine Standpauke erteilen*
ein Waschlappen sein	to be wet, be a sissy/a milksop
to be a wet blanket	*ein Dämpfer, eine kalte Dusche sein*

Page 83: The Path of Life

True Friends

The true friends involved in this exercise are 'to be the cock of the walk', 'you could have cut the air with a knife' and 'to go to the dogs'. The details of the false friends involved are as follows:

False Friends

über den Berg sein	out of the wood
to be over the hill	*auf einem absteigendem Ast sitzen, die besten Jahre hinter sich haben*
nicht die Bohne	not at all, nothing whatever
(to have) not a bean	*völlig abgebrannt sein*

über den Daumen gepeilt	at a rough guess, roughly, as a 'guesstimate'
as a rule of thumb	*als Faustregel*
auf tönernen Füßen stehen	to be on a shaky basis
to have feet of clay	*feige sein*
ins Gras beißen	to bite the dust
to bite the carpet	*in Wut/Harnisch geraten*
klar wie Kloßbrühe	crystal clear
as clear as mud	*überhaupt nicht klar*
ein blutiger Laie	an absolute beginner
a bloody liar	*ein(e) verdammter Lügner(in)*
zu Potte kommen	to finish; to come to the point
to go to pot.	*kaputt gehen*
am Rande sein	to be at the end of one's tether
to be on edge	*sehr nervös, 'hippelig' sein*
der rote Faden	the thread, the clear thread
the red tape	*der bürokratische Dschungel, Papierkrieg*
auf hoher See sein	to be on the high seas
to be all at sea	*orientierungslos sein*
der letzte Strohhalm	the last hope
the last straw	*der Tropfen, der das Fass zum Überlaufen bringt*

Language Lineage: Red tape
The red colour of 'red tape' is a reference to the red ribbons traditionally used to tie official or legal documents. Its first recorded use is just after the Great and Glorious Revolution, in 1696. As a synecdoche for 'bureaucracy, excessive adhesion to regulations' it has been in recorded use since 1837.

Field 27: *Homo Ludens*

Page 84: Free Time Activities

Sentences

Correct translations revealing the false friends would be:

1. Originally we wanted to give the two of them a mammoth *jigsaw*, but now we have bought a super book of **puzzles**.
2. She briefly *paddled* by the shore, then plucked up courage and **plunged** into the lake from a rock.
3. He **stepped** onto the stage and immediately began to *step-dance*.

4. No, she couldn't swim. Not really. But she could *do doggy-paddle*. Her brother could still only **paddle**.
5. She went straight from the sea into the amusement arcade by the beach, slouching over to the *pinball machine* in her **flippers** and goggles.
6. After they had *worked* successfully *on the jigsaw* for two hours, they **puzzled** a long time over the positioning of the final pieces.
7. Again and again, Beckham's delicate, well-placed *crosses* revealed their opponents' weakness on the right **flank**.
8. Yes, the **military** was bloody good at the *three-day event*.
9. How can we get the horses most easily from the *stalls* into the **horse-box**?
10. In those days, **dancing** at the *dance hall* was the best thing since sliced bread.
11. After you had *wrestled* with him for a few minutes, you wanted nothing more than to **wring** his neck.

Page 85: This Sporting Life

Solutions

The solutions to this exercise are: 1. a) shape b) wrestler c) keep fit 2. grandstand 3. a) do gymnastics b) handstand c) all-in wrestler 4. a) return match b) take revenge c) final d) finale 5. a) catcher 6. a) discus b) javelin c) tribune 7. turn 8. a) ringers b) league 9. a) condition b) stop-watch 10. a) queue b) cue 11. a) marbles b) football c) rugby d) cricket e) cross-county skiing f) golf g) crazy golf h) rubber

True Friends

The true friends involved in the exercise are thus 'cricket', 'discus', 'football', 'golf', 'handstand', 'fossil', 'league', 'rugby' and 'stop-watch'. The details of the false friends involved are as follows:

False Friends

der Catcher	the all-in wrestler
the catcher	*der Fänger*
das Finale	the final, the finals; the final round
the finale	*der Schlußakt*
der Knicker	(*Murmel*) the marble; (*Messer*) clasp-knife; (*Knauser*) skinflint, niggard
the knickers	*der Damenslip*
die Kondition	fitness, 'shape', stamina, (*in bester* ~) in top form
the condition	*der Zustand, die Verfassung; die Bedingung*
der Langlauf	cross-country skiing
long-distance running	*der Langstreckenlauf*
das Minigolf	crazy golf
minigolf	(very rare) *das Minigolf*
das Queue	the billiard cue

	the queue	*die Schlange, Reihe; der (Haar)Zopf*
	die Revanche	the second leg, the return match
	the revenge	*die Rache*
	der Ringer	the wrestler
	the ringer	*der hineingeschmuggelte Star*
	der Robber	the rubber
	the robber	*der Räuber*
	der Speer	(*Sport*) javelin; (*Krieg*) spear, lance
	the spear	*der Speer, die Lanze; der Spieß*
	die Tribüne	(*Zuschauer-)* the grandstand; (*Redner-*) rostrum
	the tribune	*der Tribun*
	trimmen	to keep fit
	to trim	(*Segel*) *trimmen*
	turnen	to do gymnastics
	to turn	*drehen, wenden; sich drehen/wenden gegen*
Further False Friends	*der Drache*	(*Spielzeug*) the kite; *(Märchen)* the dragon
	the dragon	*(Märchen) der Drache*

Field 28: Literature and the Theatre

Page 86: Genres and Ages

True Friends The two true friends involved in this exercise are 'classic' and 'epos/ epic'. The details of the false friends involved are as follows:

False Friends	*die Klassik*	the classical age
	the classic	*der Klassiker*
	die Lyrik	lyric poetry
	the lyrics	*der Liedtext*
	die Novelle	the novella, the Novelle
	the novel	*der Roman*
	der Novellist	the novella-writer, writer of novellas
	the novelist	*der Romancier*
	das Pamphlet	the polemic tract, the lampoon
	the pamphlet	*die Broschüre, Flug-, Druckschrift*
	die Posse	the burlesque, farce; buffoonery, tomfoolery
	the posse	AmE *das Aufgebot (an Polizei, Ordnungskräften)*
	die Prosadichtung	the prose fiction
	the prose poetry	*das Prosagedicht*
	der Roman	the novel
	the Roman	*der Römer*
	der Romancier	the novelist
	the romancer	*der/die Romanzenschreiber(in)*
	die Romantik	Romanticism
	the Romantic	*der/die Romantiker(in)*

die Sage	the saga, legend
the sage	*der Weise; Salbei*
der Schwank	the farce; the merry tale, droll story
the swank	*die Protzerei, die Angabe*
der Vers	the line of verse
the verse	*die Strophe*
verse (*ohne Artikel*)	*Verse, Lyrik*

Page 87: Anglo-American Theatre

Solutions

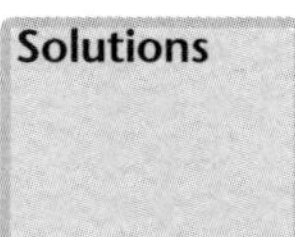

The solutions to this exercise are: 1. a) apron stage b) audience c) take their seats d) circles 2. a) plots b) chorus c) verse dramas 3. a) actors b) mimic 4. a) tickets b) stalls 5. a) character parts b) walk-on part/ mute 6. a) interval b) boxes 7. a) accolades b) uproar 8. props 9. a) Dame b) pantomime 10. spectacle 11. rehearsal

True Friends

The true friends involved in this exercise are thus 'accolade' and 'verse drama'. The details of the false friends involved are as follows:

False Friends

die Charge	(*Theater*) the character part; (*Militär*) the appointment, post; rank
the charge	*der Preis, die Gebühr; (Militär) der Angriff*
der Chor	(*Theater*) the chorus; (*Musik*) the choir
the choir	*der Musikchor*
die Dame	the lady
the Dame	*die Theaterdame; (altmod.) Schuldirektorin; brit. Standesbezeichnung*
die Fabel	(*Handlung*) the plot
the fable	*die (Tier)Fabel (bei Äsop, La Fontaine usw.)*
die Karte	the ticket
the card	*die Post-, Geburtstags-, Spielkarte*
die Loge	the box
the lodge	*das Parkwächter-, Forsthaus*
der Mime	the actor, 'Thespian'
the mime	*die Pantomime*
die Mimik	mimic art, mimicry
the mimic	*der Imitator*
der Pantomime	the mime artist
the pantomime	*engl. Weihnachtsspiel (Klamaukkomödie)*
das Parkett	the (front) stalls
the parquet	*der Parkettboden*
die Pause	the interval, intermission
the pause	*die kurze Unterbrechung*
Platz nehmen	to take a seat
to take place	*stattfinden*

die Probe	the rehearsal; (*General~*) dress rehearsal
the probe	*die Sondierung, Untersuchung; (Raumfahrt) die Sonde*
das Publikum	(*Theater*) the audience; (*Fußball usw.*) the spectators
the public	*die Öffentlichkeit*
die Rampe	(*Theater*) the apron, apron stage
the ramp	*die Laderampe, schräge Auffahrt*
der Rang	(*erster*) dress circle; (*zweiter*) upper circle; (*dritter*) gallery, the 'gods'
the rung	*die Sprosse (an der Leiter)*
die Requisiten	the props
the requisites	*das Zubehör; die Erfordernisse*
das Spektakel	uproar; noise, racket; (*Aufheben*) fuss
the spectacle	*das beeindruckende Schauspiel; das Schaustück*
der/die Statist(in)	the mute, walk-on part
the statist	*eine(r), der/die an den Nationalstaat glaubt*

Page 88: The Literary World

False Friends

The details of the false friends involved here are as follows:

die Charakteristik	the character sketch, characterization
(the) characteristic	*der Charakterzug; typisch*
das Exemplar	the copy
the exemplar	*das Vorbild, das Musterbeispiel*
die Handlung	the plot, the action
the handling	*die Behandlung, der Umgang mit*
die Kritik	the (literary) criticism; the critique
the critic	*der/die Kritiker(in)*
die Phantasie	the imagination
the fantasy	*die ungezügelte Einbildungskraft; das Hirngespinst; die sexuelle Phantasie; Fantasy-Literatur*
der Publizist	the writer, commentator, pundit
the publicist	*der Werbe- oder PR-Agent*
das Register	the index; (*Daumen~*) thumb index
the register	*das Namensverzeichnis*
die Rezension	the book-review; theatre review
the recension	*die Textversion (meistens der Bibel)*
die Schrift	the writing, piece of writing
the script	*das Drehbuch*
die Signatur	the class-mark, shelf-mark
the signature	*die Unterschrift*
die Zensur	the censorship
the censure	*der Tadel*

das Double	(*Theat.*) the understudy	**Further False Friends**
the double	*der Doppelgänger*	
fulminant	(*Theaterabend*) explosive, brilliant	
fulminating	*(nur Med.) fulminant*	
furios	rip-roaring	
furious	*wütend, in Rage*	
das Thema	the subject, the topic	
the theme	*das Motiv; (~* tune*) die Kennmelodie*	

Field 29: The Arts and the Art World

Page 89: Music

True Friends

The three true friends involved in this exercise are 'cornet', 'plectrum' and 'tambourine'. The details of the false friends are as follows:

False Friends

der Akkord	the chord; (*~Arbeit*) piece work
the accord	*die Übereinstimmung*
der Bügel	the bow; (*Steig~*) stirrup; (*Kleider~*) hanger
the bugle	*das Bügelhorn; Signalhorn; Wald-, Jagdhorn*
dudeln	to play the bagpipes
to doodle	*herumkritzeln, -schmieren, 'Männchen malen'*
das Fagott	the bassoon
the faggot	*das Reisigbündel; die Leberfrikadelle; die 'Tunte'*
die Hoboe (alt)	the oboe
the hobo	AmE *der Wanderarbeiter, Landstreicher*
die Lieder	the songs; the *lieder*
the *lieder*	*(nur) Kunstlieder (Schubert, Mahler usw.)*
die Melodie	the tune, air
the melody	*die Tonfolge, (Lied-, Sing)Weise*
die Opera	the works
the opera	*die Oper*
die Pfeife	the whistle; (*Bootsmann*) pipe
the fife	*die Querpfeife*
der Takt	the time, beat
the tact	*das Taktgefühl, der Takt*
das Tamtam	the gong
the tom-tom	*das Tomtom*
der Ton	the sound, the note
the tone	*der Klang, die Klangfarbe*
überspielen	to record, make a recording; (*Theatr.*) to overact
to overplay	*zu viel/bis zum Überdruss spielen*

Page 90: Anglo-American Art

True Friends

Among the several true friends involved in this exercise are 'medium', 'monolithic', 'motif', 'oeuvre' and 'pastose'. The details of the false friends involved are as follows:

False Friends

der Akt	(*Kunst*) the nude; (~ *der Verzweiflung*) desperate deed
the act	*die Handlung, die Tat*
die Art	(*Kunst*) the manner, style; (*Biol.*) species, kind
the art	*die Kunst; Kunstfertigkeit, Geschicklichkeit*
der/die Artist(in)	the artiste
the artist	*der/die Künstler(in)*
die Blende	(*Foto*) the shutter, the diaphragm, stop
the blend	*die Mischung*
der Blitz	the flash
the Blitz	*Bombardierung brit. Städte im 2. Weltkrieg*
die Kraft	the strength
the craft	*das handwerkliche Geschick*
der Lithograph	the lithographer
the lithograph	*die Lithographie*
das Objektiv	the view-finder
the objective	*das Ziel, die Zielsetzung*
der Photoapparat	the camera
the photo apparatus	*das Photozubehör*
der Photograph	the photographer
the photograph	*die Photographie*
die Plastik	the sculpture
the plastic	*das Plastik, der Kunststoff*

Field 30: Religious Practices

Page 91: The Religious Life

True Friends

The one true friend involved in this exercise is 'hermit'. The details of the false friends are as follows:

False Friends

das Brevier	the breviary
the brevier	*Drucktypengröße, etwa 8Pt*
die Kasualien	the (incidental) ministerial offices
the casuals	*die Freizeitkleidung, Freizeitschuhe*
die Klause	hermitage, monk's cell; (*Zuflucht*) private retreat
the clause	*der Paragraph; der Nebensatz*
die Konfession	the denomination, creed; (*selten*) confession
the confession	*die Beichte; (rare) die Konfession*

das Sekret	the secret prayer of a priest
the secret	*das Geheimnis*
sinnvoll	meaningful; sensible
sinful	*sündig, sündhaft*
der Superintendent	(*etwa*) Canon, diocesan head
the superintendent	*der Polizeichef; der Leiter, Vorsteher, Aufsichtsbeamte*
das Vatikanum	the Vatican Council
the Vatican	*der Vatikan*
das Vikariat	the office of curate
the vicarage	*das Pfarrhaus, die Pfarrei*

Page 92: The Church-Goer

True Friends

The eight true friends involved in this exercise are 'asceticism', 'ayatollah', 'Evangelist', 'liturgy', 'sacred', 'side-chapel', 'temple' and 'Upanishads'. The details of the false friends involved are as follows:

False Friends

beten	to pray
to bet	*wetten, (ein)setzen*
bigott	unduly pious/devout; (*heuchlerisch*) hypocritical
bigoted	*frömmlerisch, intolerant in kirchlicher Hinsicht*
der/die Christ(in)	the Christian
Christ	*Christus;* (the ~ child) *das Christkind*
das Christentum	Christianity
Christendom	*die Christenheit*
der Geist	the spirit; mind, intellect; (*Witz*) wit; (*Heiliger~*) Holy Ghost, Holy Spirit
the ghost	*das Gespenst;* (to give up the ~) *den Geist aufgeben*
geistlich	spiritual, religious; (*Musik*) sacred
ghostly	*gespenstisch, geisterhaft*
die Kanzel	the pulpit
the chancel	*der Altarraum, der hohe Chor*
die Kirche	the church; the Church
the kirk	*die presbyterianische Kirche in Schottland*
das Kloster	the monastery; (*Nonnen~*) nunnery, convent
the cloister	*der Kreuzgang, der gedeckte Säulengang*
die Kollekte	the collection
the collect	*ein in der anglikanischen Liturgie für bestimmte Tage vorgeschriebenes Kirchengebet, Kollekte*
die Messe	the mass, Mass; (*Leipziger usw.* ~) trade fair
the mess	*das Durcheinander; die Offiziers-, Schiffsmesse*
die Moral	morality
the moral	*die Moral der Geschichte; das Moralische*
pathetisch	solemn; impassioned, emotively charged

pathetic	*bemitleidenswert; läppisch*
der Patron	the patron saint
the patron	*der Schirmherr; der/die Kunde (~in)*
der Pope	pope of Orthodox Eastern Church
the Pope	*der Papst*
profan	secular, worldly; (*alltäglich*) mundane, humdrum
profane	*lästerlich, gottlos*
die Unrast	the unease, restlessness
the unrest	*die Unruhe(n)*
der Vikar	the curate, assistant
the vicar	*der Pfarrer; Stellvertreter des Bischofs; (~* of Christ*) der Statthalter Christi*

Language Lineage: Vicar

Both 'vicar' and *Vikar* derive from L 'vicarius' meaning a 'substitute', 'one who takes the place of, or acts instead of, another'. Nevertheless the two words go their separate ways for reasons of British esp. English church history. In C 14th, 'vicar' is found in both Chaucer and Wyclif in the sense of the 'earthly representative of God'. By 1340 it appears referring to the Pope. With the coming of the Anglican Church, however, it comes to mean first a 'person acting in place of a parson or rector *(Pfarrer)*' but then a 'representative of a community to which tithes had been appropriated'. From this meaning, it then came to be the 'incumbent of a parish from which tithes had been appropriated'. In modern English, 'vicar', 'rector' and 'pastor' are virtually synonymous, all having higher status than a mere *Vikar*.

Revision Exercises 1 (Fields 1–6)

Page 93: Exercise 1

1. Good teaching must be puzzling/intriguing. 2. Psychologists hold discussions about psychologically ill children. 3. My driving-wheel shakes/wobbles. 4. 'Fire simulator' makes its first stop in the area. 5. Preserving/Preserve the environment 6. Using new methods/prescriptions to combat ageing. 7. The oil plague becomes the boss's/premier's business. 8. There is always a first snowflake to fall, however heavy a flurry follows.

Page 93: Exercise 2

Things fall silent in autumn, eerily silent.

Everything has remained the same: nothing seems to have changed. Neither the marshland nor the ploughed fields, neither the pines up there on the hills nor the lake. Only that summer is over. The end of October. And already late in the afternoon.

In the distance a dog is howling and the earth has the fragrance of moistened leaves. It has rained long over the past weeks; now it will soon snow. The sun is gone, and the dusk is shuffling its way over the hard ground; there is a rustling sound in the stubble-field as if someone were creeping about. And with the mists comes the past. I see you again, you hills, trees and roads – we all see each other again! [...]

Revision Exercises 2 (Fields 7–12)

Page 94: Exercise 1

1. To be childlike is to ascend to childhood: to be childish is to descend into childhood. 2. The vices of the great are known as 'airs and graces'. 3. He who says what he does is vain: he who does what he says is good. 4. I guess I've got a soft spot for idiots. 5. A human being is lazy when he prefers to be annoyed than to get up. 6. Brilliance/genius is the present time become timeless. 7. Force/strength is the matter of materials. 8. All words dance attendance around truth: it/she is chaste. 9. Mockery ends where understanding begins. 10. The stupidities of the two sexes remain strictly separate(d). 11. A vain woman needs a mirror: a vain man is his own mirror. 12. Bric-à-brac/Junk is everything/anything that has outlived/forfeited its usefulness.

Page 94: Exercise 2

Translations

1. The new price system is especially attractive for senior citizens 2. Schalke make fools of themselves against Wisla Krakow. 3. In the past months there had been many indications that Gore was out for revenge and a re-match. 4. Ban on mobiles/cell phones in theatres. 5. London – world-city with the bizarre/weird means of transport. 6. Even the brightest minds have had the experience: instead of brilliant brain-waves comes a trickle of lame ideas because the think-tank control centre is working only at half-strength. This you can change.

Revision Exercises 3 (Fields 13–18)

Page 95: Exercise 1

Translations

A. Aphorisms 1. Periodicals are [. . .] the corners where literature takes a pee, but that's where all the ads are billed. 2. Risk is the bow-wave of success. 3. A meeting is a session to which many go in but from which little comes out. 4. Prospectus: illustrated simulation/pretence of (giving) information. 5. A slogan is the word that beats the competition. 6. Technology is the stored results of the long struggles against the enemies of man. Thus far it is to be praised. 7. Wages are the measure of dignity that society gives to a particular form of work. 8. 'It's always difficult to start out,' said the trainee journalist and began by writing a leading article. (*The play on words is perhaps impossible to capture here*) 9. Scholarship: tip for those with a thirst for knowledge. 10. Citizens reward honesty – even honesty that goes against the grain.

B. Headlines 1. 1. Companies take complaints seriously. 2. Wage dispute escalates. 3. Economic climate in Europe deteriorates. 4. No doubts about the solvency of the state. 5. Economies – above all in personnel costs. Town council passes budget for 2003. 6. The then seller had the trucks dispatched by his brother to Nuremberg. 7. Advertising ban on tobacco upsets the advertising sector. 8. Pensioners, white-collar workers and civil servants the most generous. 9. Headstand in fashion store gave you 20% discount. 10. Trade fair on the look-out for new ideas/blue-prints. 11. You want to be an auditor and not a mere supervisor? 12. Pessimists again at the helm. 13. Medium-sized firms lament credit conditions. 14. United Airlines facing certain bankruptcy.

Revision Exercises 4 (Fields 19–24)

Page 96: Exercise 1

A. Sentences 1. A murderer is someone who kills and who is weaker than the police. 2. A woman keeps a good eye on her sex, because for sex she gets all those things that are even more important to her than sex. 3. We transfer all our errors to our children, in whom they leave irreducible traces. 4. Such a peaceful country! The policemen there still carry sabres. 5. In Austria, people have been resigned for so long by now that it gives rise to disintegration energy. 6. When they speak of foreign policy, the Germans have hardly any other resource than morality. 7. Even cautious steps leave traces. 8. Resignedness derives from the recognition that there is no harbour and certainly no arrival but again and again a setting out with new plans, new people, new utopias, new capitulations.

B. Newspaper Texts 1. Cell phone shares celebrate rip-roaring comeback. 2. Bad marks for industrial/economic support 3. 47 per cent of all men cheat on their wives at least once. 4. Many schools in Germany bear visible signs of the financial plight of local authorities. 5. Whether the hospitals will appeal (against) the verdict is still an open question. 6. Important parts of the strategy were not put into practice. 7. Koch accuses the 'red-green' coalition of 'electoral deception/deceiving the electorate'. 8. Railway company toes the line again. 9. Against/In the face of the wind blowing from the grass roots. 10. The local authorities likewise do not consider themselves in a position to spend more on (their) human resources.

Translations

Revision Exercises 5 (Fields 25–30)

Page 97: Exercise 1

1. The morality that was good enough for our fathers is not good enough for our children. 2. The novella is a simile, the novel an example, the drama a judgement. 3. Christianity is the religion of the deepest disquiet. 4. Anyone who wants to talk with me must not just want to hear his own opinion. 5. The time of need calls apostles, not doctors/PhDs to the pulpit. 6. Lyric verse is poetry painted. 7. The Romanticism to come is [...] a piece of ice, within which a flame is burning. 8. Reading is the co-operation of the reader with the read. (*Or*: the interaction of the reader with the read.) 9. She danced to the rhythm/beat – only with the wrong partner. (*Or*: danced in step) 10. The hollow phrase is the mother tongue of politics. 11. I know that I am a kind of home-spun novelist. I am certainly not a writer of novellas/

Translations

Novellen. 12. The imagination is an eternal spring. 13. Censorship is the younger of two infamous sisters: the elder is called 'Inquisition'. 14. Criticism appears like Ate – she pursues authors, but with a limp. 15. The tune is the language of the heart. 16. The impassioned tone is a laziness of logic. 17. 'Would be dignified' is a subjunctive. (*Again the play on words is not readily rendered.*) 18. They lost the thread at the baize table of bureaucracy. (*Once again the play on words is not readily rendered.*) 19. During his lifetime, an author's books are reviewed; after his death he himself. The final review is generally somewhat more favourable. 20. Unfulfillable wishes are known as 'pious'. The assumption seems to be that only worldly wishes are fulfilled.

Revision of Revisions

Page 98: Exercise 1

Solutions

Across 2. become resigned 4. consistent 6. entrepreneur 8. jigsaw 10. pine 11. cathedral 13. get 14. complaint 15. bog 18. city centre 20. & 24. keep fit 21. avenue 23. manure 24. *see* 20 25. oar 26. meaningful 27. keep 30. grammar school 33. trial 34. solid 35. mark 37. Christian 38. pleasure

Down 1. sensitive 2. brilliant 3. checks 5. topical 7. navy 9. prescription 11. committed 12. humane 16. overlook 17. likeable 18. chair 19. reading 22. embarrassing 28. perhaps 29. copy 31. crisps 32. survey 36. hike

Page 99: Exercise 2

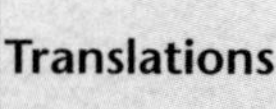

Translations

1. Another committee: senior citizens from the area/region form their Council. 2. New Year's Party – the recipes. 3. The issue became topical nationwide thanks to the campaigns/activities in the capital Wroclaw. 4. Literature: a text in a dinner jacket. Committed literature: a text in a dinner jacket with a red bow-tie. 5. People of genius do not pursue any goal: they are pursued by a goal. 6. A woman who has never been tested always thinks too well of herself and considers the victory too easy. 7. Imagination is the golden glow that lies over existence, lifting it above the grey of everyday life. 8. Even the current economic crisis is said not to affect the company as much as it does other sectors. 9. Minister demands later pensions for graduates. 10. Those who take their bearings from economic forecasts are ill-advised. 11. (Organ-)Donor from the sty. 12. Vacation on prescription – work-dodgers harm their bosses. 13. Instead of in the pulpit, many curates of the Lutheran Church land up on the scrap-heap. 14. The strength of the soul shows itself in the loftiness of its goal. 15. Love lives by miracles, not by laws.

Page 100: Exercise 3

Translations

1. Ein Gelehrter, der nichts als Bücher kennt, dürfte auch von diesen nichts wissen. 2. Ich glaube nicht, daß man von Vorlesungen genau soviel hat wie vom Lesen der Bücher, aus denen die Vorlesungen hervorgehen. 3. Letzten Endes wird der Roman eine bloße akademische Übung sein, geschrieben von Hochschullehrern, die ihn im Seminarraum benutzen, um wiederum die Findigkeit ihrer Studierenden zu testen. 4. Glaube einer Frau oder einer Grabinschrift / Oder irgend etwas anderem, das falsch ist, ehe / Du Kritikern vertraust, die selbst wund sind. 5. Das richtige Wort am richtigen Ort ist die wahre Definition von Stil. 6. Die Expansion von Wissen bedeutet, daß jedes Buch einen immer geringeren Bruchteil von all dem, was überhaupt bekannt ist, enthält. 7. Das einzig Wichtige an einem Buch ist die Bedeutung, die es für Dich hat. 8. Der Impuls zum Romanschreiben entstammt einer flüchtigen ganzheitlichen Vision vom Dasein. 9. Sie denken, es ist schrecklich, daß Wollust und Wut / mich im Alter begleiten und Aufmerksamkeit erringen. / In meiner Jugend haben sie mich nicht so gepeinigt,/ aber was habe ich denn sonst noch, um mich zum Dichten anzuspornen? 10. Adjektive sind die Verräter der Lyrik, die größten Feinde des Lyrikers. 11. Der Lyriker ist in Wirklichkeit damit beschäftigt, das Vertraute neu zu kreieren, er verschreibt sich nicht der Vermittlung von Unbekanntem. 12. Einige Rezensionen schmerzen. Das ist zwar bedauerlich, aber kein Autor hat das geringste Recht zum Herumjammern. 13. Denn der Reim ist der Strophen Ruder, mit dem sie – Schiffen gleich – ihren Kurs einhalten. 14. Die Sprache wird mit Orthographie gewürzt. 15. In vielen ihrer Sparten ist die Literatur nichts anderes als der Schatten einer guten Unterhaltung. 16. Es ist einfach so langweilig und grausig, wie wir sterben. 17. Der einzige Grund, warum ich Bücher schreibe, ist, meinem Landgut drei- oder vierhundert Morgen hinzuzufügen. 18. Ja, in den letzten zwei Wochen habe ich kaum etwas geschrieben. Ich war müßig, faul – ich habe versagt.

Literatur

Wörterbücher der „falschen Freunde"

BARNICKEL, KLAUS-DIETER, *Falsche Freunde: Ein vergleichendes Wörterbuch Deutsch-Englisch.* Heidelberg 1992.

BENNEMANN, HEINRICH, HERTING, BEATE, PRAUSE, THOMAS, *Typische Fehler Englisch.* Berlin 1994.

BREITKREUZ, HELMUT, *More False Friends: Tückische Fallen des deutsch-englischen Wortschatzes.* Reinbek 1992.

BRIDGHAM, FREDERICK, *The Friendly German-English Dictionary: A Guide to German language, culture and society through faux amis, literary illustration and other diversions.* London 1996.

HILL, ROBERT J., *A Dictionary of False Friends.* London 1982.

KIPP, HARALD, *Non-Verwexlikon: Englische Vokabeln, die am häufigsten verwechselt werden.* Bergisch-Gladbach 1986.

KÜHNEL, HELMUT, *Typische Fehler Englisch.* Berlin 1994.

PARKES, GEOFF, CORNELL, ALAN. *German-English False Friends: Reference and Practice.* 3 vols. Southampton 1989/1991/1993.

PASCOE, GRAHAM, PASCOE, HENRIETTE, *Sprachfallen Englisch: Mit Abschlusstests.* Ismaning ^{2}1998.

WHITE, A. SANDRI, *Boobytraps of the German Language.* Allenhurst, New Jersey: Aurea Publications 1988 (1966).

Zur Theorie der „falschen Freunde"

CARROLL, S. E. 'On Cognates'. *Second Language Research* 8.2, 93–119.

MALONE, JOSEPH L. 'False Friendship' *Babel* 28, 21–24.

NEUHAUS, HANS JOACHIM. 'False Friends, Frege's sense and word-formation', in: HÜLLEN, WERNER, SCHULZE R., eds. *Understanding Lexicon: Meaning, Sense and World Knowledge.* Tübingen 1988.

STEIN, DIETER. ‚Korrespondenz in kontrastiver Linguistik'. *Linguistik und Didaktik* 42 (1980), 160–167.

WANDRUSZKA, MARIO. ‚Die falschen Freunde des Übersetzers'. In: GRÄHS, LILLEBILL ET AL. *Theory and Practice of Translation.* Bern 1976, 213–34.

Zur Geschichte der „falschen Freunde"

HASCHKA, CHRISTINE. ‚Zur Entwicklungsgeschichte der „faux amis"-Forschung.' *Lebende Sprachen.* 1989.4,148–152.

Zur Didaktik der „falschen Freunde"

KUßMAUL, PAUL. *Training the Translator.* Amsterdam 1995.

Terminology

HELMUT BREITKREUZ. ‚Typen von False Friends'. In: MATTHEIER, K. J., Hrsg. *Ein Europa – Viele Sprachen: Kongreßbeiträge zur 21. Jahrestagung der Gesellschaft für Angewandte Linguistik GAL e. V.,* Frankfurt/M 1991, 224–5.

MUSOLFF, ANDREAS. ‚Echte, falsche oder gar heimtückische Freunde?' Ein Kommentar zur Metaphorik der Beschreibung von Entlehnungen. *Sprachreport* 2, 11–12.

Wegweisende Sammelbände

ARROWSMITH, WILLIAM, SHATTOCK, ROGER, Hrsg.: *The Craft and Context of Translation.* New York: Anchor Books 1964.

BEYER, MANFRED, DILLER, HANS-JÜRGEN ET AL. Hrsg.: *Realities of Translating* (= *anglistik und englischunterricht* 55/56). Heidelberg: C. Winter 1995.

BOWKER, LYNNE, CRONIN, MICHAEL ET AL. Hrsg.: *Unity in Diversity? Current Trends in Translation Studies.* Manchester: St. Jerome 1998.

BROWER, R. A. Hrsg.: *On Translation.* New York 1966.

DRESCHER, HORST W.: *Transfer. Übersetzen – Dolmetschen – Interkulturalität.* Frankfurt/M.: Peter Lang 1997.

FLEISCHMANN, EBERHARD, KUTZ, WLADIMIR, SCHMITT, PETER A. Hrsg.: *Translationsdidaktik. Grundfragen der Übersetzungswissenschaft.* Tübingen: Gunter Narr 1997.

FORSTER, LEONARD, Hrsg.: *Aspects of Translation.* London: Secker and Warburg 1958.

GERZYMISCH-ARBOGAST, GILE, DANIEL ET AL. Hrsg.: *Wege der Übersetzungs- und Dolmetschforschung.* Tübingen: Gunter Narr 1999.

SCHMITT, PETER A. Hrsg.: *Paradigmawechsel in der Translation: Festschrift für Albrecht Neubert zum 70. Geburtstag.* Tübingen: Stauffenburg 2000.

SNELL-HORNBY, MARY Hrsg.: *Übersetzungswissenschaft: Eine Neuorientierung.* Tübingen: Gunter Narr 1986.

SNELL-HORNBY, MARY, PÖCHHACKER, FRANZ, KAINDL, K. Hrsg.: *Translation Studies: An Interdiscipline.* Amsterdam: John Benjamins 1994.

WILSS, WOLFRAM Hrsg.: *Übersetzungswissenschaft.* Darmstadt: Wiss. Buchgesellschaft 1981.

WILSS, WOLFRAM, THOME, GISELA, Hrsg.: *Translation Theory and Its Implementation in the Teaching of Translating and Interpreting.* Tübingen: Gunter Narr 1984.

Einführungen in die Disziplin

BASSNETT-MCGUIRE, SUSAN: *Translation Studies.* London: Routledge 1980/1991.

BAKER, MONA: *In Other Words: A Coursebook on Translation.* London: Routledge 1992.

BELL, ROGER T.: *Translation and Translating – Theory and Practice.* London: Longman 1991.

GERZYMISCH-ARBOGAST, H.: *Übersetzungswissenschaftliches Propädeutikum.* Tübingen: Francke 1994.

KOLLER, WERNER: *Einführung in die Übersetzungswissenschaft.* Heidelberg: Quelle und Meyer 1979/1992.

SNELL-HORNBY, MARY: *Translation Studies: An Integrated Approach.* Amsterdam: John Benjamins 1988.

SNELL-HORNBY, MARY, KADRIC, MIRA Hrsg.: *Grundfragen der Übersetzungswissenschaft. Wiener Vorlesungen von Katharina Reiß.* Wien: WUV-Universitätsverlag 1993.

Beste Website

www.uni-bonn.de/~dbuncic/ffbib/subj_un.htm